A Bibliography of Family Placement Literature

A Bibliography of Family Placement Literature

Edited by John Sudbery
Stephen Hicks
Sheila Thompson
Hugh McLaughlin
Carole Bramley

with Katrina Wilson

BAAF
ADOPTION & FOSTERING

Published by
British Association for Adoption & Fostering
(BAAF)
Skyline House
200 Union Street
London SE1 0LX
www.baaf.org.uk

Charity registration 275689

British Library Cataloguing in Publication Data
A catalogue record for this book is available from the British Library

ISBN 1 903699 30 4

Project management by Miranda Davies, Editor, BAAF
Cover photographs posed by models
by Andrew Haig
Designed by Andrew Haig & Associates
Typeset by Avon DataSet Ltd, Bidford on Avon, Warwickshire
Printed by Creative Print and Design
Trade distribution by Turnaround Publisher Services, Unit 3, Olympia Trading Estate, Coburg Road, London N22 6TZ

BAAF is the leading UK-wide membership organisation for all those concerned with adoption, fostering and child care issues.

About the authors

John Sudbery is Senior Lecturer at the University of Salford and a member of the Salford Centre for Social Work Research. He is a psychotherapist and for five years was Chair of the Group for the Advancement of Psychotherapy and Psychodynamics in Social Work (GAPS). His research has investigated various aspects of the difficulties facing children and their families.

Stephen Hicks works in the School of Community, Health Sciences & Social Care at the University of Salford, where he runs the MSc in Child Care & Family Practice linked to the Post-Qualifying Child Care Award. Steve is Chair of the Northern Support Group of lesbian and gay foster carers and adopters and is co-editor of *Lesbian and Gay Fostering and Adoption* (1999).

Sheila Thompson is Senior Lecturer in the same School of Community, Health Sciences & Social Care. She has many years' practice experience in the field of fostering and adoption and is Programme Leader of the Post-Qualifying Child Care Programme, North West.

Hugh McLaughlin is the Director of Social Work and Social Policy at Salford University. Prior to moving to academia he was a social worker, team manager, service manager and Assistant Director (children and families). Hugh is a Trustee and ex-Chair of the Board of Trustees for After Adoption.

At the time of working on this book, **Carole Bramley** lectured in social work and psychology at the same university. Adopted as a child herself, her research interests lie in adoption, mental health issues and disability.

Katrina Wilson is Information Officer at BAAF. She has an MSc in Information and Library Studies from the Robert Gordon University and is a Member of the Chartered Institute of Library and Information Professionals.

Acknowledgements

We are grateful for the help of the following people, without whom this book would not have been possible: Shaila Shah and Miranda Davies at BAAF; Roy Stewart and Fergus Smith of Children Act Enterprises Ltd for checking and editing legal references in Chapter 1; librarians and other information services staff at the University of Salford; Marie Siddoo, for invaluable administrative help in the later stages of preparation of the manuscript; Mrs Ann Rothwell (who as a graduate student helped with literature searching at very short notice); Professor Steven Shardlow; and colleagues and family members who tolerated our preoccupation with this work.

Contents

Introduction

This Bibliography is intended to provide a guide to the principal literature about adoption and fostering. The first edition was published in 1988, followed by a revised version in 1994. As with previous volumes, the focus is on family placement of children who are looked after by the local authority or children placed for adoption.

The care of children who are not living with their birth parents is both a very ordinary activity and an extraordinary undertaking (Hill, 1999 – ref. 132). The literature on the subject now reflects an understanding of how diverse are the purposes and arrangements involved. It also reflects the complex overlapping perspectives and priorities of different stakeholders. A small selection of these stakeholders includes birth parents whose children are being cared for by another person, adoptive parents, adults who have been adopted, disabled children who experience regular time with another family, foster carers looking after young people who would otherwise be in secure institutions, the birth children of foster carers and administrators and policy makers who may (currently) be attempting to set out rationalised financial models of "supply, demand, average and marginal costs" of different types of family placements. Many such stakeholder groups are featured in the works listed here, including social workers who are charged with promoting and safeguarding the welfare of children and therefore supporting those who care for them in family placement.

Scope and organisation

The extent of the literature required that we set other significant limits on the scope of the Bibliography beyond the general subject of family placement.

First, its primary readership is UK based, so literature from outside the UK is included only where there are specific reasons for doing so. International perspectives are relevant sometimes because of the topic (e.g. intercountry adoptions). Some international literature sets the UK systems in perspective, highlighting the strengths and weaknesses of current systems or providing examples of innovative practice. And sometimes, key studies of particular topics are not British.

The previous edition included work up to 1993; this volume primarily considers work published since 1989 (the Children Act of that year being a significant watershed in children's welfare services). Earlier works have been included only if they are important texts, the omission of which would appear anomalous.

This still leaves a prodigious quantity of literature that far exceeds the possibility of listing. In selecting material, we have been guided by an assumption that the core readership includes members of the British Association of Adoption and Fostering (BAAF), other workers and policy makers in the field, some parents and children (of all ages) with a personal interest in the subject, and students and researchers. The selection therefore keeps areas such as psychological, social science and medical studies within proportion to a "social welfare" emphasis.

Method

There are now rigorous methods of comprehensive literature searching which combine systematic searching of databases with the use of expert knowledge. For the purposes of critical appraisal, scoping searches combine with analysis to ensure that topics are defined so that all the relevant literature in the world can expect to be located. Within this, it is then possible to isolate only those that meet specified criteria of reliability. Our topic of interest, however, was defined in advance; a scoping search using systematic methods quickly revealed that even using one database in one subtopic produced more material than could possibly be dealt with by the resources available (or presented in a work of manageable size).

Our strategy for compiling this Bibliography has therefore been a hybrid. Our professional knowledge and the outcome of consultation with relevant experts and specialist organisations have been combined with the search of comprehensive electronic databases. We have made use of the reference lists and bibliographies of books and articles, the publishing lists of key organisations and government websites. The principal databases used have been Web of Science, ChildData, CareData, Medline, PsycInfo, and Ingenta, all as at April 2003. The core search terms used have been "adop*", "foster*", "attach*" (the asterisk indicating that all terms beginning thus, such as "adoption", "adoptive", "adopted", "adopting", will be utilised). To restrict the outputs to relevant topics, a variety of additional terms were used according to the topic and the database (e.g. ChildData uses "infants", CareData uses "babies", while Medline contains a built-in limiter for specific age ranges). Our initial intention was to have read all materials annotated and included in the Bibliography. This is true of Chapters 3, 5 and 6, but was beyond our resources for the rest of the book. From the total lists of relevant literature thus obtained, we estimate that about a sixth has been included.

It follows that the Bibliography cannot be exhaustive. No doubt we have missed some important works (our predecessor observed that a bibliography is never completed, only abandoned, and we have discovered the painful reality of this), and no doubt others more expert in their fields will at times disagree with our selection. We hope that this book will be a useful resource for those intent on discovering the key works about aspects of family placement.

Structure

The literature is grouped into the following chapters, which then have a total of 38 further subheadings:

1. Family placement – the current context in the UK
2. Family placement in general; foster care
3. Adoption and permanent foster care
4. Selected schemes and care arrangements
5. Race, ethnicity, gender, sexuality, disability and family placement
6. Attachment, therapeutic help and life story work

No grouping is entirely satisfactory. Whatever divisions had been chosen, many works relate to more than one heading, and there can be argument about the social implications of choosing one organising principle rather than another; we arrived at this structure after considerable discussion. Grouping the literature into works about adoption or fostering, or about the child, the parents, the birth parents and the placing agency are other logical divisions, but all present similar difficulties, as does a chronological principle considering babies, young children and older children. There are strong arguments for not separating out sexuality and ethnicity from other aspects of identity in substitute family placement, but experience has shown that when attention has not been focused on them, poor practice can result. Furthermore, it is likely that at the present time a significant use of the book may be by people who seek the literature on these specific themes. There is a wide range of knowledge about human growth and development that is of particular relevance to family placement, but in the interests of keeping some balance in the relative size of chapters we have restricted the separate chapter to consideration of attachment and therapeutic interventions. In some chapters it has been possible to indicate the logicality of alternative organising principles by using subdivisions, and where possible we have included cross-referencing. We hope that the decisions we have made, although based on compromise, create overall a helpful work of reference.

Debates and ambiguities

The book is not a critical guide to the literature, although we have where relevant highlighted the context of publications within certain debates (for example, about "transracial" placement).

In the broader view, there are debates and analyses that are highly relevant (and may be highly charged) in relation to family placement, but in general in these areas, we have included publications only where they refer specifically to fostering or adoption. The concept of "family" is highly culturally relative, its boundaries being historically and geographically located. Moral and ideological judgements about whether same-sex couples form a family with children have been directly relevant to thinking, regulation and practice about substitute family placement. Attitudes towards learning disability, to the birth of children outside marriage and to appropriate standards of evidence in court have all made a significant impact on how and whether children are placed in "substitute" family care. "Family placement" in the UK has a particular context within a model of state intervention in family life and the existence of institutional residential care for children – matters are very different in other places with different traditions. Any reflective examination of family placement needs to take these societal dimensions into account, the diversity of family forms, the changeable social construction of moral judgements, geographical and cultural variation in the significance of "family" and social services. This Bibliography draws attention to these matters only where the literature itself explicitly does so – the reader has to use this work of reference with their own critical awareness of the relativity of the context.

We would also remind readers that the literature referred to within this Bibliography is of variable quality, and some of it displays methodological and epistemological problems or has data of limited quantity. Some authors, for example, make very broad claims or generalisations on the basis of limited or problematic data and so such claims should be treated with caution. As many of the topics covered are moral and political questions, the complex ethical questions raised cannot, and perhaps should not, be decided on the basis of the research "evidence" alone.

Electronic sources

Increasingly, people seeking information will use the internet as their starting point, and the present Bibliography comes, we suspect, at an in-between moment. A significant number of documents in this Bibliography are available online as well as in print (where we are aware of this we indicate it), and some of the resources exist only as websites. Web addresses change and "live" links on a website change to reflect this. Obviously, the web addresses printed in this book are frozen in time – generally at around September 2004.

1 Family placement – the current context in the UK

This chapter details some principal works about law, policy and regulation in the UK as they relate to family placement. It also includes some publications that locate family placement in the broader context of family support or the protection of children. The views of people who are or have been adopted or fostered figure in subsequent chapters, but a few works which indicate in general terms the priority currently afforded to children's rights to participation are included here.

Academic, training or practice materials are cited in this chapter only where they relate directly to the main material (e.g. training materials and commentaries on the Looking After Children record system). Otherwise research, practice and training materials are found in the chapter covering the area to which they refer. Therefore the government guidance about the education of looked after children is listed here, but the research about the educational attainment of children looked after will be found in Chapter 2.

The context

At the time of writing (November 2004), 60,800 children were "looked after" in public care in England, of whom 41,100 were in family placement and 3,400 were placed for adoption. The largest category of need for looked after children was "abuse or neglect" (62 per cent). These and other statistics are available on a portion of the Department for Education and Skills website (www.dfes.gov.uk/rsgateway) and from the social trends information provided by the Office of National Statistics. In Scotland, almost 11,400 children were looked after. This is about one per cent of the population under 18, but the Scottish Executive notes the considerable variation, between 0.3 per cent to 2.1 per cent in different local authority areas. Of these, 3,173 (28 per cent) were with foster carers. In Scotland, there were 373 adoption applications, of which 99 per cent were successful (of the remainder, the majority are withdrawn, not refused). Fifteen (4 per cent) Scottish adoptions were from overseas. The Scottish statistics are available from the Scottish Executive's children's statistics gateway, which lists the relevant publications – www.scotland.gov.uk/about/ED/IAC/00016135/Welcome.aspx

Law, regulations and guidance

Heading the list for England and Wales is the Adoption and Children Act 2002 which received Royal Assent on 7 November 2002. The government intends that the regulations, court rules and guidance necessary to implement it will be in place by the end of 2004, with full implementation planned for September 2005. It replaces the Adoption Act 1976 and modernises the legal framework for domestic and intercountry adoption. However, at the time of publication of this book, the Adoption Act 1976 remains in force.

Adoption policy in Scotland is a devolved matter and is the responsibility of the Scottish Executive. The Adoption and Children Act 2002 covers England and Wales but not Scotland, except in a small number of cross-border issues. At the time of writing, the Scottish Executive is reviewing adoption and fostering policy in Scotland (the law on adoption and fostering in Scotland is over 25 years old). Phase I of the review has looked at adoption practice and Phase II will consider the legal framework for adoption and fostering.

Law

001 Adoption and Children Act 2002

002 Adoption Act 1976 (as amended)

003 Care Standards Act 2000

004 Carers and Disabled Children Act 2000

005 Children Act 1989

006 The Children (Northern Ireland) Order 1995

007 Children (Scotland) Act 1995

008 The Commission for Social Care Inspection (Children's Rights Director) Regulations 2004

009 The Commissioner for Children and Young People (Northern Ireland) Order 2003

010 Commissioner for Children and Young People (Scotland) Act 2003

011 The Disability Discrimination Act 1995

012 Disqualification from Caring for Children (England) Regulations 2002

013 European Convention on Human Rights introduced to the UK by the Human Rights Act 1988 in October 2000

014 **Hague Conference on Private International Law – Convention on Protection of Children and Co-operation in Respect of Intercountry Adoption 1993** (ratified in the UK June 2003)

015 **The Protection of Children (Scotland) Act 2003**

016 **The Protection of Children and Vulnerable Adults (Northern Ireland) Order 2003**

017 **Race Relations (Amendment) Act 2000**

018 **Sexual Offences Act 2003**

019 **United Nations – Convention on the Rights of the Child 1989** (ratified in the UK December 1991)

Regulations and guidance

020 **Department of Health (1991) The Children Act 1989: Guidance and Regulations:**
- **a) Volume 3 Family placements**
- **b) Volume 6 Children with disabilities**
- **c) Volume 8 Private fostering**
- **d) Volume 9 Adoption issues London: Department of Health**

021 **Department of Health (2001) National Adoption Standards for England.** London: *Department of Health*

Adoption Standards for England that set out what users of adoption services in England can expect from agencies. The Standards include statements of values, principles and specific Standards that underpin them. The Standards apply only to domestic adoptions through adoption agencies. They have the status of "statutory guidance" issued under section 7 Local Authority Social Services Act 1970 so that local authorities should comply with them unless there are exceptional reasons – but unlike regulations, they do not apply directly with the force of law.

022 Adoption Agencies Regulations 1983 (SI 1983 No 1964) as amended by:

- **a) Adoption Agencies and Children (Arrangements for Placement and Review) (Miscellaneous Amendments) Regulations 1997 (SI 1997 No 649)**
- **b) The Children (Protection from Offenders) (Miscellaneous Amendments) Regulations 1997 (SI 1997 No 2308)**
- **c) The Children (Protection from Offenders) (Amendments) Regulations 1999 (SI 1999 No 2768)**
- **d) The Protection of Children (Access to Lists) (Prescribed Individuals) Regulations 2000 (SI 2000 No 2537)**
- **e) Local Authorities (Executive and Alternative Arrangements) (Modification of Enactments and Other Provisions) (England) Order 2001 (SI 2001 No 2237)**
- **f) The Foster Placement (Children) and Adoption Agencies Amendment (England) Regulations 2001) SI 2001 No 2992**
- **g) The Adoption Agencies (Amendment) Regulations 2003**

023 The Adoption Agencies and Children (Arrangement for Placement and Reviews) (Miscellaneous Amendments) Regulations 1997

024 The Foster Placement (Children) and Adoption Agencies Amendment (England) Regulations 2001

025 The Adoption of Children from Overseas Regulations 2001 (SI No 1251)

026 The Local Authority Adoption Service (England) Regulations 2003

027 The Voluntary Adoption Agencies and the Adoption Agencies (Miscellaneous Amendments) Regulations 2003

028 The Adoption Support Services (Local Authorities) (England) Regulations and Guidance 2003

029 The Intercountry Adoption (Hague Convention) Regulations 2003

030 The Adoption (Bringing Children into the UK) Regulations 2003

031 The Registration of Foreign Adoptions Regulations 2003

032 The Adoption Support Services (Local Authorities) (England) Regulations 2003 accompanying guidance

033 **Department of Health (1998) Local Authority Circular LAC(98)20 – Adoption: Achieving the right balance**

034 **The Independent Review of Determinations (Adoption) Regulations 2004**

035 **Department of Health (2002) Fostering Services National Minimum Standards and Fostering Services Regulations**
This document contains the fostering service regulations and national minimum standards applicable to fostering services. Together, these regulations and standards form the basis of the regulatory framework under the *Care Standards Act 2000 (CSA)* for the conduct of fostering services.

036 **The Fostering Services (Wales) Regulations 2003**

037 **Commission for Social Care Inspection**
www.csci.gov.uk
Care Standards are referred to in various sections of this book. This website gives a guide to the operation of the Commission for Social Care Inspection, including its responsibilities in the regulation and inspection of fostering and adoption services.

Related studies, guides and other resources

038 **Aldgate J and Statham J (2001) The Children Act Now: Messages from research.** London: *Department of Health*
A review of 24 research studies commissioned by the

Department of Health to evaluate the implementation of the Children Act 1989. They include studies about the care of children looked after by local authorities, contact and leaving care, plus a guide to key principles of the Act. The review makes links between the research findings and the intention of initiatives such as Quality Protects in England, Children First in Wales and the Government's Objectives for Children's Social Services.

039 **Allen N (2003) Making Sense of the New Adoption Law.** Lyme Regis: *Russell House Publishing*
This guide for social workers and social welfare agencies summarises the origins of the Adoption and Children Act 2002, outlines its main themes and in successive chapters explains provisions relating to: the effects of adoption; "open adoption" (not referred to in the Act, but an established feature of practice); the provision of adoption services and regulatory standards; adoption agencies; baby adoption; adoption of looked after children; assessment of adopters; adoptions with a foreign element; and access to information after adoption.

040 **BAAF Scotland (2001) Adoption Procedure and Practice: Scotland.** London: *BAAF*
Summarises law and regulation and includes training materials for panel members, practitioners and managers in Scotland.

041 **Borthwick S and Lord J (2003) Fostering Panels: Guidance for local authorities, fostering agencies and panel members in England.** London: *BAAF*
This guide brings together the key messages in regulations, standards and inspections about fostering

panels for members of panels as well as foster carers, managers and workers in fostering agencies. The guidance includes pointers to best practice and is applicable to all fostering service providers: local authority, independent, or voluntary agencies. Also see ref. 26.

042 **Brophy J, Wale C J and Bates P (1999) Myths and Practices: The use of experts in child care proceedings.** London: *BAAF*
The first England and Wales survey of the use of experts explores the range of practices by courts, guardians ad litem, local authorities and parents. Detailed analysis of 557 cases identifies the major specialists providing expert evidence and emerging patterns.

043 **Clarke Hall and Morrison on Children (2002).** London: *Butterworths*
This comprehensive encyclopaedia (produced in five loose-leaf volumes) gathers together all the legislation, circulars and guidance notes that relate to every aspect of child law, including useful procedural tables, checklists, precedents and flowcharts. Expert commentary and analysis explain and clarify the law throughout and ensure that the reader is fully aware of its practical implications. The work is kept up to date through three revised issues a year and regular monthly bulletins that keep the subscriber informed of the latest legislation and cases. Also see Hershman and McFarlane – ref. 048.

044 **Cullen D and Lane M (2003) Child Care Law: A summary of the law in England and Wales (4th edition).** London: *BAAF*
Quick reference guide to the law in England and Wales

relating to the care of children. Designed to provide a basic framework, it presents a summary of main statutes, regulations and court rules and contains sections on: parents, parental responsibility and private family life; private arrangements for the care of children; child protection; children looked after by local authorities; reviews; representations and complaints; the courts; and adoption.

045 **Department of Health (2002): Adoptions of Children Looked After (2002–03)**
Provides a range of statistics about children adopted, set out in the context of performance assessment indicators for local authorities. Available online through the following web address, which also gives links to a number of other statistics about children in care:
www.dfes.gov.uk/vsgateway/DB/SBU/b000425/index.shtml

046 **Department of Health (2003) The Adoption Site.**
www.dfes.gov.uk/adoption/lawandguidance/adoption/law.htm
This government website introduces all matters relating to adoption under the headings: introduction to adoption, adoption reforms, improving practice, law and guidance, links and addresses, and intercountry adoption.

047 **Duncan W (2000) 'The Hague Convention on Protection of Children and Co-operation in Respect of Intercountry Adoption', in Selman P (ed.) Intercountry Adoption: Developments, trends and perspectives.** London: *BAAF*
This account is given by the Deputy Secretary General of the Hague Conference on International Private Law. It

covers the principles of the Convention, the context in which it needed to be developed and a summary of its operating principles. Footnotes provide some quotations from significant text of the Convention.

048 **Hershman D and McFarlane A (2003) Children Act Handbook 2002.** London: *Jordan Publishing*
A handbook to the Children Act 1989, updated annually.

049 **Hershman D and McFarlane A (2004) Children Law and Practice.** London: *Family Law/Jordans*
Together with *Clarke, Hall & Morrison on Children* (ref. 43), this is generally regarded as the leading reference work on the subject. A similar loose-leaf format allows for regular updates.

050 **Lord J, Barker S and Cullen D (2000) Effective Panels: Guidance on regulations, process and good practice in adoption and permanence panels.** London: *BAAF*
A 60-page guide to law and regulation affecting the roles and responsibilities of adoption panel members, together with guidance on good practice.

051 **Performance and Innovation Unit (2000) Prime Minister's Review of Adoption.** London: *The Cabinet Office*
This study was commissioned by the Prime Minister as part of a major review of adoption. The remit was to provide an initial assessment of the main problem areas, identify options and make recommendations for government policy on the use of adoption for children in the care of local authorities. The study team from the PIU drew on research evidence and contributions from a wide range of

organisations involved in the field. The report contains recommendations to the government and was issued for consultation as part of the process of developing policy.

052 **Adoption and Permanence Taskforce Annual Report, October 2001; Adoption and Permanence Taskforce Second Annual Report, October 2002.**
www.dfes.gov.uk/adoption/adoptionreforms/taskforce.shtml
The Adoption and Permanence Taskforce was set up with the aim of supporting councils in improving their performance on planning for and delivering permanence for looked after children, maximising the use of adoption as an option for meeting the needs of looked after children and providing effective support to all parties affected by adoption, and providing a source of advice and expertise to inform policy development and implementation on adoption and permanence.

053 **Plumtree A (1997) Child Care Law: Scotland – a summary.** London: *BAAF*
This handy reference guide reflects all the changes introduced by the Children (Scotland) Act 1995 and aims to provide a basic framework of the law.

054 **Plumtree A (1999) Getting it Right: Social work reports in adoption proceedings in Scotland.**
London: *BAAF*
Provides comprehensive advice on the preparation and writing of reports for courts in a range of cases: freeings, agency adoptions, non-agency adoptions, Convention adoptions and section 49 applications. Topics covered include over-arching principles, legal requirements, sources of information, some questions answered, layout

of reports, Sheriff Court and Court of Session rules.

055 **Smith F and Brann C with Cullen D (2004) Fostering Now: Current law including regulations, guidance and standards.** London: *BAAF*
Produced in a similar format to *Adoption Now* (ref. 000), this small, compact reference book covers all the legal aspects related to fostering at the time of writing. They include fostering services and registration regulation, fees and inspection regulations and all aspects of the National Minimum Standards for fostering.

056 **Smith F, Stewart R and Cullen D (2003) Adoption Now: Current law including regulations, guidance and standards.** London: *BAAF*
Comprehensive pocket-sized guide to law, regulations, guidance and standards, designed for use by 'all those in England and, unless otherwise indicated, Wales, whose work with children and their families does or might involve adoption'.

The Looking After Children (LAC) system

057 **Bell M (1998) 'The Looking After Children materials: a critical analysis of their use in practice',** *Adoption & Fostering*, 22:4, pp. 15–23
Discusses the use of the LAC materials, based on their use by social work students and practitioners. Overall, the practitioners were positive, reporting their value for the child in recording a detailed history, and in providing a structure for care planning which incorporated the views of all parties. Concerns were raised that the records were not necessarily the most effective or child-

centred way of collecting information, that the questioning could be intrusive and that the forms risked placing some artificial boundaries around some key professional decisions. Explores the extent to which an external agenda for practice has the benefits the promoters suggest, and considers whether an essentially bureaucratic system for recording complex and individualistic judgements can double up as a sensitive practice tool.

058 **Garrett P M (1999) 'Mapping child care social work in the final years of the twentieth century: a critical response to the "Looking After Children" system',** *British Journal of Social Work*, 29:1, pp. 27–47
Offers a critique of the Looking After Children Assessment and Action records. The article suggests the LAC system does not acknowledge the extent to which it is rooted in a particular social and political context: an 'individualised' view of 'troublesome children' and their parents, and operational models of social work from the late 1990s.

059 **Garrett P M (2002) '"Yes Minister": reviewing the "Looking After Children" experience and identifying the messages for social work research',** *British Journal of Social Work*, 32:7, pp. 831–46
A further critique of the LAC system in relation to the argument that it is based on 'objective' research, with particular focus on the Assessment and Action Records.

060 **Smith F and Brann C (2000) Looking After Children: Good parenting, good outcomes.** London: *Children Act Enterprises Ltd*
www.caeuk.org

A pocket-sized guide produced in partnership with the Department of Health.

061 **Wheelaghan S, Hill M, Borland M, Lambert L and Triseliotis J (1999a) Looking After Children in Scotland, Social Work Research Findings No 30.** Edinburgh: *The Scottish Office*
Available online at www.scotland.gov.uk/cru/resfinds/swr30-00.htm
An accessible summary of the findings from the research published in full as Wheelaghan *et al* (1999b).

062 **Wheelaghan S, Hill M, Borland M, Lambert L and Triseliotis J (1999b) The Looking After Children Materials: An evaluation of the Scottish pilot.** Edinburgh: *The Stationery Office*
An evaluation of six Scottish local authorities that introduced the Looking After Children (LAC) materials. Despite certain teething problems, the materials were assessed as a helpful innovation. When used well, the LAC records provide carers with fuller information than has previously been available to them, and enhance their roles, but researchers found some important longer-term practical and communication issues. Effective use of the records is time consuming. Requiring workers to complete information forms 'retrospectively' (i.e. on children already looked after) tends to lead to resentment. The forms can promote engagement with young people. For some the formal layout is off-putting and the timing for raising an issue may not be right. The introduction of LAC highlighted some long-standing difficulties in service organisation or delivery.

Education Protects

Research and practice guidance concerning the education of children in care can be found in Chapters 2 and 3.

063 Department for Education and Employment (DfEE) (2000a) Guidance on the Education of Children and Young People in Public Care. London: *DfES*. Also available online (last visited April 2004) at www.dfes.gov.uk/educationprotects

The joint Department of Health (DH)/DfEE Guidance on the Education of Children and Young People in Public Care (schools must designate a specific teacher to advocate for young people in care and ensure that the guidance is carried out) intended to tackle the under-achievement of children in residential and foster care, aiming to bring their attainment closer to that of their peers. Each child in care should have a Personal Education Plan (PEP) that needs to be initiated by the social worker in conjunction with the young person, teacher and parent. Emphasises the need for high expectations and reiterates that all government departments (including education) are responsible for being "corporate parents". A summary of key messages to schools is also available online (see below).

064 Department for Education and Employment (2000b) Education Protects: Guidance on the education of children and young people in public care: summary for social workers. London: *Department for Education and Employment*
www.dfes.gov.uk/qualityprotects/docs/social.doc

A four-page online summary of key messages to schools from the joint DH/DfEE Guidance on the Education of

Children and Young People in Public Care. A summary for foster carers is also available at www.dfes.gov.uk/qualityprotects/docs/foster.doc

065 **Department for Education and Skills (2004) Education Protects.**
www.dfes.gov.uk/educationprotects
Website for the Education Protects initiative, bringing together statements of rationale, policy documents, relevant research, targets and indicators, and an events diary.

Choice Protects

Choice Protects is a government programme to improve fostering placement choice and stability for looked after children.

066 **Department of Health (2003) Choice Protects.**
www.dfes.gov.uk/choiceprotects
The programme is the responsibility for the Minister for Children, who is within the Department for Education and Skills (DfES), so that this website address is likely to change. The website gives links to relevant publications, accounts of new initiatives and funding, and links to statistical sources. It sets out values and policy options, and presents discussion papers and recent research about fostering. It provides contact details for the Choice Protects project team. Choice Protects also publishes regular update bulletins, available online at
www.dfes.gov.uk/choiceprotects/bulletins.

The Integrated Children's System

The following websites provide information about the Integrated Children's System (ICS). This has been developed by the Department of Health and the Welsh Assembly with the intention of helping social services managers and practitioners improve the outcomes of their work with children and families.

067 www.dfes.gov.uk/integratedchildrenssystem/

068 www.dfes.gov.uk/integratedchildrenssystem/ppt/the-policy-context.ppt

The ICS is intended to take further previous developments such as the Assessment Framework and the LAC materials. The Department for Education and Skills describes it as offering a single approach to undertaking the key processes of assessment, planning, intervention and review, based on an understanding of children's developmental needs in the context of their families and communities. It is strongly emphasised that these are common processes for all agencies. The development of the ICS was first signalled in *Learning the Lessons* (Department of Health, 2000) the government's response to the Waterhouse report, *Lost in Care*, and it is now integral to the development of the Children's National Service Framework.

Managing the supply and demand of placements

069 Audit Commission, Social Services Inspectorate and National Assembly for Wales (2003a) Making Ends Meet: Managing the supply of placements.

www.joint-reviews.gov.uk/money/children/4-26.html

Audit Commission guidance about good practice and best value in foster placements. Advocates a strategic approach to, and gives outline guidance about: developing the council's own placements; broadening the type of placements used (kinship care and specialist foster care); and securing best value from independent providers. Identifies 'beacon councils' in this field and gives links to two 'good practice examples'.

070 **Audit Commission, Social Services Inspectorate and National Assembly for Wales (2003b) Costing Children's Placements.**
www.joint-reviews.gov.uk/money/children/4-28.html
Advice about managing and commissioning foster placements in a particular financial model.

071 **Audit Commission, Social Services Inspectorate and National Assembly for Wales (2003c) Corporate Parenting.**
www.joint-reviews.gov.uk/money/children/4-210.html
A guide, particularly for councillors, about standards in relation to their corporate parenting responsibilities. Sets out a wide range of personal, leadership, corporate and financial responsibilities for councillors, with links to relevant documents.

072 **Beecham J (2000) Unit Costs: Not exactly child's play: a guide to estimating unit costs for children's social care.** London/Totnes/Canterbury: *Department of Health/Dartington Social Research Unit/Personal Social services Research Unit at the University of Kent.*
www.pssru.ac.uk/pdf/B062.pdf
This guide sets out to provide a model of costing (about unit costs, supply and demand, average and marginal

costs) that is intended to be persuasive to financial managers and policy makers whilst doing no violence to the work of social services professionals and the lives of children and carers. It is intended to make the model and procedures accessible and comprehensible to a wide readership of local authority staff, researchers and trainers.

Child migrants

073 www.children.doh.gov.uk/childmigrants/Index.htm
Earlier this century, several thousand British children (usually in the care of voluntary organisations) were sent to former Dominions – mainly Australia, Canada and New Zealand – under several schemes involving the British government, the governments of the receiving countries, and the voluntary organisations which operated the schemes. This site contains details of the initiatives to help former British child migrants, specifically the information index set up to help child migrants find their families and the support fund 'to assist people without means' to re-unite when they have found their family.

Interventions to safeguard and promote the welfare of children

Family placement takes place within a context of promoting and safeguarding the welfare of children. A guide to the literature on this subject would be a library rather than a bibliography; the following references are offered as the briefest of guides.

074 **Department of Health (2000) Framework for the Assessment of Children in Need and Their Families.** London: *The Stationery Office*
The statutory framework within which services are provided to children in need. The title applies both to a single book and to a pack of four books that also includes "practice guidance". All are set out clearly and accessibly.

075 **Department of Health, Home Office and Department for Education and Employment (1999) Working Together to Safeguard Children: A guide to interagency working to safeguard and promote the welfare of children.** London: *The Stationery Office*
The framework for interagency and interdisciplinary work to protect children from abuse or neglect. Available online at www.children.doh.gov.uk/quality5.htm

076 **Bullock R and Little M (2002) 'The contribution of children's services to the protection of children', in Browne K D, Hanks H, Stratton P and Hamilton C (eds.), Early Prediction and Prevention of Child Abuse: A handbook.** Chichester: *John Wiley & Sons*
Recognises that much social intervention on behalf of children in need, whatever their circumstances, is provided not only by social workers but also by health, education and police professionals. Nevertheless, much of the core work and research is carried out within the field of the social services. Highlights the need for changing definitions of intervention because the changing pattern of children's services has invalidated previously held assumptions. Reviews referral processes, inter-agency co-operation, and research on the contribution of services that look after abused and neglected children away from home – highlights the growing know-

ledge base derived from scientifically designed studies and reviews future problems and challenges in child protection.

077 **Cloke C and Davies M (eds.) (1995) Participation and Empowerment in Child Protection.** London: *Pitman*
A collection of contributions that examine the issues and argue for the greater involvement of children and young people in the planning and intervention processes surrounding child protection.

078 **Family Rights Group (undated) Family Group Conferences.** London: *Family Rights Group.* www.frg.org.uk/FGC/FGC.asp.
Family group conferences are decision-making forums that focus on the welfare of the child. They are a mechanism that enables the formal state systems to work in partnership with informal family and community systems, recognising the knowledge and expertise of family and informal systems and professional systems. The process strengthens families and respects and affirms each family's unique cultural experience. See also the references in Chapter 6 to kinship care. FRG has established a Family Group Conference Network (May 1999) to promote FGCs and share practice experience.

079 **Frost N, Lloyd A and Jeffrey L (eds.) (2003) The RHP Companion to Family Support.** Lyme Regis: *Russell House Publishing*
Provides accounts of family support written from academic, policy and practice perspectives. Also contains contributions from local authority perspectives and from

the voluntary sector. Includes: a review of concepts of 'family' relevant to the other areas in this chapter; descriptions of policy and practice developments within the statutory and voluntary sectors; plus nine accounts of practice in varied settings and across a variety of problem areas.

080 **Hetherington R, Cooper A, Smith P and Wilford G (1997) Protecting Children: Messages from Europe.** Lyme Regis: *Russell House Publishing*

An ingenious study design allows for a comparison of the approaches to intervention in families in eight different European systems of child protection. There are commonalities but the English system (at the time of the study) emerges with several very distinctive features that would not universally be seen as positive. The cross-European perspective is thought-provoking about ways of improving approaches to intervention in families to protect children.

081 **Hill M (ed.) (1999) Effective Ways of Working with Children and their Families, Research Highlight in Social Work 35.** London: *Jessica Kingsley*

Reviews the evidence about different ways of working effectively with children and their families. Provides an initial survey of the types of research evidence available and the range of service areas and methods covered in the book. Specialist chapters then focus on different methods and areas of practice, including foster care.

082 **Little M, Axford N and Morpeth L (2003) 'Children's services in the UK 1997–2003: problems, developments and challenges for the future',** *Children & Society*, 17:3, pp. 205–14

Reviews the first five years of New Labour government in the UK: Have promises with respect to children in the UK been delivered, and have developments made any real and potentially lasting difference? It shows that there has been extensive service development, mainly beyond the Department of Health, and directed at targets such as improving preventive services in relation to children's social and psychological problems (for example, Sure Start, Children's Fund, the Youth Justice Board). There has been considerable effort to improve assessment and administrative data. Argues that the approach of providing predominantly low-level interventions to large groups may now need re-thinking.

083 **Smith F (2004) Child Protection: A pocket-sized guide.** London: *Children Act Enterprises Ltd*
www.caeuk.org

Statistics: children in need and children in care

084 **National Statistics Office.** www.statistics.gov.uk
General starting point for official statistics. Navigate through hierarchical links beginning at
www.statistics.gov.uk/CCI/nscl.asp?ID=6285
Links to statistics on Adoptions, Care Orders, Child protection, Disabilities of children looked after; Foster placements and Respite care for children.

085 **Department of Health (2004) Children Looked After by Local Authorities: Year ending 31 March 2003, England and Volume 1: Commentary and national tables.** London: *Department of Health*

086 **Ivaldi G (1998) Children Adopted from Care: An examination of agency adoptions in England–1996.** London: *BAAF*

This ground-breaking study analysed the Department of Health's Children Looked After database to provide the first-ever accurate picture of the pattern of local authority adoptions.

087 **Ivaldi G (2000a) Surveying Adoption: A comprehensive analysis of local authority adoptions 1998–1999.** London: *BAAF*

Ivaldi's second important study provides a comprehensive picture of the numbers, characteristics and histories of looked after children who were adopted in England during 1998–99.

088 **Ivaldi G (2000b) Children and Families in the Voluntary Sector: An overview of child placement and adoption work by the voluntary adoption agencies in England 1994–98.** London: *BAAF*

Scrutinises crucial areas of child placement and adoption work by voluntary adoption agencies, and looks at their specific contribution.

089 **Northern Ireland Department of Health, Social Services and Public Safety (2003) 'Community Statistics – 1 April 2002–March 2003.** Belfast: *Department of Health, Social Services and Public Safety (DHSSPS)*

090 **Scottish Executive (2003) Children's Social Work Statistics 2002–2003.** Edinburgh: *Scottish Executive*

Includes statistics on children looked after and the number of these in family placement. Available online at www.scotland.gov.uk/stats/bulletins/00287-00.asp

091 Scottish Executive (2003) Adoption applications in Scotland. Edinburgh: *The Scottish Executive*
Statistics on the number of adoption and freeing order applications in Scotland.

092 Welsh Assembly (2003) Personal Social Services Statistics: Wales 2003. Cardiff: *National Assembly for Wales*

093 Welsh Assembly (2003) Local Authority Performance Statistics: Social services year ending 31 March 2003 (Statistical Release 59/2003). Cardiff: *National Assembly for Wales*

2 Family placement in general; foster care

This chapter covers subjects that are generically relevant to all forms of family placement. It also lists publications about foster care that do not feature in other chapters. The publications therefore include:

- Those which apply to both adoptive and foster placements.
- Generic works about children in state care. Obviously, these will usually exclude adoption. A number of them refer to foster care in the context of (or in comparison with) residential care.
- Works which are about foster care as a whole – e.g. proposals for standards and regulations.

References specific to permanent placement are included in the next chapter, and various specialist topics are considered in Chapters 4, 5 and 6. Law and regulation are listed separately in Chapter 1.

The books, articles and reports that follow cover a great variety of areas in many different combinations. References about practice include specific topics such as HIV or more general studies of the social worker's responsibilities in relation to children's attachment needs. There are works for use by foster carers and texts about direct work with children.

Although there are still many gaps in our empirical knowledge, there is a significant tradition of research studies of family placement, now including formal reviews using systematic methods such as those by Wilson *et al* (2003) – ref. 193. Studies analyse the varied purpose of different types of placement and how effectively placements actually achieve these purposes. A number of studies report comparisons between different forms of foster care or compare residential and foster care or foster care and adoption.

Many of the publications examine specific issues: contact between children and their birth parents and, in the case of foster care, the impact of such contact on the likelihood of reunification; the educational achievement and health of children who are looked after or adopted; abuse in family placement and its frequency, compared with that of children in their birth families; and the impact of a foster child on the carers' own children. Some of these studies are exploratory, many look for correlations with outcomes (or disruption) and a number make policy recommendations in the light of their findings. They study the different patterns of family placement from the point of view of children, birth parents, adoptive/ foster carers, agencies and then outwards to other stakeholders – the children in birth or placement family, the school, policy makers. Many of the issues need to be considered in the light of the literature in later chapters, for example, the work by Cosis Brown (refs. 657 and 658) in Chapter 5 about assessment and subsequent work with gay and lesbian people.

Increasing numbers of studies aim to present the views of the children or adults involved; we include first-person accounts and works written for and by children, adoptive parents and foster carers.

Although policy and regulatory documents are listed in the previous chapter, many of the publications make policy recommendations, and this chapter includes works whose main purpose is to campaign for change in policy and organisation.

Where to start

The Social Care Institute of Excellence (SCIE), the Quality Protects Programme and Research in Practice (RIP) now rival the excellent example of the Joseph Rowntree Foundation in producing eminently readable, brief and authoritative digests of research alongside the fully referenced reports. The Quality Protects research briefings can be accessed through the Research in Practice web pages (www.rip.org.uk). During the period in which the Bibliography has been in preparation, these organisations have produced important research reviews about family placement (e.g. Wilson *et al* 2004 reviewing 'success in foster care' – ref. 194).

For those with internet access, the Fostering Information Service (www.fostering.org.uk) is relevant at all levels of interest, from first tentative thoughts about fostering, through the assessment process, to briefings about the latest policy or finance changes. The Fostering Network (www.thefostering.net) and BAAF (www.baaf.org.uk) are similarly helpful sources. Each organisation provides introductory leaflets.

General

094 Aldgate J and Simmonds J (1998) Direct Work with Children: A guide for social practitioners. London: *Batsford*

This concise introduction to direct work with children has proved a valuable and popular practice guide for social workers at all levels, and an essential text for social work students. It considers the importance of developing a framework for direct work, the assessment of children's needs, separation and loss, work with emotionally damaged children, permanency planning for older children, racial issues, creative work with adolescents, meeting the needs of workers, introducing direct work with children to area teams, and ending relationships successfully.

095 **BAAF (ed.) (1998) Exchanging Visions: Papers on best practice in Europe for children separated form their birth parents.** London: *BAAF*
This collection of papers from BAAF's first-ever European conference reflects a wide variety of workshop topics, from social policy and the status of children in society to improving the quality of foster care. Contributors include Ravinder Barn, Felicity Collier, Matthew Colton, Annick-Camille Dumaret, Marjut Kosonen and Walter Lorenz.

096 **Baldry S and Kemmis J (1998a) 'What is it like to be looked after by a local authority?',** *British Journal of Social Work*, 28:1, pp. 129–36
A research note of a survey undertaken with young people looked after by a London authority. Describes how the survey was integrated into Quality Assurance systems in the authority. The respondents were ethnically diverse and mainly in foster placements, a significant number in placements with private agencies outside the borough. Most of the young people were positive about their placement and, in relation to the social workers, valued listening, getting things done and showing a genuine interest in them.

097 **Baldry S and Kemmis J (1998b) 'The quality of child care in one local authority: a user study',** *Adoption & Fostering*, 22:3, pp. 34–41

Expanded article based on the above research note and taking into account other studies.

098 **Barber J G, Delfabbro P H and Cooper L L (2001) 'The predictors of unsuccessful transition to foster care',** *Journal of Child Psychology & Psychiatry*, 42:6, pp. 785–90

The placement movements of 235 children entering foster care over a 12-month period were followed up four months after referral into care. Baseline and follow-up measures of the 170 children who were still in care at follow-up were also compared. Results indicated that adolescents with mental health or behavioural issues were the least likely to achieve placement stability or to display improved psychological adjustment in care. In fact, unsatisfactory transition to foster care was found to be so prevalent among these children that conventional foster family care should be considered unsuitable for them. The paper concludes that there is an urgent need for a wider range of alternative care options for the adolescent population.

099 **Batty D (ed.) (1991) Sexually Abused Children: Making their placements work.** London: *BAAF*

This collection of papers discusses a wide range of issues about placement and work with children who have been abused, preparation and support of carers and implications for medical and education services.

100 **Batty D and Wrighton P (1996) Your Child and Foster Care: A guide for birth parents considering private fostering.** London: *BAAF*

Designed to help all parents who may be unable to care for their children and may have to find a private foster carer.

101 **Beek M and Schofield G (2004) Providing a Secure Base in Long-term Foster Care.** London: *BAAF*

Meeting the children's social services objective of 'ensuring that all children are securely attached to carers capable of providing safe and effective care for the duration of childhood' is a major challenge for children in foster care and their carers. Such children have often built defences that make them hard to reach emotionally and need the experience of sensitive parenting and a secure base to heal their sense of hurt and build self-esteem. This study records progress over three years of the group first met in *Growing Up in Foster Care* (ref. 385). The authors describe the varied ways in which foster carers were reaching out to the children, many of whom were beginning to relinquish some of their more troubled behaviours and to accept the possibility that they were loved and lovable.

102 **Benedict M I and White R B (1991) 'Factors associated with foster care length of stay',** *Child Welfare*, 70:1, pp. 45–58

A study that examines factors influencing length of placement.

103 **Berridge D (1997) Foster Care: A research review.** London: *The Stationery Office*

An overview of 20 years' research on foster care primarily focused on the UK. The report analyses the complexity of foster care and provides a summary of the evidence about foster children, placements, parents and families, foster carers, agencies and social workers. The overview compares the situation to 20 years previously and identifies major themes and omissions.

104 **Berridge D (1999) 'Work with fostered children and their families', in Hill M (ed.) Effective Ways of Working with Children and their Families, Research Highlight 35.** London: *Jessica Kingsley*

Reviews the evidence about different ways of working effectively with children living in foster homes. The chapter is part of a book looking at research evidence about the totality of work with children and families. Provides a summary of the context, a review of the nature of the evidence available and a brief summary of the main messages from research in relation to: child-related factors; social networks, parental contact and care careers; and placement-related factors. Recommendations focus on the need to improve the status of foster care.

105 **Biehal N and Wade J (1999) 'Taking a chance? The risks associated with going missing from substitute care',** *Child Abuse Review*, 8:6, pp. 366–76

An empirical study carried out in four local authorities. Subjects were over 200 young people who absented themselves from care arrangements. The study identifies different types of absence, categorises the risks to which the different groups were exposed, and discusses risk management and the difficulty of making realistic assessments of risk.

106 **Bond H (2004) Fostering a Child: A guide for people interested in fostering.** London: *BAAF*

This short guide helps to dispel outdated myths about who can and who can't foster. The author describes the sorts of children needing to be fostered and why, their legal status, who can foster, who to approach if you want to apply, selection, training and getting started, fees and allowances, and what happens when a child moves in and when they return home. Includes a full list of fostering agencies and other useful organisations.

107 **Bond H and Pickerden J (eds.) (2000) The Need to Know: Meeting the communication needs of children in public care: research findings and recommendations for good practice.** London: *Who Cares? Trust*
Highlights the extent to which the review system is the major conduit through which a young person's "voice" is heard organisationally, and how dependent this therefore is on the quality of relationship with the social worker. Foster carers were found to have less involvement in the process.

108 **Bullock R, Little M and Millham S (1998) Secure Treatment Outcomes: The care careers of very difficult adolescents.** Aldershot: *Ashgate*
Discussions and analyses in this book are in the context of the late 1990s, the research data coming from a longitudinal study of over 200 adolescents admitted to long-stay secure treatment units in the 1980s. All the young people were characterised as "very difficult". The book models the life routes (of young person and family), the processes (decisions made by professionals and courts), the career route (the living experiences of the young people consequent upon processes) and the eventual outcomes. The authors conclude that when factors are modelled in this way, outcomes are highly predictable.

109 **Clark H B, Lee B, Prange M and McDonald B A (1996) 'Children lost within the foster care system: Can wraparound service strategies improve placement outcomes?',** *Journal of Child and Family Studies*, 5:1, pp. 39–54

Examines the effectiveness of the "wraparound" approach in better meeting the needs of children in foster care. "Wraparound services" are community based and are creatively tailored to the needs of an individual child, even if the services are part of universal services. "Wraparound" plans are "culturally competent", engage formal, community and informal resources, and are devised by a group of four to ten people, including the child and parents. Services are unconditional – they continue when the needs of the child or family change and are not contingent on "good behaviour". The study found statistically measurable advantages in placement stability. See also refs. 110 and 111.

110 **Clark H B, Prange M, Lee B, Boyd L, McDonald B A and Stewart E (1994) 'Improving adjustment outcomes for foster children with emotional and behavioural disorders: early findings from a controlled study on individualised services',** *Journal of Emotional and Behavioral Disorders*, 2, pp. 207–18

A study focusing specifically on the needs of foster children with emotional and behavioural difficulties. See also refs. 144 and 146.

111 **Clark H B and Hieneman M (1999) 'Comparing the wraparound process with features of positive behavioral support: What we can learn?',** *Journal of Positive Behavioral Interventions*, 1:3, pp. 183–86

Compares a wraparound approach with other interventions about behavioural difficulties. See also refs. 109 and 110.

112 **Cleaver H (1999) 'Contact: the social worker's experience',** *Adoption & Fostering*, 21:4, pp. 34–40
This paper examines issues and practices in relation to contact between foster children and their parents. It looks particularly at the social work task and difficulties, considering the influence of the courts, balancing the needs of children and their parents, supervision, timing, and venue of contact. See also ref. 113.

113 **Cleaver H (2000) Fostering Family Contact.** London: *The Stationery Office*
Presents the findings and discusses the implications of a study of contact in fostering. This involved a retrospective study of social work records in a particular year (in all, over 300 social workers participated) and a prospective study of 32 children. Cleaver reports and analyses a range of factors – for example, although the goal of care is placement stability, sometimes a well-judged change of placement promotes contact and results in better continuity and stability overall; the venue of contact has a significant effect on its value; factors associated with successful contact include continuity of social work support and involvement of foster carers in planning and arrangements; children with more secure attachment before placement tend to have better contact during it (which raises methodological problems in assessing why placements with good contact tend to be more successful than those without).

114 **Corlyon J and McGuire C (1999) Pregnancy and Parenthood: The views and experiences of young people in public care.** London: *National Children's Bureau*

Explores the experiences of young women who become pregnant or parents while in, or soon after leaving, public care. Presents the findings of a three-year study and examines the extent to which they were prepared for parenthood and supported once they became mothers. Also compares the views of a group of young people in care who are neither pregnant nor parents, with those of a group living with their families.

115 **Curtis P A, Alexander G and Lunghofer L A (2001) 'A literature review comparing the outcomes of residential group care and therapeutic foster care',** *Child and Adolescent Social Work Journal*, 18:5, pp. 377–92

Describes the evidence relating to the effectiveness of programmes designed to treat children and young people in residential group care and therapeutic foster care.

116 **Davis E, McKay B, McStae L, Pringle K and Scott S (1991) 'Fostering young people who have been sexually abused', in Batty D, Sexually Abused Children: Making their placements work.** London: *BAAF*

Discusses the support provided through a Crisis and Assessment Placement Service to carers of young people who have been sexually abused.

117 **Department of the Environment, Transport and the Regions (2000) 'Social services: improving standards for children in foster care', in DETR,**

Beacon Council Scheme Round 2 Theme Research. London: *DETR*

Six concise research summaries about the organisation of fostering, including: factors relevant to defining the tasks of foster care; what difficulties authorities face in carrying out these tasks; how successfully foster care meets its tasks; and improving the performance of foster care. Recommendations focus on issues such as placement choice, attention to what precedes and follows foster care, selection, support and training of foster carers. Available online at:
www.odpm.gov.uk/stellent/groups/odpm_localgov/documents/pdf/odpm_locgov_pdf_604823.pdf

118 Department of Health (1991) Patterns and Outcomes in Child Placement. London: *HMSO*

A publication designed to disseminate the results of childcare research. It was published shortly after the introduction of the Children Act 1989, and was written by the team that also produced the guide to Principles and Practice for the Act. Reviews over 50 studies and is structured around the promotion of the child's welfare, partnership and planning.

119 Department of Health (1998) Caring for Children Away from Home: Messages from research. Chichester: *John Wiley & Sons*

This summary of a programme of research is presented as part of a sequence which includes refs. 038 and 118 in this Bibliography and *Child Protection: Messages from Research* (Department of Health, 1995). The book reviews 12 research studies commissioned by the Department of Health, about topics such as secure units (see ref. 108), leaving care (see refs. 286–289), sexually abused and abusing children (see refs. 122 and 251) and absence from care (see 105), and variations between children's homes. The book is primarily about residential care, but its finding are relevant to understanding the experiences and needs of many children who are in family placement, and understanding the systems which have impacted on them.

120 **Fahlberg V (1994, 5th reprint 2004) A Child's Journey through Placement.** London: *BAAF*
A classic text on the experience of children in care and the management of their journey. Includes sections on attachment and bonding, child development, separation and loss, minimising the trauma of moves and direct work with children.

121 **Fanshel D, Finch S J and Grundy J F (1990) Foster Children in Life Course Perspective.** New York: *Columbia University Press*
US study of the Casey Family Program, an early agency specialising in the provision of long-term foster care and the examination of issues affecting it. Contains narrative accounts of past and current users of the service, including accounts of the lives of foster children after they left care, and gives some indication of the philosophy underlying this programme. Includes indications of the extent of physical punishment and sexualised approaches experienced by children, and reports the recommendations made by the people who had used the agency's services.

122 **Farmer E and Pollock S (1998) Sexually Abused and Abusing Children in Substitute Care.** Chichester: *John Wiley & Sons*

Examines how sexually abused and abusing children are managed in foster and residential care. Based on a UK study which drew data from 250 case files and interviews with 40 children, their parents and caregivers. The study identifies patterns of care, of risks and of needs. It uses the study to identify evidence on effectiveness and to make recommendations for good practice.

123 Farmer E, Moyers S and Lipscombe J (2001) The Fostering Task with Adolescents: Report to the Department of Health. Bristol: *School for Policy Studies, University of Bristol*

Study of parenting approaches of 68 foster carers responsible for adolescents, highlighting strategies that significantly affected the placement outcomes. Identifies implications for policy and practice.

124 Fernandez E (1996) Significant Harm: Unravelling child protection decisions and substitute care careers of children. Avebury: *Ashgate*

Documents the child's experience in substitute care from the perspective of child welfare workers and the biological parents and illustrates the use of "event history analysis" to identify those children in care who are in need of special attention.

125 Fisher T, Sinclair I, Gibbs I and Wilson K (2000) 'Sharing the care: the qualities sought of social workers by foster carers', *Child & Family Social Work*, 5:3, pp. 225–34

Material drawn from the larger study – Sinclair *et al*, 2000 (see refs. 173 and 174). Describes the qualities sought of social workers by foster carers and the relationship between these qualities and the likelihood that carers will continue fostering; carers view social workers as a vital source of support.

126 **Fletcher B (1993) Not Just a Name: The views of young people in foster and residential care.** London: *National Consumer Council*
Consumer survey of over 600 children and young people in care. Indicates the importance of directly involving children and young people in planning, decision making and recording about them, and shows how professionals often underestimate their abilities to participate.

127 **Gardner H (1996) 'The concept of family: perceptions of children in family foster care',** *Child Welfare*, 75:2, pp. 161–82
This study of Australian children in substitute family care found that the children consistently regarded their foster family rather than their birth family as "family". See also refs. 131 and 146.

128 **Gilligan R (2000) 'The importance of listening to the child in foster care', in Kelly G and Gilligan R (eds.) Issues in Foster Care: Policy, practice and research.** London: *Jessica Kingsley*
Argues for the importance of prioritising the voice as well as the welfare of the child. Starts from the UN Convention on the Rights of the Child and covers topics such as children's preoccupation with birth parents and siblings, reasons why they are in care, the future, concerns about powerlessness, bullying, etc.

129 **Hayden C, Goddard J, Gorin S and van der Spek N (1999) State Child Care: Looking after children?** London: *Jessica Kingsley*

This account of state care in the UK is based on four empirical research studies. The chapters include: a general account of "coming into care", both residential and family based; developments in foster care, including professional foster care; and issues of behaviour, education and aftercare – each dealt with in relation to residential and substitute family care.

130 **Head A and Elgar M (1999) 'The placement of sexually abused and abusing siblings', in Mullender A (ed.), We Are Family: Sibling relationships in placement and beyond.** London: *BAAF*
Presents the findings of a detailed study involving 51 children from 24 families. Issues surrounding separation, sexually abusive behaviour, contact and caring for siblings together are discussed.

131 **Heptinstall E, Bhopal K and Brannen J (2001) 'Adjusting to a foster family: children's perspectives',** *Adoption & Fostering*, 25:4, pp. 6–16
Studies the views of family life held by children who are in foster or residential care. Comparisons with children living with at least one birth parent show that in some respects looked after children's perspectives of family life reflect their adverse early experiences, while in other ways their interpretation of their situation is based on common perceptions they share with other children. See also ref. 127.

132 **Hill M (ed.) (1999) Signposts in Fostering: Policy, practice and research issues.** London: *BAAF*
A collection of papers previously published in BAAF's quarterly journal, *Adoption & Fostering*. Includes contributions on local authority fostering in Wales;

specialist fostering; developing leaving care services; recruiting and retaining foster carers; gender, sex and sexuality in the assessment of prospective carers; assessing Asian families in Scotland; involving birth parents in foster care training; using respite care to prevent long-term family breakdown; short-term family-based care for children in need; meeting the needs of sibling groups in care; fostering as seen by the carers' children; the role of social workers in supporting and developing the needs of foster carers; education of children in foster care; the health of children looked after by the local authority; foster carers who cease to foster; and the implications of recent childcare research findings for foster care.

133 Hill M (ed.) (2002) Shaping Childcare Practice in Scotland: Key papers in adoption and fostering. London: *BAAF*

This collection brings together seminal papers that have contributed to shaping childcare practice in Scotland since 1980. First published in BAAF's *Adoption & Fostering* journal, these cover trends in child placement philosophy, children's legislation in Scotland, perspectives on adoption, post-adoption services and issues, perspectives on foster care, placement outcomes and assessment and meeting children's needs.

134 Jackson S (2002) 'Promoting stability and continuity in care away from home', in McNeish D, Newman T and Roberts H (eds.), What Works for Children? Effective services for children and families. Buckingham: *Open University Press*

This chapter is a forceful promotion of the need to create stability for children cared for by the state. It examines the meaning of "stability", the evidence for its significance and what works to promote it. Argues that "continuity of care" should be the default position in decision making, highlighting research that the average number of placements for children in care in the UK increased between 1995 and 2000 (see refs. 135 and 136).

135 **Jackson S and Thomas N (1999) On the Move Again? What works in creating stability for looked after children?** Ilford: *Barnardo's*
Reviews the research as at 1999 about stability for looked after children, identifying factors associated with stability and instability.

136 **James G (1994) The Children Act 1989, Contact Orders Study: Experiences in local authorities of public law applications involving issues of contact for children with their parents and families.** London: *Department of Health*
Report from the Social Services Inspectorate about the views and decisions of local authority staff and guardians ad litem in relation to court work involving contact issues (excludes work which was solely concerned with private law).

137 **Jonson-Reid M and Barth R P (2000) 'From placement to prison: the path to adolescent incarceration from child welfare supervised foster or group care',** *Children and Youth Services Review*, 22:7, pp. 493–516
A US longitudinal study of outcomes for young people in residential or foster care. Examines the incidence of imprisonment for serious or violent offences as a post-

discharge outcome. Children/young people first placed between the ages of 12 and 15 and those with multiple placements had a higher risk of incarceration for a serious or violent offence during adolescence. The risk for different ethnic groups changed according to gender and the type of foster care experience. Makes recommendations for future research and service delivery. A study quoted in Wilson *et al* (2003 – ref. 193).

138 Kagan R (1996) Turmoil to Turning Points: Building hope for children in crisis placements.
New York: *W W Norton*
A comprehensive US overview, using an ecological model, of work to create safety for vulnerable children, particularly those placed in foster care in emergency situations. Emphasises partnership with families, proactive involvement of parents and use of community networks in the context of case conferences and protection plans.

139 Kalland M, Pensola T H, Meriläinen J and Sinkkonen J (2001) 'Mortality in children registered in the Finnish child welfare registry: population-based study', *British Medical Journal*, 323:7306, pp. 207–8
This Finnish study found that children in foster care are more likely to die from causes such as suicide, accidents or substance misuse than other children.

140 Kapp S A and Propp J (2002) 'Client satisfaction methods: input from parents with children in foster care', *Child and Adolescent Social Work Journal*, 19:3, pp. 227–45
An article concerned with the evaluation of the service

experience of parents who have had their children placed in foster care. The authors describe the methods used to develop a client satisfaction instrument. The psychometrics of the instrument, the information generated from its use, a descriptive profile of the satisfaction scores of the respondents, some relationships between apparently distinct aspects of client satisfaction and service implications are described.

141 **Kapp S and Vela H (2004) 'The unheard client: assessing the satisfaction of parents of children in foster care',** *Child & Family Social Work*, 9:2, pp. 197–207

Outlines the development of an instrument designed to measure the satisfaction of parents whose children have been placed in foster care and discusses the information it generated.

142 **Kelly G and Gilligan R (eds.) (2000) Issues in Foster Care: Policy practice and research.** London: *Jessica Kingsley*

Nine papers present an overview of fostering. In particular, they analyse the importance of long-term foster care, outcome studies, safety and protection from abuse, managing children's behaviour and "relative care" (examining the differences between relative care and traditional foster care and between relative care and informal family network care). Also see ref. 362.

143 **Kelly G (2000) 'Outcome studies of foster care', in Kelly G and Gilligan R (eds.),** as above

Presents a summary of the outcomes of foster care identified in research and the issues involved. Includes a study of variables such as the length of care, outcomes for "professional foster care", the impact of family contact during placement and the influence of values on research outcomes and their interpretation.

144 Kerr K (2000) 'Managing children's behaviour in foster care', in Kelly G and Gilligan R (eds.), as above

Focuses on "Applied Behaviour Management" (an ABC approach) with little discussion of emotional experience or development related to the occurrence of foster care, its antecedents and sequels (although this is dealt with elsewhere in this edited collection).

145 Kirton D (2001) 'Love and money: payment, motivation and the fostering task', *Child & Family Social Work*, 6:3, pp. 199–208

This UK study is based on interviews with 20 female carers and explores the place of payment within foster care. Kirton charts how carers perceive their task as "parenting" or "a job", whether and how they experience payment as compensation or as an appropriate reward for their skills. Also examined are the ways in which remuneration may impact upon the practice of foster care, for example in decision-making over the taking or ending of placements and the provision of aftercare support for care leavers. The study highlights the distinctive nature of foster care as an institution that straddles the public and private domains, and examines the resulting complexities. It concludes by suggesting that while payment issues provide important threads that run throughout foster care, their influence is ultimately limited by the latter's base within the family.

146 Kufeldt K, Armstrong J and Dorosh M (1995) 'How children in care view their own and their foster families: a research study', *Child Welfare*, 74:3, pp. 695–715

A study about the meaning of "family" to children living in foster care. See also refs. 127 and 131.

147 Lambert C (2001) Promoting Resilience in "Looked After Children". Norwich: *University of East Anglia*

Addresses the question of why it is that some children arrive at adaptive outcomes despite risk and adversity while others fail to do so. Particular emphasis is placed on children in the public care system who are looked after, in order to discover the ways in which their life chances can be improved by using a resilience-led approach to practice.

148 Leathers S J (2002) 'Foster children's behavioral disturbance and detachment from caregivers and community institutions', *Children and Youth Services Review*, 24:4, pp. 239–68

US statistical study examining correlations between behavioural difficulties of children and certain of their experiences in foster care, characterised as "community participation". The latter included features such as attachment to caregivers, involvement in schools and churches, and few moves. Some correlations were found, with different factors for girls and boys; placement movement was correlated with behavioural difficulties for both.

149 **Lewandowski C A and Pierce L (2002) 'Assessing the effect of family-centred out-of-home care on reunification outcomes',** *Research on Social Work Practice*, 12:2, pp. 205–21
A research study examining the effectiveness of one family-centred approach developed by Missouri's Department of Family Services.

150 **Maluccio A N, Ainsworth F and Thoburn J (2000) Child Welfare Outcome Research in the United States, United Kingdom and Australia.** Washington, DC: *Child Welfare League of America*
Includes comparisons of outcome research about foster care in the USA, Australia and the UK. Reviews studies of treatment foster care and kinship foster care as well as studies of adoption and family reunification.

151 **Marsh P and Triseliotis J (eds.) (1993) Prevention and Reunification in Child Care.** London: *BAAF/Batsford*
Collection of papers exploring a range of topics including partnership, family support (including respite care), the differing experiences of black and white children and families, support groups and children and parents in the care system.

152 **McNeish D, Newman T and Roberts H (eds.) (2002) What Works for Children? Effective services for children and families.** Buckingham: *Open University Press*
Part of an initiative to promote evidence-based social care. The first section of the book is devoted to research about the care of children away from their birth parents; includes chapters on the evidence about family place-

ment services, about promoting stability and continuity in care away from home and about leaving care.

153 **Morris S and Wheatley H (1994) Time to Listen: The experiences of young people in foster and residential care: a ChildLine study.** London: *ChildLine*

Reports on an analysis of calls made to ChildLine by 676 young people in care and the results of 63 interviews face to face. Includes accounts from young people as well as recommendations to local authorities.

154 **Mullender A (ed.) (1999) We are Family: Sibling relationships in placement and beyond.** London: *BAAF*

Taking decisions about separating or keeping groups of brothers and sisters together is one of the most challenging tasks facing childcare social workers. They try to balance a mix of competing needs and perspectives while struggling to find suitable placements. This anthology brings together findings from a range of research studies, together with the first-hand accounts of siblings, adopters and professionals to offer an evidence-base for these complex decisions.

155 **National Foster Care Association (1999a) Code of practice on the recruitment, assessment, approval, training, management and support of foster carers.** London: *NFCA*

Produced by a sub-group of the UK Joint Working Party on Foster Care, this code of practice sets out the measures necessary to protect vulnerable children in foster care. It is designed to be used by anyone working in or responsible for the delivery of foster care services, whether in a local authority, independent or voluntary agency. See also refs. 156 and 157 below.

156 **National Foster Care Association (1999b) Report and Recommendations of the UK Joint Working Party on Foster Care.** London: *NFCA*
The UK Joint Working Party on Foster Care was formed in order to promote and improve the quality of foster care in the UK, with the backing of the Department of Health and the Scottish Office. Taking in the views of all stakeholders, including fostered children, the working party produced a code of practice, a good practice guide and proposed National Standards. This report makes a number of recommendations on the future of services for vulnerable children and young people including the introduction of regulation for fostering services.

157 **National Foster Care Association (1999c) UK National Standards for Foster Care.** London: *NFCA*
The Standards include 25 good practice benchmarks covering children, foster carers and local authorities, among them measures intended to ensure better educational outcomes for children, preparation, training, ongoing support and regular reviews of foster carers and improved complaints procedures.

158 **Newton R R, Litrownik A J and Landsverk J (2000) 'Children and youth in foster care: disentangling the relationship between problem behaviors and number of placements',** *Child Abuse and Neglect*, 24:10, pp. 1363–74
This US study followed a sample of 415 fostered young people in California who remained in placement for at least five months. The results suggest that lack of

stability in placements contributes negatively to both the internalising and externalising behaviour of foster children, and that children who experience numerous changes in placement may be at particularly high risk. The conclusion that behaviour problems are both the cause and a consequence of placement disruption is hardly new, but the article also sheds light on whether poor outcomes in state care are the result of prior family experiences or are caused by the "care" experience.

159 **Packman J and Hall C (1998) From Care to Accommodation: Support, protection and control in child care services.** London: *The Stationery Office*
Examines some of the key changes introduced by the Children Act 1989 and their impact on families, children and social services departments.

160 **Padbury P and Frost N (2002) Solving Problems in Foster Care: Key issues for young people, foster carers and social services.** London: *The Children's Society*
Based on a research study of 61 young people (aged 8–18) in foster care, their carers and social workers in three local authorities. The study investigated how problem-solving was undertaken by the participants and how managers and policies were influenced by the outcomes. The concerns of the young people were more acute about issues specific to being in care than to concerns generic to all young people. The majority of young people and carers felt well supported, but a significant minority did not. For each group who participated in the research, the report lists factors that worked and those that did not assist in problem-solving. In relation to (service) feedback and

complaint mechanisms, it was found that these exist but are not working well.

161 **Palmer S E (1990) 'Group treatment of foster children to reduce separation conflicts associated with placement breakdown',** *Child Welfare*, 69:3, pp. 227–38
Describes group work with young people in substitute care and uses the material from the therapeutic work to highlight the issues which were consistently poorly addressed (or not tackled) by the social work agencies.

162 **Perez-del-Aguila R, Holland S, Faulkner A, Connell D and Hayes S (2004) Overview and Survey of Effectiveness of Interventions to Promote Stability and Continuity of Care for Looked After Children: Final report.** Cardiff: *Cardiff University School of Social Sciences*
Report of a project involving telephone interviews with local authorities and voluntary agencies that set out to examine how managers responded to the challenge of providing stable care for vulnerable children.

163 **Pithouse A, Jones E, Crowley A, Smail P and Butler I (2000) A Study of the Placement of Looked After Children in Wales.** Cardiff: *Cardiff University School of Social Sciences*
Presents the results of a study examining the number of children in public care in Wales and the services they receive.

164 **Pithouse A and Parry O (1997) 'Fostering in Wales: the all-Wales review',** *Adoption & Fostering*, 21:2, pp. 41–9

Reviews fostering services as at 1994 across the then eight Welsh county councils, highlighting both the commonalities and variations in approaches to family support and family placement.

165 **Rhodes K W, Orme J G and Buehler C (2001) 'A comparison of family foster parents who quit, consider quitting and plan to continue fostering',** *Social Service Review*, 75:1, pp. 84–114

US study examining why some foster carers continue while others stop. Reasons for stopping include poor agency support, poor communication with social workers, lack of authority in decision making and difficulties with children's behaviour. In comparison with continuing foster parents, the foster carers who stopped reported less training and fewer "mentor arrangements" with existing foster carers; those who plan to cease reported greater need for financial and childcare support than continuing and former foster parents. There are comparable concerns in US and UK foster care, but there are also a number of differences between the contexts.

166 **Rowe J, Hundleby M and Garnett L (1989) Child Care Now: A survey of placement patterns.** London: *BAAF*

Although only just within the time limits of this bibliography, this study is included because of the detailed picture it provides. Among the findings: 27 per cent of placements planned as long term disrupted in the first year (4 per cent of preschool placements, 38 per cent of

14–15-year-olds); in comparing outcomes for specialist and general placements for adolescents, 50 per cent of specialist placements 'achieved their goals'. There were also fewer planned short-term placements in the specialist provision.

167 Roy P, Rutter M and Pickles A (2000) 'Institutional care: risk from family background or pattern of rearing?', *Journal of Child Psychology & Psychiatry*, 41:2, pp. 139–49

A report of the findings of a study comparing the relative importance of risk from early family backgrounds with the risk associated with different patterns of care. A group of children placed in residential care was compared to a group in foster care. Levels of hyperactivity/inattention were high in both substitute care groups but highest in the residential group. The authors argue that against a background of genetic and early environmental risk, residential care is more likely to lead to a pattern of hyperactivity/inattention. This article is important in influencing the debate about the role of genetics and environment.

168 Sellick C and Thoburn J (1996) What Works in Family Placement? Ilford: *Barnardo's*

One of a series of publications intended to promote evidence-based practice in social work. Surveys the range of tasks undertaken in family placement and analyses the nature and sources of evidence in this field. Indicates the range of outcome measures which can be used (client outcome measures, satisfaction measures and service outcome measures) and different possible study designs. Presents its main findings according to "task-focused temporary foster care" and "long-term family placement". Published in 1996, this is updated by Sellick and Thoburn, 2002 below.

169 **Sellick C and Thoburn J (2002) 'Family placement services', in McNeish D, Newman T and Roberts H (eds.), What Works for Children? Effective services for children and families.** Buckingham: *Open University Press*
Supplements and updates Sellick and Thoburn (1996). Reviews research under the headings of Temporary (supplementary) Foster Care and Permanent Family Placement. Provides a research-based profile of "supplementary care" (e.g. it is the most common type of placement for looked after children, the increasing importance of kinship care and up to half of children are placed with single carers). Summarises findings about recruitment (e.g. success is associated with targeted schemes), assessment, training, support and policy. Examines permanent placement in relation to the decision-making process (e.g. age at placement is a determining factor, delay in the process is usually less so) and the (generally inconclusive) studies about practice.

170 **Shaw C (1998) Remember My Messages: The experiences and views of 2000 children in public care in the UK.** London: *Who Cares? Trust*
Original report of study also listed below as Shaw (2003). A national questionnaire survey (by the Who Cares? Trust) of 2,073 young people and children aged 8–20 in care. In a clear, easy-to-read presentation, the report provides quantitative analysis of answers about education, health and other aspects of the care system. Includes messages about what would have made the experience better.

171 **Shaw C (2003) 'Remember My Messages: The experience and views of 2000 children in public care in the UK', in Reynolds J, The Managing Care Reader.** London: *Routledge*
See also Shaw (1998) ref. 170.

172 **Shemmings D (ed.) (1999) Involving children in family support and child protection.** London: *The Stationery Office*
Presents research findings and ideas for developing practice in 18 short chapters.

173 **Sinclair I, Baker C, Wilson K and Gibbs I (2003) What Happens to Foster Children: Final report to the Department of Health.** York: *Social Work Research and Development Unit*
See Sinclair *et al* (2000) ref. 174.

174 **Sinclair I, Wilson K and Gibbs I (2000) Supporting Foster Placements: Reports 1 and 2.** York: *University of York, Social Work Research and Development Unit*
Part of a series of works that set out to model the factors that contribute to foster care success. Examines over 500 foster placements in seven English local authorities. (Twenty-four per cent were single carers, of whom 55 per cent were from minority ethnic groups; short-term unplanned placements were less successful than planned placements, but after the placements lasted a year this was not so; 30 per cent of short-term carers had placements lasting over a year; more than 50 per cent of children referred for placement had behavioural or emotional problems and ten per cent were disabled or had health problems.) The study used statistical analysis to identify relevant factors and to report on what

contributed to success or otherwise of placements. Overall, the researchers report how impressed they were both with the children's appraisal of their placements and the commitment of the carers. They analyse the different types of foster care which will continue to be needed and set out a model that uses children's contributions, carers' contributions and "matching, fit and interaction". See also refs. 173, 175–177.

175 Sinclair I, Wilson K and Gibbs I (2001) '"A life more ordinary": what children want from foster placements', *Adoption & Fostering*, 25:4, pp. 17–26

Based on their own study findings, the authors discuss the criteria that foster care needs to meet if it is to fulfil the requirements of looked after children. Analysis of 150 postal questionnaires from foster children showed five main preoccupations: the care they received from their foster families; the relationship between their feelings for their foster and their birth families; their contact with and prospects of return to their birth families; the predictability of their care careers and their own say in them; and the "ordinariness" or lack of it in their lives. Despite these common preoccupations, the children varied widely in what they wanted (e.g. whether they wanted to return home). See also refs. 174, 176, 177 and 193.

176 Sinclair I and Wilson K (2003) 'Matches and mismatches: the contribution of carers and children to the success of foster placements', *British Journal of Social Work*, 33:7, pp. 871–84

Further publications from the work of this group to model the factors that contribute to successful fostering. Data collected on 472 foster children identified a number of characteristics that were associated with successful placements. These included: encouraging the child to feel that they have chosen the placement; the child's characteristics (e.g. difficult behaviours and lack of obviously appealing characteristics were seen as problematic and as a matter for training); the importance of foster carers as the keys to a successful placement has important implications for their selection, training and support. Also see refs. 174, 175, 177 and 193.

177 Sinclair I, Wilson K and Gibbs I (2004) Foster Placements: Why they succeed and why they fail. London: *Jessica Kingsley*
Publication in book form of findings from this group. It includes accounts from children, carers and social workers, and discussion of ways that support can be tailored to the individual needs and characteristics of the child. Also see refs. 173–176 and 193.

178 Thoburn J, Sellick C and Philpot T (2004) What Works in Adoption and Foster Care? London: *BAAF*
This revised volume from Barnardo's "What Works" series aims to help managers and practitioners in family and childcare social work to make practical decisions, based on sound evidence about where to place children and what sort of practice is most likely to bring about the desired outcomes for children, birth relatives, foster carers and the adoptive family.

179 Triseliotis J (1989) 'Foster care outcomes: a review of key research findings', *Adoption & Fostering*, 13:3, pp. 5–17
Highlights changes in fostering philosophy and in the light of this, reviews studies relating to long-term and

short-term foster care, intermediate and mainstream fostering. Identifies predictive factors that are child related, foster-placement related, birth related and agency related. Available online at:
195.195.162.66/dbtw-wpd/documents/articles/0003243.txt

180 **Triseliotis J, Borland M and Hill M (1998a) 'Foster carers who cease to foster',** *Adoption & Fostering*, 22:2, pp. 54–61
Despite the long history of formal fostering in Britain, no systematic study had been carried out to ascertain the rate of annual losses incurred when carers leave the services and to establish reasons for this. This article is based on a wider study of foster care and foster carers in Scotland that tried to rectify the situation. See also refs. 165 and 181–183.

181 **Triseliotis J, Borland M and Hill M (1998b) Fostering Good Relations: A study of foster care and foster carers in Scotland: interim report of a study of foster carers, Social Work Research Findings 22.** Edinburgh: *Scottish Executive Central Research Unit*
Interim report of first phase of a study examining foster care and foster carers in Scotland. The study aimed to explore issues of recruitment and retention of carers. This first phase involved a postal survey in 1996 of 822 active and 96 former foster carers about their characteristics, experiences and views of the fostering services (see Triseliotis *et al*, 1999a and 1999b). Available online at:
www.scotland.gov.uk/cru/documents/rs22-01.htm

182 **Triseliotis J, Borland M and Hill M (1999a) Fostering Good Relations: A study of foster care and foster carers in Scotland, Social Work Research Findings 34.** Edinburgh: *Scottish Executive Central Research Unit*
Reports on an important study, carried out in 1997. The first part (ref. 181) reported on 835 foster carers in Scotland. The second part focuses on the organisation and structure of fostering services in 32 local authorities. Includes findings about policy, recruitment, assessment, financial issues and quality systems (see also ref. 183). Summary available online at:
www.scotland.gov.uk/cru/resfinds/swr34-00.htm

183 **Triseliotis J, Borland M and Hill M (1999b) Delivering Foster Care.** London: *BAAF*
Report of the study which is the subject also of refs. 181 and 182 above. Involving 835 foster carers and 32 local authorities, the book examines the characteristics, motives and social circumstances of active and former foster carers; investigates retention and loss; describes the experience of fostering, including contact issues between parents and children; and evaluates post-placement support and general experiences of the fostering service. The organisational study examines organisation, structure and policies, recruitment, assessment and matching of children, financial issues and quality systems.

184 **Triseliotis J, Borland M, Hill H and Lambert L (1995) Teenagers and the Social Work Services.** London: *HMSO*
Based on a three-year study that examined programmes of care and supervision for 116 teenagers aged 13–17

who became subject to social services intervention. Includes discussion of the problems and expectations set, the evaluation of services by key participants and the identification of important policy, practice and training implications.

185 **Triseliotis J, Sellick C and Short R (1995) Foster Care: Theory and practice.** London: *Batsford*
The authors provide a valuable overview of the foster care field by bringing together many strands of theory and practice into one accessible volume. All aspects of the field are examined, including the institution and practice of foster care, recruitment and training of foster carers, the assessment of foster carers and working with families towards reunification.

186 **Utting W, Rose N and Pugh G (2001) Better Results for Children and Families: Involving communities in planning services based on outcomes.** London: *NCVCCO*
Argues for a change in service development to allow more co-ordination between education, health and social services.

187 **Vuchinich S, Ozretich, R A, Pratt C C and Kneedler B (2002) 'Problem-solving communication in foster families and birth families',** *Child Welfare*, 81:3, pp. 571–94
Compares parent–child problem-solving communication within foster families and within birth families. Found that patterns within foster families in general were similar to those within "low-risk" birth families.

188 **Warren D (1999) 'Setting new national standards for foster care',** *Adoption & Fostering*, 23:2, pp. 48–56
Discusses the background and implications of the Foster Care Standards initiative, launched in England in June 1999.

189 **Waterhouse S (1997) The Organisation of Fostering Services: A study of the arrangements for delivery of fostering services by local authorities in England.** London: *National Foster Care Association*
Examining fostering arrangements in 94 English local authorities, the study demonstrated a deficit in the number and range of foster carers available. The growth in kinship care is documented. Recommendations are made about the factors associated with good practice, stability and foster carer retention.

190 **Watson A and Jones D (2002) 'The impact of fostering on foster carers' own children',** *Adoption & Fostering*, 26:1, pp. 49–55
Presents the results of a survey of over 100 children of foster parents. Highlights the negative effects on some children and emphasises the importance of family placement staff and other childcare social workers paying attention to the needs of the birth children of foster carers.

191 **Wheal A (ed.) (1999) The RHP Companion to Foster Care.** Lyme Regis: *Russell House Publishing*
Topics range from studies of the changing perception of childhood to current issues in fostering. These include educational achievement of children in care, identity issues, organisation of fostering services, fostering of

siblings, professional foster care, child protection and training.

192 **Wheal A (2000) The Foster Carer's Handbook.** Lyme Regis: *Russell House Publishing*
This handbook has been produced for foster and residential carers in England and Wales who are looking after children under 11. Written in an accessible style, with checklists and practical exercises for the young people to use, it aims to help carers understand and implement many of the requirements of the Children Act 1989. Prepared in consultation with BAAF, CCETSW and NFCA.

193 **Wilson K, Petrie S and Sinclair I (2003) 'A kind of loving: a model of effective foster care',** *British Journal of Social Work*, 33:8, pp. 991–1003
This paper is built on a statistical study that analysed factors leading to successful placements (see also refs. 173–177). A model of successful foster caring is developed focusing on three aspects of the foster placement: those relating to the child, the foster carer and the interaction between the two. In particular they develop the notion of responsive parenting characterised by handling attachment, reinforcing socially acceptable self-esteem and identity and handling difficult behaviour appropriately as key variables.

194 **Wilson K, Sinclair I, Taylor C, Pithouse A and Sellick C (2004) Fostering Success: An exploration of the research literature in foster care.** London: *SCIE*
Makes use of nearly 300 studies to review the research about the outcomes or consequences of foster care. The

authors worked with three consultation groups of foster carers and young people throughout the study. Also available online at www.scie.org.uk, both in full and in summary form.

195 **Wilson K, Sinclair I and Gibbs I (2000) 'The trouble with foster care: the impact of stressful "events" on foster carers',** *British Journal of Social Work*, 30:2, pp. 193–209

This study reports on a postal survey of 950 foster carers designed to document the proportions who had experienced one or more of six stressful "events": breakdowns or disruptions, allegations, relationship with birth parents, family tensions, "tug of love" cases and other disagreements with social workers. More than three-quarters of those who had fostered for five years had experienced at least one of these events. In relation to allegations the overwhelming response was that it was not so much the allegation itself but lack of information, exclusion from the proceedings and poor feedback that distressed foster carers the most.

196 **Wright L E and Seymour C (2000) Working with Children and Families Separated by Incarceration: A handbook for child welfare agencies.** Washington, DC: *Child Welfare League of America*

Examines the impact of parental incarceration in the USA and suggests ways in which families can be preserved and supported.

197 **Youth Justice Board (2003) Young People who Sexually Abuse.** London: *Youth Justice Board*

Principles and practice in working with adult sex offenders cannot simply be transferred to working with young people because there is a danger that it excludes the developmental aspect of their offending. This guide emphasises that to reduce the likelihood of a young person re-offending, it is necessary to explore their abuse through an "holistic" approach, through consideration of their entire life – their environment, their home, their school and their community. When working with young people who sexually abuse it is essential that a multi-agency approach is adopted, using provision and colleagues from a range of other services including the NHS, social services and probation. See also refs. 122 and 251.

Health and mental health

Many outcome studies consider the health and emotional well-being of children who are fostered. Studies that focus exclusively on these areas are grouped in this section. In addition, most of the references in Chapter 6 are relevant to the emotional well-being and emotional distress of children in family placement.

198 Arcelus J, Bellerby T and Vostanis P (1999) 'A mental health service for young people in the care of the local authority', *Clinical Child Psychology and Psychiatry*, 4:2, pp. 233–45
Describes the development and results of a direct access mental health service for children and young people living in residential or foster care.

199 BAAF (1999) Hepatitis and HIV: Issues related to substitute care, foster care, residential care and adoption, Practice Note 39. London: *BAAF*

A leaflet in the Practice Notes series from BAAF, providing information on issues about HIV and AIDS in relation to substitute care.

200 **Butler I and Payne H (1997) 'The health of children looked after by the local authority',** *Adoption & Fostering*, 21:2, pp. 28–35
Presents findings from a local study of the form and practice of statutory medical examinations for children looked after by the local authority.

201 **Dimigen G, Del Priore C, Butler S, Evans S, Ferguson L and Swan M (1999) 'Psychiatric disorder among children at time of entering local authority care: questionnaire survey',** *British Medical Journal*, 319:7211, pp. 675
This study reports a survey of 89 children aged 5–12 who entered care and for whom health assessments were requested over a nine-month period in Glasgow. Nearly 40 per cent showed elevated levels of "conduct disorder" or depression and 27 per cent showed "very elevated" scores on both. "Very high" levels of depression were more common in those entering residential than foster care. The study was part of the planning for an early intervention programme.

202 **McCann J, James A, Wilson S and Dunn G (1996) 'Prevalence of psychiatric disorders in young people in the care system',** *British Medical Journal*, 313:7071, pp. 1529–30
This study examined a cohort of all children aged 13–17 looked after in Oxfordshire and compared measures of psychiatric disorder in this group with a randomly chosen group matched for age, sex and school/GP

practice. Researchers found high levels of problems, including undiagnosed potentially treatable conditions.

203 **Mather M (ed) (2002) 'Promoting children's health', Special Issue.** *Adoption & Fostering*, 26:4
Includes articles on the interface between medicine and social work in working with looked after children, the role of the specialist nurse, vaccination and immunisation and constructing mental health services for looked after children.

204 **Mather M, Batty D and Payne H (2000) Doctors for Children in Public Care: A resource guide advocating, protecting and promoting health.** London: *BAAF*
A resource guide (with training materials) for doctors and other health professionals looking after children in public care. Links to the requirements of Quality Protects and 'promotes good health and well-being using a holistic approach'. Among the issues addressed are the health needs of looked after children, statutory health needs assessment, planning for better health, listening to young people's views, adult health issues including those that are controversial, the role of primary health care and the GP as medical adviser, confidentiality and medical record-keeping; and the role of the medical adviser in the looked after children system. Includes service specifications and practice standards for medical advisers to looked after children.

205 **Mather M, Humphrey J and Robson J (1997) 'The statutory medical and health needs of looked after children: time for a radical review?',** *Adoption & Fostering*, 21:2, pp. 301–10

The authors argue that, despite specific UK legislation and the considerable resources allocated to meeting the health needs of looked after children over the years, there are a number of elements hindering the system. They identify these by first analysing the medical examinations of looked after children carried out in one London borough over a two-year period. This analysis is followed by a review of key findings from a survey and a series of group discussions with young people, aimed at establishing concerns and priorities from the point of view of themselves as "consumers".

206 **Meltzer H, Gatward R, Corbin T, Goodman R and Ford T (2003) The Mental Health of Young People Looked After by Local Authorities in England: The report of a survey carried out in 2002 by the Survey Division of the Office for National Statistics on behalf of the Department of Health.** London: *The Stationery Office*
The first part of the report focuses on the prevalence rates of mental disorders among young people looked after by local authorities. The second part shows the way in which children and adolescents with particular disorders vary from those without that disorder on a range of factors including their background, personal and familial characteristics, physical health, use of services and social functioning. Available online at: www.statistics.gov.uk/downloads/theme_health/ChildrensMentalHlth.pdf

207 **Meltzer H, Lader D, Corbin T, Goodman R and Ford T (2004a) The Mental Health of Young People Looked After by Local Authorities in Scotland: The report of a survey carried out in**

2002/2003 by the Office for National Statistics on behalf of the Scottish Executive. London: *The Stationery Office*
Presents the findings of the first national survey of the mental health of looked after children and young people in Scotland. The survey involved 355 looked after children aged between 5 and 17 years and was intended to examine the prevalence of mental disorders and the impact on children and service providers. Available online at:
www.statistics.gov.uk/downloads/theme_health/Mentalhealth_Scotland.pdf

208 **Meltzer H, Lader D, Corbin T, Goodman R and Ford T (2004b) The Mental Health of Young People Looked After by Local Authorities in Wales: The report of a survey carried out in 2002/2003 by the Office for National Statistics on behalf of the Welsh Assembly Government.** London: *The Stationery Office*
Presents the findings of the first national survey of the mental health of looked after children and young people in Wales. This involved 149 looked after children aged between 5 and 17 years and was intended to examine the prevalence of mental disorders and the impact on children and service providers. Available online at:
www.statistics.gov.uk/downloads/theme_health/mentalhealth_Wales.pdf

209 **Payne H (2000) 'The health of children in public care',** *Current Opinion in Psychiatry*, 13:4, pp. 381–88
Reviews the risk factors for children entering public care and explores what health services can do to meet their needs and improve outcomes.

210 **Payne H and Butler I (1998) 'Improving the health care process and determining health outcomes for children looked after by the local authority',** *Ambulatory Child Health*, 4:2, pp. 165–72
Argues that the health needs of children in care are not adequately met and proposes that an identified person, such as a medical adviser, should be given responsibility for monitoring and meeting such needs.

211 **Payne H and Butler I (2003) Promoting the Mental Health of Children in Need, Quality Protects Research Briefing 9.** London: *Department of Health*
A research briefing examining the type, prevalence and risk factors associated with mental health issues and psychiatric illness in children. Describes service responses that can contribute to resilience and good mental health. Available online at:
www.rip.org.uk/publications/documents/QPB/brief9.pdf

212 **Phillips R (ed.) (2004) Caring for Children Exposed to Parental Substance Misuse: Implications for family placement.** London: *BAAF*
This collection replaces and extends the earlier *Bruised before Birth*, now out of print. Contributors attempt to provide answers to the questions raised by increased awareness of the effects on children of drugs, alcohol and other substances used by parents, especially by mothers during pregnancy. They consider the impact – psychological, social, behavioural and genetic – on children exposed to parental substance misuse and tackle the challenges posed in parenting children damaged in this way.

213 Richardson J and Joughin C (2000) The Mental Health Needs of Looked After Children. London: *Gaskell*

A wide-ranging research-based guide for professionals and carers responsible for children in care. The guide includes a list of relevant organisations and explains the current organisation of mental health services for young people. It emphasises prevention and the importance of interagency co-ordination. The book gives an overview of the mental health needs that may arise for children in care or accommodated.

214 Stein E, Evans B, Mazumdar R, Rae-Grant N (1996) 'The mental health of children in foster care: a comparison with community and clinical samples', *Canadian Journal of Psychiatry*, 41:6, pp. 385–91

Report of a Canadian study to determine whether the characteristics of children in care were more similar to general community profiles or to "clinical" samples. The "care" sample comprised 248 children, the "community" sample 1,751 and the "clinical" sample 654 referred to a children's mental health service. The study found that the children in care were more similar to the "clinical" sample. (Note that this study is wrongly dated as 1977 in some databases.)

Education

Works listed in the first part of this chapter frequently refer to education – for example, Hill (1999 – ref. 132), Wilson *et al* (2003 – ref. 193), Wheal (1999 – ref. 191). Organisational and policy perspectives are included in publications such as those from the Department of the Environment, Transport and the

Regions (2001 – ref. 117), and in the relevant section of Chapter 1 (refs. 63–65). Studies specific to permanent placements (such as Aldgate *et al* (1992 – ref. 337) are located in Chapter 3. A good place to start for many purposes is Morgan (1999 – ref. 236).

215 **Aldgate J, Heath A and Colton M (1992) The Educational Progress of Children in Foster Care, Report to the ESRC.** Oxford: *University of Oxford*
Investigated the educational progress over three years of 49 fostered children in the care of one local authority. The comparison group was a group of children living in their own homes whose families were clients of the Social Services Department. Highlighted that the educational difficulties of children may be longstanding, that social workers may tend to overestimate the educational progress of children in their care (possibly because they conflate "lack of behaviour problems in school" with "reasonable educational progress") and that systematic attention is a duty of the "corporate parent".

216 **Aldgate J, Heath A, Colton M and Simm M (1993) 'Social work and the education of children in foster care',** *Adoption & Fostering*, 17:3, pp. 25–34
Further reports based on the ESRC study (ref. 198). Explores the extent to which social workers advocate the educational needs of children and young people in foster care. Describes the priority which education-related work had within their activities for children, the reality for children of this aspect of "corporate parenting" within foster placement (including educational outcomes) and the educational expectations of social workers, teachers and foster carers. Reprinted in Hill (1999 – ref. 132).

217 **Blome W W (1997) 'What happens to foster kids: educational experiences of a random sample of foster care youth and a matched group of non-foster care youth',** *Child and Adolescent Social Work Journal,* 14:1, pp. 41–53

US longitudinal study comparing 167 children in care with a matched "community" sample. The study covered six years and there was only a small loss to the sample over that period. Blome reports that the study group "dropped out" of school earlier, had lower qualifications, presented more discipline problems, experienced more educational disruption and had less financial support to stay in education than the comparison group.

218 **Bullock R, Little M and Millham S (2001) 'Children's return from state care to school', in Jackson S, Nobody Ever Told Us School Mattered: Raising the educational attainments of children in care.** London: *BAAF*

The authors argue that preoccupation with children's separation from and return to the family should not result in neglect of the wider contexts of their experience. Many children rejoining their families have to enter new schools. Sometimes the stigma and insecurities of the past make these negotiations difficult for the young person, particularly if compounded by unease and tensions within the family. As schooling is central to so many aspects of a child's life, its neglect is likely to cause widespread problems for returning children.

219 Cairns K and Stanway C (2004) Learn the Child: Helping looked after children to learn: a good practice guide for social workers, carers and teachers. London: *BAAF*

A resource pack that looks at ways in which teachers, foster carers, social workers and other professionals can help looked after children to learn and discusses how trauma affects children and the impact on behaviour and learning. The book includes a set of case studies and is accompanied by a CD-ROM of PowerPoint presentations and handouts.

220 Colton M, Heath A and Aldgate J (1995) 'Factors which influence the educational attainment of children in foster family care', *Community Alternatives: International Journal of Family Care*, 7:1, pp. 15–36

Argues that the early experiences of children in public care seriously affect their educational attainment and that more than average parental input is required to overcome this early disadvantage.

221 Dixon B (2003) Education: A carer's handbook. Manchester: *National Teaching and Advisory Service*

This comprehensive guide through the complexities of the education system is designed to help the foster carers who directly look after children in care. It includes practical information on special needs provision, inclusion/exclusion, who to contact in school, as well as a glossary of common acronyms and abbreviations.

222 **Fletcher B (1996) Who Cares? about Education: The education of children who are looked after by local authorities: a guide for school governors.** London: *Who Cares? Trust*
The Who Cares? Trust has made education for children in care one of its priority development areas. This is a guide to good practice and regulation designed for school governors.

223 **Fletcher B (1998) Who Cares? about Education: The education of children who are looked after by local authorities: a guide for elected members.** London: *Who Cares? Trust*
See previous ref. This is designed to present facts, issues, good practice and regulations for councillors.

224 **Fletcher-Campbell F (1997) The Education of Children who are Looked After.** Slough: *National Foundation for Educational Research*
Another milestone towards the policy developments in the late 1990s of Quality Protects/Education Protects and Children First. This book reports descriptive statistical data from a national survey of all local education authorities, results from 14 more in-depth studies and detail from a second phase of research which examined six areas as case studies of practice. This further material includes information from the education support services created specifically for this area of responsibility, from Social Services Departments and from carers. Summarises issues and conclusions about good practice and makes recommendations.

225 **Fletcher-Campbell F and Hall C (1990) Changing Schools? Changing People? The education of children in care.** Slough: *National Foundation for Educational Research*
NFER-sponsored study which followed the work of Jackson and others (see ref. 230) by researching the facts about the educational attainments of children in care. It describes the problems which exist and establishes plans for the action required to improve the situation.

226 **Heath A, Colton M and Aldgate J (1989) 'The educational progress of children in and out of care',** *British Journal of Social Work*, 19:6, pp. 447–60
Early findings from a longitudinal study of foster children (see 227), the control group being children whose families received social work support at home (regarded as a more relevant control group than the community samples of studies such as ref. 259).

227 **Heath A, Colton M and Aldgate J (1994) 'Failure to escape: a longitudinal study of foster children's educational attainment',** *British Journal of Social Work*, 24:3, pp. 241–60
Highlights the low educational attainment of children cared for away from home. In particular, it demonstrates that even those children who are cared for in long-term, settled placements in middle-class environments do not escape from this disadvantage. A history of child abuse before entering care is shown to be a negative indicator. In order to address these difficulties the chapter argues for extra educational provision to be provided for children in foster care.

228 **Hibbert H (2003) Education Matters: For everyone working with children in public care.** London: *Who Cares? Trust*

Gathers together information on a range of topics relating to the education of children in care, with the aim of improving educational outcomes and experiences. Includes information on stability, literacy, special education needs, education planning and inter-agency working as well as details of current projects and programmes.

229 **Hunt R (2000) The Educational Performance of Children in Need and Children Looked After, Quality Protects Research Briefing 1.** London: *Department of Health*

Written in clear, practical language, the Briefing summarises research about the educational attainment of children in need and looked after by local authorities. Reviews what education can do and outlines current duties and initiatives relating to local authorities and education in this area. Sets out "what helps" in relation to specific vulnerable groups, including children who are looked after, with straightforward guidance for frontline workers and organisations. Also available online through www.rip.org (click through "our publications"; last viewed January 2004) and www.rip.org.uk/publications/documents/QPB/QPB1.PDF

230 **Jackson S (1994) 'Educating children in residential and foster care',** *Oxford Review of Education*, 20:3, pp. 267–79

A review article introducing a special issue with papers by Sinclair, Garrett, Bullock, Colton, Heath, Stein and others. Children in foster care were shown to achieve consistently less well than those in their own families. Follow-up comparison with children in care who are successful in education shows the significance for later life chances and the review emphasises the specific state responsibility to address any earlier educational disadvantage experienced by children in care. Refers to the contrasting findings with adopted children and reports the problems caused *within* the educational environment.

231 **Jackson S (1998) 'Educational success for looked after children: the social worker's responsibility',** *Practice*, 10:4, pp. 47–55

Research over the past 20 years shows the educational disadvantage experienced by children in care. This article presents the social worker's responsibilities for improving the situation, drawing on the author's research on high achievers who have been in care (see refs. 233 and 237). It presents the case that the promotion and support of looked after children's education must be a central part of social workers' role.

232 **Jackson S (ed.) (2001) Nobody Ever Told Us School Mattered: Raising the educational attainments of children in care.** London: *BAAF*

Collection of research papers on educational attainment of children in care which have been influential in the growth of awareness of this issue, some of which are listed elsewhere in the bibliography. Original chapters discuss the impact of recent government initiatives, innovations in policy and practice, issues raised in research and ideas from overseas. Other topics include creating a care environment that promotes learning, how social workers can be encouraged to make education a priority, how looked after children can be kept in mainstream schooling and how their life chances can be improved.

233 **Jackson S and Martin P Y (1998) 'Surviving the care system: education and resilience',** *Journal of Adolescence*, 21:5, pp. 569–83

The studies described in this article sought to trace a group of more successful people who had grown up in care, using educational achievement as a marker. A risk and resilience framework was used to identify the protective factors which enabled them to achieve a life trajectory very different from that of their siblings and peers. From their own accounts, success in education was a crucial factor, contrasting markedly with the educational problems documented for many other children in care. The implications for childcare practice and decision making are discussed.

234 **Jackson S and Sachdev D (2001) Better Education, Better Futures: Research, practice and the views of young people in public care.** Ilford: *Barnardo's*

This book brings together research and some innovative policy and practice initiatives implemented by social work, social services and education staff from across the four nations of the UK in education for children and young people in care. Includes the views and experiences of some young people who are or have been in care.

235 **Martin P and Jackson S (2002) 'Educational success for children in public care: advice from a group of high achievers',** *Child & Family Social Work*, 7:2, pp.121–130

This article examines the opinions of 38 high-achieving

young people who spent at least a year in residential or foster care on what they think are the best ways to enhance the educational experience of looked after children. They highlighted the importance of foster carers, residential workers, social workers and teachers in providing academic support and encouragement. Negative stereotypes and low expectations of children in care among professionals and care providers were major obstacles to their educational success. Many speak warmly of help received from teachers and foster carers but on entering higher education they are often on their own, the majority facing severe problems. They stressed the need for continuing financial support and adequate year-round accommodation.

236 **Morgan S (1999) Care About Education: A joint training curriculum for supporting children in public care.** London: *National Children's Bureau*
The curriculum arose from a project working with education and social services staff, foster carers and young people in care. The project identified good practice and produced educational and training materials.

237 **Rosenfeld L B and Richman J M (2003) 'Social support and educational outcomes for students in out-of-home care',** *Children and Schools*, 25:2, pp. 69–86
US study investigating the relationship between out-of-home placement, student perception of support and school performance. Identifying eight types of social support, the researchers found that students placed out of home or identified as "at risk" educationally reported fewer types of support than other students. At-risk young people perceived more support from their neighbours and

less support from their teachers, peers and adult caretakers than other students. Students in out-of-home care did not perform as well in school as others. Discusses the implications of the findings for school social workers.

238 Sandiford P (1996) Improving Educational Opportunities for Looked After Young People: A good practice guide for teachers. London: *National Children's Bureau*
Outlines key legislation and the essential elements of good practice.

239 Sandiford P (1999) Personal Education Plan for Children and Young People in Public Care. London: *National Children's Bureau*
Pack of three booklets designed to provide social workers, teachers, foster carers and others working directly with children and young people in public care with a tool for educational planning and development.

240 Sinclair R (1998) The Education of Children in Need. Dartington: *Research in Practice*
An accessible review of research sponsored by the National Children's Bureau and Research in Practice highlighting the needs of vulnerable children, including those looked after by the local authority. Available online at: www.rip.org.uk/publications/documents/research reviews/SINCLAIR.PDF

241 Stein E (1997) 'Teachers' assessments of children in foster care', *Developmental Disabilities Bulletin,* 25:2, pp. 1–17
Canadian study comparing foster children with a community comparison group on a wider range of school

functioning measures than used by most studies. Found the expected significant differences, but also reports the differences evident between boys and girls. The study emphasises the values of teachers' perspectives and puts forward pointers to how their input could operate more effectively (for example, reducing their evident drive to bring in further play therapy and remedial specialists), emphasising the value of a case management approach. It tends not to explore the role of policy initiatives such as "Looking After Children", Quality Protects and Education Protects characteristic of the UK approach. See also Stein *et al*, 1996 – ref. 214.

242 Valios N (2003) 'Could do better?', *Community Care*, Issue 1470, 1 May, pp. 28–31
Argues that a decline in educational results for looked after children has led the government to lower its targets. Comments on release of figures from the Office for National Statistics showing that just 41 per cent of looked after children achieved one GCSE or GNVQ pass in 2001, a decline of four per cent on 2001 (the national rate for other children stood at about 98 per cent) and includes comments from young people in care.

243 Who Cares? Trust (1999) Equal Chances Information Pack – Finding the facts: an audit of education of looked after children and young people. London: *Who Cares? Trust*
First publication of the "Equal Chances" initiative of Who Cares?. The initiative is designed to improve the educational achievements of children in care.

244 **Who Cares? Trust (1999) Equal Chances: Acting on the facts – a practice guide.** London: *Who Cares? Trust*
Describes a range of practical solutions that local authorities can use to improve the education attainments of children in care.

245 **Who Cares? Trust/National Literacy Association (2001) Right to Read: Promoting the benefits of reading to children and young people in public care – project findings and recommendations for good practice.** London: *Who Cares? Trust*
This report promotes the benefits of reading to children and young people in public care. Based on a pilot study of five local authorities undertaken in 2000, it gives project findings and recommendations to encourage reading for pleasure. The project has produced a list of recommendations for local authorities, among these: that the professionals in contact with children in care must be trained to support their literacy development (including working with teachers and libraries); and libraries must work with social services to make links with children in care. Includes policy recommendations for local authorities corporately.

246 **Zetlin A, Weinberg L and Kimm C (2003) 'Are the educational needs of children in foster care being addressed?',** *Children and Schools*, 25:2, pp. 105–19
US study examining the commitment to and activity about the education of children in foster care. Authors used data from case files, caregivers and caseworkers in one (large) child welfare agency. In general, the study found scant knowledge of educational progress or the needs of the children in the agency's care and little attention to maintenance of educational records. Offers

suggestions and strategies to improve the agency procedures, to better prepare caseworkers and to work collaboratively with the schools.

247 **Zima B T, Bussing R, Freeman S, Yang X, Belin T R and Forness S R (2000) 'Behavior problems, academic skill delays and school failure among school-aged children in foster care: their relationship to placement characteristics',** *Journal of Child and Family Studies*, 9:1, pp. 87–103
This US study of 302 fostered children aged 6–12 found that about 27 per cent were in the "clinical" range for behavioural problems and 23 per cent showed "severe delay", while 14 per cent were excluded from school. It is a statistical paper oriented towards planning and research, indicating the wide variation in existing empirical data. It correlates the findings with placement characteristics (such as the level of the foster parents' education, number of placements experienced by the child, whether placement is kinship or not). The analysis of results is complex, but not always in the direction that might be expected.

Abuse and allegations of abuse in foster care

A review of the research about abuse within family placement, its incidence, comparison with its incidence in families of origin and the factors involved in differential reporting rates is given by Wilson *et al*, and Gallagher – refs. 194 and 253. There are a number of references in Chapter 5 to the issues specific to disabled children, e.g. refs. 725 and 741. In general, works that focus on restorative or therapeutic work have been located in Chapter 6. Several of the studies listed earlier in the chapter about the experience of foster carers refer to their experience of the investigation of allegations of abuse – see for example, ref. 195. Many general works about foster care refer also to abuse – e.g. refs. 121, 129, 132 (see 249 below), 142 (see 259 below) and 191.

248 Benedict M I, Zuravin S, Brandt D and Abbey H (1994) 'Types and frequency of child maltreatment by family foster care providers in an urban population', *Child Abuse and Neglect*, 18:7, pp. 577–85

This US study compared abuse by foster carers to that which happened to children living in their own family. It found that there were three times as many reports of abuse in foster care; 20 per cent of these were substantiated compared with 35 per cent when a child was living with their birth family. There were different patterns of abuse, "physical abuse" being more common in foster care compared with "neglect" in other situations. Discusses possible differences in criteria for reporting and substantiation. See also refs. 253, 255 and 258. A commentary on the significance and interpretation of these statistics is provided in ref. 194.

249 Boushel M (1994) 'Keeping safe: strengthening the protective environment of children in foster care', *Adoption & Fostering*, 18:1, pp. 33–9

Well-publicised examples of sexual abuse by carers have reawakened anxieties about children's safety in out-of-home care. It is suggested that a more comprehensive approach to assessment and support of the child's "protective environment" is needed.

250 **Colton M and Vanstone M (1996) Betrayal of Trust: Sexual abuse by men who work with children – in their own words.** London: *Free Association Books*
In-depth interviews with men serving prison sentences for sexually abusing children in their trust. All the men expressed a wish to contribute to child protection and the book considers the implications of their accounts for the treatment of offenders and the protection of potential victims of abuse.

251 **Farmer E and Pollock S (2003) 'Managing sexually abused and/or abusing children in substitute care',** *Child & Family Social Work*, 8:2, pp. 101–12
Based on the work described at more length in ref. 122, the material in this article is particularly relevant to the management of sexualised behaviour in placement.

252 **Fever F (1994) Who Cares? Memories of a childhood in Barnardo's.** London: *Warner*
The author is a ("user") inspector with the Social Services Inspectorate. 'Life in care', he says, 'is one long process of homelessness'. A moving and articulate account of life from being a baby brought into the care of Barnardo's – some good carers but many incompetent or abusive. As an adult, he finds that his file records contain 'blatant lies' and 'vast chunks of my experience had gone unwritten'.

253 **Gallagher B (1999) 'The abuse of children in public care',** *Child Abuse Review*, 8:6, pp. 357–65
Part of a special issue of the journal devoted to children in public care. Presents the range of themes to be addressed – the extent and nature of abuse, the dynamics of its investigation and prevention – and analyses the complexity in each area.

254 **Hewitt P (2003) The Looked After Kid: My life in a children's home.** Edinburgh: *Mainstream*
The author was taken into care as a baby. He describes a placement with a foster family where he was regularly beaten and humiliated. At ten years old, after enduring years of this destructive anger and abuse he rebelled and was moved to "an orphanage". Set in the 1970s, this volume addresses the emotional struggle faced by some children in residential care. It seeks to address the feeling of fear and rejection that the author experienced in his childhood and youth.

255 **Hobbs G, Hobbs C and Wynne J (1999) 'Abuse of children in foster and residential care',** *Child Abuse and Neglect*, 23:12, pp. 1239–52
A retrospective study of 158 children in Leeds, fostered or in residential care. Forty-one per cent of the abuse was by foster carers, 23 per cent by birth parents and 20 per cent by other children. Analyses the characteristics of the children, their physical and mental health and the nature and management of the abuse. A "significant proportion" of abuse within foster care was severe, including death. The authors discuss the implications of regarding this group of children as an "at risk" group (rates of abuse are analysed as 3.9/1000 children in the birth family, 39.5/1000 in foster care and 23/1000 in residential care).

256 **Macaskill C (1991, reprinted 1994) Adopting or Fostering a Sexually Abused Child.** London: *Batsford*
Macaskill describes the findings of a 1989 research project covering 80 placements of abused children. She discusses the implications for everyone involved, from the trauma of allegations and helping children talk about

their experiences, to the impact on other children in the family.

257 **Minty B (1991) 'True and false disclosures, true and false denials: believing and disbelieving children's allegations of abuse',** *Practice*, 5:3, pp. 196–213
Reviews the literature and gives examples of untrue allegations made by children and parents.

258 **Minty B and Bray S (2001) 'Allegations against foster carers: an in-depth study',** *Child Abuse Review*, 10:5, pp. 336–50
Allegations against 22 foster carers were studied, with less than ten per cent being substantiated. Six allegations were found to be untrue and ten investigations were inconclusive. The article analyses the processes involved, highlighting that standards are higher for foster carers than others, that carers frequently received no written statement of the allegation or the outcome, and that they were not permitted to give their account of what happened in the case conference or serious incident meetings. Argues that these processes violated foster carers' human rights. See also ref. 195.

259 **Nixon S (2000) 'Safe care, abuse and allegations of abuse in foster care', in Kelly G and Gilligan R (eds.) Issues in Foster Care: Policy, practice and research.** London: *Jessica Kingsley*
This chapter summarises what is known about the nature and extent of abuse in foster care and goes on to examine the impact on the different individuals involved. Looks at various approaches to prevention and investigation, and reviews good practice for every stage.

260 Nixon S and Verity P (1996) 'Allegations against foster families', *Foster Care*, 84, pp. 11–14
Describes social worker and agency perspectives on accusations made against foster carers. See also ref. 262.

261 Sexty C (1999) 'Protecting foster children: review of the Protection from Offenders Regulations', *ChildRight*, 153, pp. 14–15
Discusses the impact of regulations introduced to prevent children from being placed with convicted child abusers and shows that the outcomes can be unfair to foster carers and contrary to the interests of children.

262 Verity P and Nixon S (1995) 'Allegations against foster families: survey results', *Foster Care*, 83, pp. 13–16
Reports the findings of a survey of carers' expectations and experiences of allegations and investigations. See also ref. 260.

263 Waterhouse R (1999) Lost in Care: Report of the tribunal of inquiry into the abuse of children in care in the former County Council areas of Gwynedd and Clwyd since 1974. London: *The Stationery Office*
Report of the Waterhouse inquiry with conclusions and recommendations in full.

Works by and for children or carers

See also ref. 046 (about law). Further relevant publications are listed in a separate section in Chapter 3 dealing with permanent placements and in Chapter 6, listed as publications about interventions and therapy. Refs. 691 and 692 are of particular interest in relation to disabled children. Refs. 252 and 254 relate particularly to abuse. The voice of the child and their participation in research is now accorded a high priority and many further research-based publications set out to present that voice (e.g. refs. 128, 146, 385 and 389).

264 Alton H (1987) Moving Pictures: Trigger pictures to help children talk about moves in their life. London: *BAAF*
A pack of 16 pictures covering a variety of topics, such as 'different types of family homes', 'different standards and rules' and 'family arguments'. Contains guidelines for use and three sets of the 16 picture cards.

265 Argent H and Lane M (2004) What Happens in Court? A guide for children. London: *BAAF*
A user-friendly guide to help children understand the role that a court might play in their lives, based on the story of a seven-year-old who goes into foster care. Includes information on 'who's who' in court, the various court orders that may be made and explains matters relating to adoption. Available in English and Welsh.

266 Byrne S and Chambers L (1998) Feeling Safe: Tina's Story. London: *BAAF*
Part of BAAF's "My Story" series for children, this book focuses on a girl who has to go into foster care following abuse in the home.

267 Byrne S and Chambers L (2001) Waiting for the right home: Daniel's Story. London: *BAAF*
This 24-page story is designed for use with children in foster care. Its central character is in an uncertain

situation: he has been removed from home because of violence and is currently in a short-term foster family. Includes worksheets for the child's use.

268 **Camis J (2003) We are Fostering.** London: *BAAF*
A life story workbook designed to help birth children who share their homes with foster children. Provides information on the processes involved in fostering and adoption and space for drawings, photographs and a record of feelings.

269 **Cockburn V (ed.) (2000) It's Mad that's All: A collection of poems about being looked after.** London: *Foster Carers Association*
Poems in which children in public care express their feelings about families, changes, teachers and carers, trying to connect and life and death.

270 **Creech S (2003) Ruby Holler.** London: *Bloomsbury Children's Books*
Dallas and Florida have lived in the Boxton Creek Home longer than any other residents. They have a reputation for rule-breaking and for being difficult to place – every foster home they've been put in has sent them back – so when an elderly couple invite them to stay at Ruby Holler, they do not expect it to turn out well. But they'd reckoned without Tiller and Sairy Morey whose unusual lifestyles, patience and unobtrusive parenting turn out to be just right for Dallas and Florida. This sensitive novel takes a look at fostering from both sides and explores how apparently bad behaviour may not be as unreasonable as it looks. Suitable for ages ten to adult.

271 **Foxon J (2002) Nutmeg Gets Cross.** London: *BAAF*
Part of a series of stories for children who have been adopted based on Nutmeg the squirrel. Tackles especially the anxious, angry or confused feelings that may be experienced after adoption. Includes practice guidelines for adults, highlighting some of the themes and emotional implications of the story.

272 **Foxon J (2003) Nutmeg Gets a Letter.** London: *BAAF*
Another Nutmeg story book designed for post-adoption work with children. This story focuses on the child's questions about why they can no longer live with their birth parent(s) and validates both positive and negative feelings about this. Includes practice guidelines written by Hedi Argent and a feature on contact issues and arrangements. Designed especially for use by adoptive parents with their children.

273 **Herbert S (1991) I Miss My Foster Parents.**
Washington, DC: *Child Welfare League of America*
Written by a child who was adopted and experienced first hand the anxiety of leaving his foster family. Stefon describes the fear and how he feels when he and his sister Latisha leave their foster home and go to live with their new adoptive family. For ages 4 to 12.

274 **Kahn H and Rawlings S (2002) Tia's Wishes.**
London: *BAAF*
A story for children about to be adopted featuring a young girl. Includes various resources (including magic wand, scared bear, stickers, glitter glue and a special pen) to assist them to talk about their situation, their wishes, their fears and the likely reality. Intended for ages 4 to 10.

275 **Kahn H and Rawlings S (2003) Tyler's Wishes.** London: *BAAF*
Similar story featuring a young boy. Includes various resources (including stickers, wishes box, magic wand) to assist them to talk about their situation, as above. Intended for ages 4 to 10.

276 **Lingard J (1999) Tom and the Tree House.** London: *Hodder*
Tom's adoptive parents are delighted when the doctors are proved wrong and his mum becomes pregnant. But Tom is worried. This baby is really theirs in a way he can never be; surely they will love her more than him? A child's novel about a particularly sensitive situation. Suitable for ages 6 to 9.

277 **Little J (2000), Willow and Twig.** New York: *Viking*
This prize-winning book tells the story of two children, Willow and her brother Twig, who are left alone when their mother disappears. They move to their grand-mother's country home where a crew of animals and an eccentric family help them to deal with and understand Twig's wild behaviour. A book that fostering families and the children who live with them can relate to and enjoy.

278 **MacLiver C and Thom M (1990) Family Talk.** London: *BAAF*
A booklet with three sets of 18 picture sheets for children whose family is adopting or fostering. Designed to be used with the whole family together encouraging children to ask questions and express their views.

279 **Naik A (1999) Your Rights.** London: *Hodder*
A paperback for children and young people with guidance on a wide variety of matters, including explanations about courts and care orders.

280 **National Foster Care Association (1992) My Book About Me.** London: *NFCA*
This book is designed for use by social workers or foster carers with children who have recently joined a foster family. It is made up of a series of sections, each of which gives the child the opportunity to fill in the text, colour and add relevant photos. Creates a chance to review together the significant events in a child's life and their current situation.

281 **Orritt B (1999) Dennis Duckling: Going into care.** London: *BAAF*
This little book tells the story of Dennis, an appealing duckling, who has to leave his family as they can no longer look after him. He goes to live on a new pond where he begins to make new friends and is cared for by grown-up ducks. Suitable for use with very young children.

282 **Shah S (2003) Fostering: What it is and what it means; a guide for children and young people.** London: *BAAF*
Covers different types of fostering, how children come to be fostered, birth parents and contact, school and health questions, and much more. There are quizzes about real life and fictional people who were fostered, plus contact addresses and phone numbers (with space to record information specific for an individual child).

283 **Velthuijs M (2001) Frog Finds a Friend.** London: *Andersen Press*

Although this picture book doesn't mention the word "adoption", it tells the story of Frog taking a lost teddy bear into his home. Through Frog's love and attention, Bear learns to talk and play and eventually becomes very much part of the local community. When he suddenly decides he doesn't really belong there, he sets out to go back to the place he came from. Frog is heartbroken but eventually Bear comes back because he has decided that this is where he really belongs. A potentially useful book for talking about feelings in an unobtrusive way; children can talk about how Bear and Frog feel rather than having to talk about themselves.

284 **Wilson J (2002) Dustbin Baby.** London: *Random House*

Written in the first person, this highly readable account of the mixed emotions of an abandoned child provides children and adults with an insight into how it feels to be "in care".

Leaving care and after

Law, guidance and statutory initiatives about leaving care have improved dramatically over the last ten years. Typical guidance and support documents for young people leaving care, as well as those who care for them, are provided by First Key (now known as the National Leaving Care Advisory Service). Practice guidance is given in accessible form by various publications by Stein, Biehal and Ward, and the topic is covered by many of the resources in the first section of this chapter, e.g. refs. 114, 132, 152 and 183. Good starting points are Wade (2003 – ref. 310), which is concise and clear, or Wheal (2002 – ref. 311), a more substantial consideration of various issues. In addition, studies of outcomes, health and education often make reference to leaving care.

285 **Action on Aftercare Consortium (1996) Too Much Too Young: The failure of social policy in meeting the needs of care leavers.** Ilford: *Barnardo's*
A study from the mid-1990s documenting the failure of social policy in meeting the needs of care leavers in relation to education, employment, accommodation, the penal system and finance support, and making recommendations in each policy area. Like refs. 286–289 and many of the other works in this section it is one of the studies acknowledged by the government to have influenced the Children (Leaving Care) Act 2000.

286 **Biehal N, Clayden J, Stein M and Wade J (1992) Prepared for Living? A survey of young people leaving the care of three local authorities.** London: *National Children's Bureau*
As well as documenting resilience, this study highlights the greater likelihood of young parenthood and the increased risks of unemployment, homelessness, prostitution, drug and alcohol misuse, admission to psychiatric care, crime and suicide to which the most vulnerable children in society are exposed.

287 **Biehal N, Clayden J, Stein M and Wade J (1995) Moving On: Young people and leaving care schemes.** London: *HMSO*
Report of the Department of Health-funded research study of leaving care. Surveys 183 young people (nearly a third from foster care) in four leaving care schemes, their social workers and other staff. Documents the

challenges and experiences of care leavers over a period of two years. The study provides evidence that specialist schemes can be more effective in improving outcomes, but that this needs to be integrated into the whole continuum of services – both in the young person's past and in the range of services now used. Highlights the need to capitalise on the family resources of young people, and to enable them easily to access non-stigmatising support as they are setting up a home, establishing a career and possibly becoming parents.

288 **Biehal N and Wade J (1996) 'Looking back, looking forward: care leavers, families and change',** *Children and Youth Services Review*, 18:4/5, pp. 425–45
Draws on the findings of a four-year study of leaving care services in England funded by the Department of Health. Reports on patterns of family contact for care leavers and the quality of their relationships with their families and considers the continuing informal support that both biological and substitute families can offer to care leavers. The new families that many care leavers create through early parenthood and the continuing support needs of these young parents are also discussed.

289 **Biehal N and Wade J (1999) '"I thought it would be easier": the early housing careers of young people leaving care', in Rugg J (ed.) (1999) Young People, Housing and Social Policy.** London: *Routledge*
Reports on the issues of housing and homelessness facing young people leaving care in the context of a book looking at the full range of young people's early housing histories. Sets this in the perspective of the range of government policy initiatives aimed at young people and offers a critique of relevant aspects of social policy.

290 **Cheung S Y and Heath A (1994) 'After care: the education and occupation of adults who have been in care',** *Oxford Review of Education*, 20:3, pp. 361–75
This study documented the poor educational attainment and economic participation of young people leaving care, and the negative implications of this for subsequent careers, emphasising that the shortcomings during the period in care are exacerbated by additional penalties afterwards. Part of the special issue of this journal devoted to the educational attainment of children in care.

291 **Department of Health/Centrepoint (2002) Care Leaving Strategies: A good practice handbook.** London: *DH*
A handbook developed for local authorities following the Children (Leaving Care) Act 2000. Based on work by Centrepoint with seven London boroughs, it provides good practice guidance and checklists about providing for the housing and other support needs of young people leaving care. Available online at:
www.dfes.gov.uk/qualityprotects/pdfs/care_strategies.pdf

292 **Dodd T and Hunter P (1992) The National Prison Survey 1991: A report to the Home Office of a study of prisoners in England and Wales carried out by the social survey division of OPCS.** London: *HMSO*
Wilson, Sinclair *et al* (2004 – ref. 194) quote from this report that about 38 per cent of the prison population have spent a period in care, compared with approximately two per cent of the general population (cautioning that this is not the same as saying that this proportion of a cohort of care leavers will spend time in prison).

293 **First Key (1987) A Study of Black Young People Leaving Care.** Leeds: *First Key*

In the context of the other research in this section, this survey highlighted the specific issues faced by young black people leaving care, including cultural and identity questions arising from being black in a predominantly white system of care.

294 **First Key (1996) Standards in Leaving Care: Report of the national working group.** Leeds: *First Key*

Now known as the National Leaving Care Advisory Service, First Key's codification of standards were influential in leading to the provisions of the Children (Leaving Care) Act 2000 and its associated Regulations.

295 **Fry E (1992) After Care: Making the most of foster care.** London: *National Foster Care Association*

Examines the contribution that could be made to after-care services by greater recognition and integration of the support provided by foster carers, currently regarded as "informal support".

296 **Garnett L (1992) Leaving Care and After.** London: *National Children's Bureau*

One of a number of significant research studies about the living situation and life chances of care leavers that influenced later policy and legislation.

297 **Hai N and Williams A (2004) Implementing the Children (Leaving Care) Act 2000: The experience of eight London boroughs.** London: *National Children's Bureau*

This summary of research findings examines the experience of the Children (Leaving Care) Act 2000 with regard to young people, staff and managers, Pathway Plans, Personal Advisers and performance indicator outcomes. It gives details of a project that commenced in October 2001 and involved eight local authorities. The aims of the project were to work with the local authorities in introducing the new legislation, to monitor the implementation of the Act and to evaluate its impact on services and care leavers.

298 **Hayden C, Goddard J, Gorin S and van der Spek N (1999) 'Leaving care', in Hayden C, Goddard J, Gorin S and van der Spek N (1999) State Child Care: Looking after children?** London: *Jessica Kingsley* (see ref. 129)
This chapter, written before the introduction of the Children (Leaving Care) Act, sets the four studies of the authors (including one of 376 foster carers, one of 186 children in care and one of 143 care leavers) in the context of the policy issues and findings of other studies reported in this section of the Bibliography.

299 **Hutson S (1997) Supported Housing: The experience of young care leavers.** Ilford: *Barnardo's*
This report is based on a three-year study of care leavers at a Barnardo's project in Cardiff. It describes young people's experiences and views in respect of accommodation, support, education, training, work, benefits, poverty and gender, and incorporates recommendations for policy and practice.

300 **Marsh P and Peel M (1999) Leaving Care in Partnership: Family involvement with care leavers.** London: *The Stationery Office*
Based on a study funded by the Department of Health

involving 39 young men and 48 young women, around 14 per cent of whom had a heritage other than white European. The main message is that much more could be done to ensure that the resources of family networks are available to young people leaving care. The networks were potentially more extensive than social workers realised, the young people were often at a point where they identified with and wished to use the family networks, and there was often important capacity within those networks (social workers tended to focus mainly on parents, neglecting the wider family context).

301 **National Children's Home (1993) A Lost Generation? A survey of the problems faced by vulnerable young people living on their own.** London: *National Children's Home*
This report, written by C Abrahams and T Lobstein, includes a section focusing specifically on care leavers.

302 **Saunders L and Broad B (1997) The Health Needs of Young People Leaving Care.** Leicester: *Centre for Social Action, De Montfort University*
A peer research study which involved young people as core members of the research group. The aims were to identify the unmet health needs of care leavers. Reporting the findings from a basic sample of 50 care leavers, the study indicated how "basic survival" measures in difficult circumstances were often more important to the young people than "healthy living". Factors implicated in (emotional and social) health for this group were compared with those for the more general population of young people.

303 **Smith C (1998) Leaving Care: Messages from young people.** London: *Royal Philanthropic Society*
Study of care leavers' experiences.

304 **Social Services Inspectorate (1997) When Leaving Home is also Leaving Care: An inspection of services for young people leaving care.** London: *Department of Health*
Report based on inspection of nine local authorities. Highlights good and bad practice and how well those authorities are living up to the responsibilities placed upon them by the Children Act 1989. The views of young people themselves are brought together in the form of a letter to Directors of Social Services. Strategies and guidance are suggested to enable both statutory and voluntary organisations to work towards developing policies that will be more effective in helping young people move to an independent life.

305 **Stein M (1997) What Works in Leaving Care?** Ilford: *Barnardo's*
Reviews what is known from research about the effectiveness of leaving care services. In the context of the issues highlighted by other studies in this section (the most vulnerable people at an earlier age being required to tackle more complex problems with fewer supports), it draws on studies mainly completed in the last 20 years to consider the range of services offered in relation to accommodation, personal and financial support, education and employment. Discusses theoretical frameworks and policy implications, and highlights gaps in research, particularly of outcome studies, studies using comparisons with the general population and those which distinguish different groups within care leavers.

306 **Stein M and Wade J (2000) Helping Care Leavers: Problems and strategic responses.** London: *Department of Health*

National Summary as at 1999 of statistics and policy issues relating to leaving care. Provides a literature review of the nature and difficulties involved. The aims and objectives of local authorities supporting care leavers are discussed along with the issues that affect local authority responses to the problems of care leavers. Outlines the development of leaving care schemes and areas of best practice. Cites numerous references.

307 **Strathdee R and Johnson M (1994) Out of Care and on the Streets: Young people, care leavers and homelessness.** London: *Centrepoint*

A briefing paper which discusses evidence showing that young people leaving care are twice as likely to become homeless and find themselves sleeping on the streets.

308 **Taussig H N, Clyman R B, and Landsverk J (2001) 'Children who return home from foster care: a 6-year prospective study of behavioral health outcomes in adolescence',** *Pediatrics*, 108:1: E10

This "leaving care" study differs from the others in this section in referring to subjects who were 7–12 years old when they left care at the beginning of the study. One hundred and forty-nine foster children were interviewed five months and six years after returning from placement. Compared with children who stayed in care, children who were reunited with their biological families showed more self-destructive behaviour, more substance use, more arrests, more internalising behaviours and total behaviour problems, and were more likely to have

lower grades and to have dropped out of school. Available online at:
www.pediatrics.aappublications.org/cgi/content/full/108/1/e10

309 Wade J (1997) 'Developing leaving care services: tapping the potential of foster carers', *Adoption & Fostering*, 21:3, pp. 40–49
Drawing on the four-year study of specialist leaving care services funded by the Department of Health (see refs. 265–268), this paper pays particular attention to the implications for and potential role of foster carers. It situates moving on from substitute care or accommodation in the context of broader youth transitions to adulthood. Three key dimensions of transition for a sample of care leavers are discussed: the timing and nature of their moving on; their early education and employment careers; and their ability to develop networks of social support.

310 Wade J (2003) Leaving Care, Quality Protects Research Briefing 7. London: *Department of Health*
Part of the 'Research in Practice – Making research count' initiative, this briefing reviews the experiences of leaving care, outlining especially the problems that can arise and specialist initiatives for care leavers and the policy/legislation framework. Explains how this area of responsibility fits into government and Quality Protects priorities. The research briefing is available with full references or in a more summary form highlighting only key resources. Accessible online at:
www.rip.org.uk/publications/documents/QPB/brief7.pdf

311 **Wheal A (ed.) (2002) The RHP Companion to Leaving Care.** Lyme Regis: *Russell House Publishing*
Sets the specific challenges for many young people leaving care in the context of the general societal picture of young adulthood.

Training

More than any other subject, the publications relevant to training occur in every section of the Bibliography. In relation to disabled children and therapeutic and direct work with children, some cross-references are given at the end of this section. References about the training of carers and social workers about the abuse of children are included in the current section, but see also ref. 660 about gendered abuse and ref. 722, for example, about the abuse of disabled children. Relevant policy publications prioritising training by the National Foster Care Association (now the Fostering Network) are refs. 155–157 above. Morgan (1999 – ref. 236) – is a joint training curriculum for teachers, social workers and carers arising from an interdisciplinary project about education that included young people in foster care. Refs. 312 and 611 refer specifically to the training of Asian carers.

Many references designed for children and carers are useful as training resources – see refs. 264–284 (this chapter) and refs. 475–497 (Chapter 3). Excellent step-by-step guidance for prospective foster carers, from first thoughts through each stage of the assessment process, is to be found online at www.fostering.org.uk. In relation to adoption, see also refs. 046, 467–474.

312 **Almas T (1991) Fostering and Adoption in Asian families: A guide for the preparation and training of Asian adoptive and foster families.** Bradford: *Barnardo's*

A pack of training materials about the preparation of Asian adults to be foster carers or adoptive parents, based on the author's work in Bradford.

313 **Butler I and Roberts G (2003) 'Looking after', in Butler I and Roberts G, Social Work with Children and Families: Getting into practice (2nd edition).** London: *Jessica Kingsley*

An example of training materials designed to promote an understanding of looking after children, suitable for initial training with a wide variety of people including foster carers, social workers or residential staff.

314 **Gilchrist A and Hoggan P (1996) 'Involving birth parents in foster carer training',** *Adoption & Fostering*, 20:1, pp. 30–34

This article describes and discusses the involvement of birth parents in ongoing training for approved foster carers. The inclusion of birth parents is seen as beneficial for both foster carers and birth parents. To undertake this work properly requires resources which are intensive both in terms of finance and worker time.

315 **Gilligan R (2001) Promoting Resilience: A resource guide on working with children in the care system.** London: *BAAF*

This resource guide for social workers and carers begins with a resumé of theoretical ideas underpinning the concept of resilience. Its strength is the translation of these ideas into practical suggestions and strategies for practitioners. These in turn are interwoven with quotations from young people that add a powerful dimension to the narrative.

316 **Hellett J and Simmonds J (2003) Parenting a Child who has been Sexually Abused: A training programme for foster carers and adopters.** London: *BAAF*

A training programme about sexual abuse for use with foster and adoptive carers, 'based on the premise that children can be helped to recover from their experiences of abuse in a family environment, where their caregivers are actively engaged with them in assisting their recovery'. Includes guidance for trainers, video, handouts and overheads.

317 **Jewett C (1994) Helping Children Cope with Separation and Loss (2nd edition).** London: *BAAF*

A clear and sensitive work for use by adults (parents, carers or practitioners) responsible for children who have suffered loss.

318 **Lindon J and Lindon L (1994) Caring for Young Children: A workbook for early years workers.** Basingstoke: *Macmillan*

Provides information on key areas of the development and care of young children including contact and communication, health and well-being and playing with babies and children. Also covers the core units for the NVQ/SVQ level 2 awards in child care and education.

319 Lowe K (1999) 'Training for foster carers', in Wheal A (ed.) The RHP Companion to Foster Care. Lyme Regis: *Russell House Publishing*

Discusses the changing face of foster care training as it became a more central issue towards the end of the 1990s.

320 Miller J (1997) Never Too Young: How young children can take responsibility and make decisions: a handbook for early years workers. London: *The National Early Years Network/Save the Children*

A spiral-bound A4 handbook designed for use with adults who have responsibilities for young children. Takes adults through their own current attitudes and behaviours, then looks at ways of enhancing children's participation. Includes a wide range of resource and activity suggestions.

321 Minnis H and Devine C (2001) 'The effect of foster carer training on the emotional and behavioural functioning of looked after children', *Adoption & Fostering*, 25:1, pp. 44–54

The Foster Carers' Training Project was a three-year research project which examined the effect of training foster carers on the emotions and behaviour of the children they were looking after. The research produced useful quantitative findings, but the training itself also provided rich information about foster carers' communications and interactions with the children in their care.

322 **Minnis H, Devine C and Pelosi T (1999) 'Foster carers speak about training'**, *Adoption & Fostering*, 23:2, pp. 42–47

This article describes a qualitative pilot study of a training programme aimed at helping foster carers to develop their skills in communication and to increase their ability to cope with their foster children's feelings and behaviour (ref. 321).

323 **National Foster Care Association/National Extension College (2000) Caring for Children and Young People.** London: *NFCA/NEC*

Standards-based training that links to NVQ level 3. Each of 12 workbooks relates to a unit in the NVQ and Scottish NVQ, and contains background material, practical activities and case studies.

324 **Open Learning Foundation (undated) 'Working with children being looked after by the local authority', in DipSW Social Work with Children and Families.** London: *Open Learning Foundation*

In the Open Learning Foundation's social work materials, the module on social work with children and families includes a section on working with children being looked after by the local authority (undergraduate level, 20 credits). These learning materials are available for use by members of academic institutions who pay an annual subscription.

325 **Pithouse A, Hill-Tout J and Lowe K (2002) 'Training foster carers in challenging behaviour: a case study in disappointment'**, *Child & Family Social Work*, 7:3, pp. 203–14

This article sets out key features of an investigation

conducted into the impact of training foster carers in techniques to manage challenging behaviour. The results suggested that training, as designed and delivered, had limited impact on child conduct and carer capacity, but that it was perceived very positively by foster carers who said they used it in practice. Further details published in *Adoption & Fostering,* 27:1, 2003, pp. 47–56.

326 Richardson B, Foster V A and McAdams III C R (1998) 'Parenting attitudes and moral development of treatment foster parents: implications for training and supervision', *Child and Youth Care Forum*, 27:6, pp. 409–31

A quantitative study of 103 "specialist" foster carers identified that those with higher levels of moral reasoning were more likely to report more nurturing and appropriate parenting attitudes. This suggests the need for foster carers' assessment, training and support programmes to consider psychological maturity and developmental training and supervision models, as opposed to expecting foster carers to present themselves already equipped.

327 Sanchirico A and Jablonka K (2000) 'Keeping foster children connected to their biological parents: the impact of foster parent training and support', *Child and Adolescent Social Work Journal,* 17:3, pp. 185–203

Reports on a study that examined whether specific training and support increased the capacity of foster carers to support the relationship between child and birth parent. The findings were generally positive.

328 **The Fostering Network (2003) The Skills to Foster: A foundation for quality care.** London: *The Fostering Network*
A national training course for people interested in becoming approved foster carers. The course recognises fostering as a profession and focuses on the skills needed to be an effective carer.

Training and disability

Many of the works in Chapter 5 about disability are of direct value in training. Where publications could be listed with equal relevance in this section or in Chapter 5, we have tended to keep them in Chapter 5. Works of particular use in the training of carers, practitioners, managers or committee members are by Argent *et al* (refs. 690–692) and information refs. such as 727. Ref. 740 relates particularly to the abuse of disabled children; 829 and 838 to life story work.

Training and therapeutic interventions with children

Again, many of the works in Chapter 7 about therapeutic and practice developments (refs. 791–840) are relevant to training, and could equally have been listed in the present section.

Classic studies

Under this heading are a small selection of studies that are still referred to, but were published before 1989, falling outside the time limits of this Bibliography.

329 **Berridge D and Cleaver H (1987) Foster Home Breakdown.** Oxford: *Blackwell*

Study of the factors associated with disruption in fostering, including findings such as that sibling groups fared better, short-term placements were less vulnerable and organisation of fostering services within the local authority was not a determining factor.

330 **Fisher M, Marsh P, Phillips D and Sainsbury E (1986) In and Out of Care: The experiences of children, parents and social workers.** London: *BAAF*

A client study of the experiences of workers and clients at admission to care, movements within care and discharge from care incorporating 331 interviews with parents, siblings, social workers, residential workers and carers.

331 **Kahan B (1979) Growing up in Care: Ten people talking.** Oxford: *Blackwell*

Record of group discussions with young adults who grew up in care.

332 **Millham S, Bullock R, Hosie K and Haak M (1986) Lost in Care: The problems of maintaining links between children in care and their families.** Aldershot: *Gower*

A study by the Dartington Research Unit (1980–83) of 450 children entering local authority care and the problems some experienced in maintaining links with their families. Over a two-year period the care careers of all children were traced, whatever their status, age or duration in care.

333 **Parker R (1966) Decisions in Child Care: A study of prediction in fostering.** London: *Allen & Unwin*

The study showed a clear association between placement breakdown and the presence of the foster carers' own children of a similar age in the home – findings subsequently reinforced by a range of other studies.

334 **Rowe J and Lambert L (1973) Children Who Wait: A study of children needing substitute families.** London: *Association of British Adoption Agencies*
The classic study which introduced UK social workers to the idea of "drift" and the need for a radical approach to placement planning.

335 **Sinclair R (1984) Decision-making in Statutory Reviews on Children in Care.** Aldershot: *Gower*
A study of almost 300 reviews of the cases of children placed in foster care in three social work districts in one local authority.

336 **Triseliotis J (ed.) (1988) Groupwork in Adoption and Foster Care.** London: *Batsford*
Papers in this edited collection focus on a variety of topics, among them: the preparation and assessment of families, children's needs, post-adoption groups, specialist fostering and preparing adolescents.

3 Adoption and permanent foster care

Permanency planning has been an important feature of recent childcare practice. This is reflected in the literature, which relates to the children themselves, their birth parents, their adoptive or foster families and the agencies responsible for the placement. Permanency policies have been developed within the framework of the Children Act 1989, which places the first priority, other things being equal, on securing permanence for children within their birth family. Research confirms that where retention or restoration to the birth family is not possible adoption provides a positive option both for infants and late-placed children.

Publications in this chapter refer to both adoption and permanent foster care. There has been considerable debate about whether permanence can be provided within the foster care system. In a recent review, Triseliotis (2002 – ref. 392) argued that while adoption appears to create a greater sense of security and belonging, the difference in outcome rates between these two forms of family placement is narrowing.

In selecting references a key issue has been "currency". The aim has been to include recent practice developments and research. However, this of course incorporates the experiences of adults, some of whom were adopted or relinquished their children for adoption many decades ago.

The writings that follow refer to both infants and children placed later in their childhood. Needless to say, the various research studies use different definitions of "late placed", just as in outcome studies they use different measures of success. Research studies examine the various stages of the placement process and from different perspectives. The literature reports and expresses the views of adoptive and foster parents, birth family members, foster and adopted children, adopted adults and adults who have grown up in foster care. We have paid particular attention to issues in relation to openness and contact and sibling placements because of their relevance to current placement practice.

Howe (1998b – ref. 360) reminds us that while research has increased our understanding of children's needs 'social practices are irredeemably moral and political practices which, though heavily informed by science have, in the final analysis, to be conducted using the art of sound argument'. Nowhere is this more true than in the permanent placement of children away from their family of birth.

Permanence: needs and outcomes

This section lists generic works about permanence – the needs of children, the dynamics of placement, the organisation of services and the outcomes of permanent placement.

See also refs. 611–651 about race, ethnicity and placement; 652–687 refer to gender, sexuality and adoption, and 689–745 refer to disability.

337 Aldgate J, Colton M, Ghate D and Heath A (1992) 'Educational attainment and stability in long-term foster care', *Children & Society*, 6:2, pp. 91–103

A research study of long-term foster care examining the interplay between educational attainment, the child's history, current placement status and contact with the birth family. Levels of educational attainment in the study group compared unfavourably with the general population but favourably with the sample of similarly high-risk children in the community. The authors conclude that the type of placement (long-term foster care/adoption) seemed less important than the expectation of stability.

338 Beckett C, Groothues C and O'Connor T G (1998) 'Adopting from Romania: the role of siblings in adjustment', *Adoption & Fostering*, 22:2, pp. 25–34

An analysis of the role of siblings in the adjustment of adopted children and their families. The data are drawn from a wider research project into the adoption of children from Romania. This is not therefore a study of UK adoptions and the findings cannot necessarily be assumed to be the same. They point to the complex interaction between different variables in adoption outcomes. The variables examined included the age between siblings and the nature of sibling relationships, e.g. birth and adopted child or two unrelated adopted children. Some families found the task of bringing together birth and adopted children more challenging than they had anticipated. Others emphasised the positive effect of a child with very different attributes joining the family network.

339 Beek M and Schofield G (2002) 'Foster carers' perspectives on permanence: a focus group study', *Adoption & Fostering*, 26:2, pp. 14–27

A report of focus groups set up to establish the views of caregivers about the role of long-term fostering in providing permanency for children. A number of themes were identified: parenting and parental autonomy, family membership, fostering as a family until adult life, the role of the birth family and support from the local authority.

340 **Beesley P, Hutchinson B, Millar I and de Sousa S (2003). Preparing to Adopt: A training pack for preparation groups.** London: *BAAF*

This training programme sets out a comprehensive approach to preparing adopters and provides agencies with an agreed common curriculum. Issues covered include how children learn to feel secure, overcoming the effects of neglect and abuse, keeping family links alive, building resilience in children and the matching process. The course aims to enable prospective adopters to gain an appreciation of what adoption means, the roles of all those involved and to consider the implications of adoption for themselves.

341 **Berridge D (2000) 'Placement stability', Quality Protects Research Briefings.** London: *Department of Health*

Provides evidence of factors that contribute to stability in foster and kinship care, residential care and restoration. The latter reflects a philosophy that places the return of the child to their birth family as the first permanency option. Concludes with key points for practitioners. Available online at
www.rip.org.uk/publications/documents/QPB/QPB2.pdf

342 **Brodzinsky D and Schechter M (eds.) (1990) The Psychology of Adoption.** New York: *Oxford University Press*

A significant collection of contributions from leading researchers from various disciplines exploring adoption. A number focus on infant placements. However, they lend insight into the meaning of adoption, which has relevance to the placement of older children. Of particular significance is the "stress and coping model of adoption adjustment", developed by Brodzinsky, a theoretical framework for understanding children's adaptation to adoption.

343 **Byrne S (2000) Linking and Introductions: Helping children join adoptive families.** London: *BAAF*
Each of the key stages in placing children for adoption has its own particular challenges. This guide addresses the vital phase of linking children with new families prior to placement. It provides a child-centred framework for thinking through the major stages of linking and introducing children to potential families, and explores the challenge of assessing needs and strengths as well as balancing and minimising risk.

344 **Cairns B (2004) Fostering Attachments: Long-term outcomes in family group care.** London: *BAAF*
Brian Cairns describes the family group environment that he and his wife Kate (see below) developed as foster carers during a period of nearly 20 years. Their house was officially designated a voluntary children's home in 1975, but it was also their family home until 1994. Their family included their three natural children and a further 12 children they fostered. The understanding was that the children who came to join the Cairns family could stay until they were ready to move on as independent adults. Cairns describes how he and Kate sought to make this carefully planned family environment work as a therapeutic network modelling the parenting of traumatised and sometimes difficult children. Drawing on personal experience, he explores issues of health, education, identity, family and social relationships, social presentation, emotional and behavioural development, self-care skills, the carers' and the birth children's experiences.

345 Cairns K (2002) 'Making sense: the use of theory and research to support foster care', *Adoption & Fostering*, 26:2, pp. 6–13

Written by an experienced social worker/trainer, who with her partner and birth children offered permanence through specialised foster care to 12 children (see above). The article describes a number of theoretical ideas that helped the family to make sense of the behaviour and feelings of these troubled children living with the family. Written in a clear and pragmatic style, accessible to social workers and carers.

346 Dance C, Rushton A and Quinton D (2002) 'Emotional abuse in early childhood: relationships with progress in subsequent family placements', *Journal of Child Psychology & Psychiatry*, 43:3, pp. 395–407

An analysis of data from two studies of late-placed children looking specifically at those who had been rejected by their birth family and placed with the intention of permanence in middle childhood. The authors use the term "preferential rejection" to refer to children who have been the focus of negativity and rejection not experienced by their siblings. Findings suggest that these children are more likely to experience poor outcomes, particularly if this is combined with "false affection" on the part of the child and lower levels of sensitivity in the new parent.

347 Douglas A and Philpot T (eds.) Adoption: Changing families, changing times. London: *Routledge*

The editors have drawn together contributions from all those with an interest in adoption: adopted people; birth parents and adoptive parents; practitioners and managers in the statutory and voluntary sectors; academics and policy makers. Chapters on research and policy are interspersed with those from people with first-hand experience of being adopted, becoming an adoptive parent or giving up a child for adoption.

348 **Dumaret A C, Coppel-Batsch M and Couraud S (1997) 'Adult outcome of children reared for long-term periods in foster families',** *Child Abuse and Neglect*, 21:10, pp. 911–27

A French family study of 63 adults aged over 23 who had been looked after for at least five years in foster families, their families of origin having been described as 'severely psychosocially dysfunctional'. Researchers assessed that 'intergenerational repetition of child placement behaviours significant in the previous generation had practically disappeared'. The results also highlighted the substantial therapeutic and child-rearing support provided by the staff of the foster care agency.

349 **Fratter J, Rowe J, Sapsford D and Thoburn J (1991) Permanent Family Placement: A decade of experience.** London: *BAAF*

An important large-scale study of children with special needs placed in permanent families. The data were collected when the children had been in placement between 18 months and six-and-a-half years. Disruption is the outcome measure used. A complex multi-variant analysis enabled risk, protective and neutral factors to be identified. The overall disruption rate was 21 per cent but with a marked variation according to age of placement.

350 **Gibbons J, Gallagher B, Bell C and Gordon D (1995) Development after Physical Abuse in Early Childhood: A follow-up study of children on child protection registers.** London: *HMSO*

A carefully designed retrospective study of children placed on registers operated by the NSPCC following physical abuse. Children were followed up ten years later and compared to a comparison group. Forty per cent of the studied children had a poor outcome compared to 19 per cent of the comparison group. Outcomes for children in foster/adoptive care were compared with the children restored to their birth families. In contrast with previous studies the most significant factor affecting poor outcome was not age of placement but critical and punitive styles of parenting within the current placement. However, the direction of causation is not clear.

351 **Gilligan R (1997) 'Beyond permanence: the importance of resilience in child care placement practice and planning',** *Adoption & Fostering*, 21:1, pp. 12–20

The author argues that a child's need for permanence should be considered within a wider philosophy based on an understanding of resilience. He identifies the three building blocks of resilience: a secure base, self-esteem and a sense of self-efficacy. This provides a framework for practitioners which enables them to draw on a wide range of resources and protective factors within the child's family, social and educational networks.

352 **Hadley Centre for Adoption and Foster Care Studies (2002) What Do we Know about Permanent Sibling Placement?, Briefing Paper.** Bristol: *The Hadley Centre for Adoption and Foster Care Studies, University of Bristol*

A substantive research review about permanent placement of siblings away from their birth families. It looks in particular at the effects of sibling placement on placement disruption and how important children feel their siblings are to them (see also ref. 380). A summary and review of the book is available online via the "evidence bank" resource of Research in Practice: www.rip.org.uk

353 **Heptinstall E, Bhopal K and Brannen J (2001) 'Adjusting to a foster family: children's perspectives',** *Adoption & Fostering*, 25:4, pp. 6–16

Reports the findings of a small-scale, qualitative study examining children's response to foster care. The sample is part of a larger study examining children's perspectives of family life. The study is based on a sociological approach to childhood, emphasising children as active participants who create and attribute meaning to their situation. Although the experience of the foster children differed in some important respects from children in other family settings, they shared ideas about the central role children play in family life and had a common tendency to live for the present.

354 **Hill M and Shaw M (eds.) (1998) Signposts in Adoption: Policy, practice and research issues.** London: *BAAF*

An anthology of seminal papers published in BAAF's quarterly journal, *Adoption & Fostering*. The collection provides an overview of many of the key debates surrounding adoption including permanence, resilience, openness, attachment, ethnic and cultural issues, outcome research and post-adoption support.

355 **Hindle D (2000) 'Assessing children's perspectives on sibling placements in foster or adoptive homes',** *Clinical Child Psychology and Psychiatry*, 5:4, pp. 613–25

This article, written by a child psychotherapist, emphasises the need to understand the perspective of children when making complex decisions in relation to sibling placements. She describes an assessment model that provides a framework within which children's interactions, verbal and non-verbal communication and play can be observed. This enables practitioners to consider the children's shared and individual needs. The model is illustrated by reference to case examples.

356 **Hodges J and Tizard B (1989a) 'IQ and behavioural adjustment of ex-institutional adolescents',** *Journal of Child Psychology & Psychiatry*, 30, pp. 53–76;
Hodges J and Tizard B (1989b) 'Social and family relationships of ex-institutional adolescents', *Journal of Child Psychology & Psychiatry*, 30, pp. 77–98

These two articles report the findings of a significant prospective study of children who, following an early history of residential care, were placed for adoption, returned to their birth families or remained in residential care. The study addresses the important question of the reversibility of the effects of early deprivation, particularly in the area of primary attachment experiences. In general, more favourable outcomes were associated with adoption. At 16 years of age, despite considerable developmental recovery, the institutionalised children as a whole had retained some problems, especially in relationships with peers and at school, and some anxious behaviour but not at the level of clinical diagnosis.

357 **Howe D (1996) Adopters on Adoption: Reflections on parenthood and children.** London: *BAAF*
Based on interviews with 120 adoptive families, this book provides a voice for the adopters' experiences. Initial chapters focus on why people want to adopt, the experience of being assessed and comments on the current patterns of adoption. The book then moves on to focus on the experiences of adopting babies, achieving secure attachments and some of the difficulties of anxious-to-please children, angry children, uninvolved and wary children and the experiences of birth mothers, biology and beliefs.

358 **Howe D (1996) 'Adopters' relationships with their adopted children from adolescence to early adulthood',** *Adoption & Fostering*, 20:3, pp. 35–43
Findings of a study based on interviews with adoptive parents when their children had reached early adulthood. The aim was to collate information about the children's pre-placement experiences, achievements and problems during adolescence. Analysis of the data led to the identification of three groups: children placed as infants, children placed following a relative good start in their birth family, and children placed after a history of adversity. The child's early history appeared to be more significant than their age at placement.

359 Howe D (1998a) Patterns of Adoption: Nature, nurture and psychosocial development. Oxford: *Blackwell*

This important and authoritative book has made a major contribution to our understanding of the processes and outcomes in adoption, both of infants and late-placed children. Howe begins with an analysis of the complex interaction between genes and environment in the development of children. He examines the influence of genetic and environmental influences in infant adoption and the broader range of pre- and post-placement factors in late adoptions. He argues that an understanding of the nature of risk and resilience, vulnerability and protection helps us to make sense of these findings. Another major element of the book is the way the author has used attachment theory to provide insight into the behaviour and responses of adopted children. The identification of different patterns of behaviour (secure, anxious, angry) and the way these are linked to early experiences offer helpful information for carers and practitioners.

360 Howe D (1998b) 'Adoption outcome research and practical judgement', *Adoption & Fostering*, 22:2, pp. 6–15

Howe uses a basic framework of pre-placement and post-placement influences on final outcomes to review the research into the long-term developmental outcomes of children placed for adoption. However, given the complex interactions between children and their environments, he argues that assessing the risk and protective forces that may affect a child's development requires the reasoning skills of the philosopher as well as the investigative skills of the scientist.

361 **Katz L (1999) 'Concurrent planning: benefits and pitfalls',** *Child Welfare*, 78:1, pp. 71–87

This article reviews the development of concurrent planning projects, which were established to reduce the delay in the placements of young high-risk children. While acknowledging the benefits to the children of this form of placement practice the authors argue that practitioners need to be aware of the pitfalls that can undermine its effectiveness. See also Monck *et al* – ref. 368.

362 **Kelly G and Gilligan R (eds.) (2000) Issues in Foster Care: Policy, practice and research.** London: *Jessica Kingsley*

This book draws on the expertise of a number of different contributors to examine current policy, practice and research in relation to foster care. There is a specific chapter in relation to long-term foster care. However, readers are reminded to examine research evidence critically and to be aware of how research findings are influenced by the value base of the researcher. This, it is argued, is of particular relevance to the long-term fostering/adoption debate. Also see ref. 151.

363 **Livingston Smith S and Howard J A (1994) 'The impact of previous sexual abuse on children's adjustment in adoptive placement',** *Social Work*, 39:5, pp. 491–501

In a study of nine- to ten-year-old adopted children, the researchers found a higher risk for adoption disruption (74 per cent compared with 43 per cent) among children who had previously been sexually abused than for those who had not. This was attributed in part to problematic behaviours that either worsened or did not improve after placement. Although sexual acting out decreased among the sexually abused children, this behaviour was very troubling to many adoptive parents. Those children were assessed as having greater difficulties attaching to new parents. Researchers noted that in many cases previous sexual abuse had not been identified.

364 **Lord J and Borthwick S (2001) Together or Apart? Assessing brothers and sisters for permanent placement.** London: *BAAF*
This book highlights factors that affect decisions on whether siblings are placed together or separately, and considers when, how and by whom key decisions are made. The authors look at the needs of new permanent families and make suggestions about recruitment, preparation and support of families taking sibling groups.

365 **Lowe N, Murch M, Bader K, Borkowski M, Copner R, Lisles C and Shearman J (2002) The Plan for the Child: Adoption or long-term fostering.** London: *BAAF*
The findings of a research project commissioned by Quality Protects to examine factors influencing the choice of long-term fostering or adoption as the preferred permanency option and the reason for delays in implementing plans. The authors conclude that age, birth family contact, history of abuse, ethnicity and gender are all factors that influence the decision-making process. Examining possible reasons for the wide variation between authorities in the use of adoption, they challenge practitioners and policy-makers to consider the meaning of terms like "permanence". They argue that more consideration needs to be given to defining and supporting a

range of options for children that can provide them with the stability they need without necessarily severing all contact with the birth family.

366 **McAuley C (1996) 'Children's perspectives on long-term foster care', in Hill M and Aldgate J (eds.) Child Welfare Services: Developments in law, policy, practice and research.** London: *Jessica Kingsley*
Reports on the experiences of 19 children aged four to 11 living in 16 foster families. After two years the children still carried a considerable number of unresolved issues including the importance of wider social networks such as school and the loss of contacts with family members. Of particular importance was the finding that after two years the children were still in the early stages of building relationships with their new foster family.

367 **Minty B (1999) 'Outcomes in long-term foster family care',** *Journal of Child Psychology & Psychiatry*, 40:7, pp. 991–99
A detailed annotation focusing on outcomes for children placed in long-term foster care in the UK, USA, Canada and France. The author argues that the outcome for long-term foster care is 'generally much better than current professional prejudice suggests' (p. 997). Early decision-making and later discharge appear to be associated with better outcomes, as is the absence of "conduct problems". The recruitment of skilled carers and the commitment to provide them with appropriate support are key issues.

368 **Monck E, Reynolds J and Wigfall V (2003) The Role of Concurrent Planning: Making permanent placements for young children.** London: *BAAF*

Based on a small-scale study to evaluate the introduction of concurrent planning, taking into account the needs of the children and the views of birth parents and carers. Compared to a comparison group of children placed through more traditional means the timescales for achieving permanence were considerably shorter, but the young age of the children needs to be born in mind. The report provides useful details of how concurrent planning services work and how they may be developed in the future.

369 **Morgan P (1998) Adoption and the Care of Children: The British and American experience.** London: *Institute of Economic Affairs*

In what is essentially an indictment of local authorities' poor track record in looking after children, Morgan argues that childcare legislation and practice should be re-organised so that adoption becomes the first, not the last, option for children who cannot live with their parents. She shows how the objections to adoption have changed over the years, from fears that it would undermine primogeniture, or encourage immorality by giving unmarried mothers an easy way out, to 'the more modern obsession with matching racial profiles'. Despite these objections, studies have shown that adoption has extremely good outcomes and she insists that 'there is no such thing as an unadoptable child'.

370 **Morris A (1999) The Adoption Experience: Families who give children a second chance.** London: *Jessica Kingsley*

Adopters tell it like it is on every part of the adoption process, from the moment of first deciding to adopt to feelings about children seeking a reunion with their birth families or simply leaving home. Includes a chapter on the legal aspects of adoption and useful information and addresses.

371 **Mullender A (ed.) (1999) We are Family: Sibling relationships in placement and beyond.** London: *BAAF*
See ref. 154.

372 **Owen M (1999) Novices, Old Hands and Professionals: Adoption by single people.** London: *BAAF*
Reports the findings of a study set out to establish the views of single adoptive parents and their adopted children. The sample comprised successful single applicants who had adopted children with a range of specific needs including physical and learning disabilities, children who had experienced an adverse early history or black or dual-heritage children who were considered to need a culturally appropriate placement. The study was based primarily on semi-structured interviews and information derived from files. The report describes the anxieties experienced by single applicants in relation to the approval process. It also documents how families were able to meet the needs of children with a range of different needs. Factors associated with poorer outcomes mirrored the findings of wider studies including age at placement and a history of adversity.

373 Parker R, Ridgway J and Davies C (eds.) (1999) Adoption Now: Messages from research. Chichester: *John Wiley & Sons*

An overview of studies commissioned by the Department of Health to identify the principal messages from research about adoption policy and practice. The studies include consideration of outcomes, predictive and risk factors, selection and preparation of families, legal and court proceedings, issues of organisation, policy and management and identification of support needs. A recurrent theme is the need to listen to the voice of the child. A summary account of the review is available online via the "evidence bank" resource of Research in Practice: www.rip.org.uk (accessed December 2003).

374 Pavao J M (1998) The Family of Adoption. Boston: *Beacon Press*

This book by an adopted person and social work academic demonstrates that there are predictable and understandable developmental stages and challenges for all adopted people. A powerful work which emphasises that adoption is about finding families for children, not finding children for families.

375 Quinton D, Rushton A, Dance C and Mayes D (1998) Joining New Families: A study of adoption and fostering in middle childhood. Chichester: *John Wiley & Sons*

A significant prospective study of 61 children placed in permanent families between the age of five and nine years following a history of neglect/abuse. The children were followed up in the first 12 months of placement. Poor outcomes were associated with children placed singly within established families, overactive/restless behaviour and low parental responsiveness. Sensitive parenting was particularly important for the more difficult children but did not necessarily lead to a reduction in behavioural problems. By 12 months two-thirds of the children had developed a satisfactory relationship with one or both parents.

376 Roy P, Rutter M and Pickles A (2000) 'Institutional care: risk from family background or pattern of rearing?', *Journal of Child Psychology & Psychiatry*, 41:2, pp. 139–49
See ref. 167.

377 Rushton A (2003) The Adoption of Looked After Children. London: *Social Care Institute for Excellence*
The remit of this knowledge review is to map the literature on the adoption of children from care, to identify the extent of research-based knowledge, to note the gaps in the evidence and to make broad recommendations for future research. The review of 66 studies charts the growth in research over the last 40 years and elucidates how this has increased the complexity of the questions to be answered.

378 Rushton A and Dance C (2003) 'Preferentially rejected children and their development in permanent family placements', *Child & Family Social Work*, 8:4, pp. 257–67
A report of the findings of an analysis of data in relation to a sample of children, all of whom were placed singly in families with the intention of permanence in middle childhood. The sample was drawn from two wider studies of late-placed children. The aim was to examine the children's history, the sensitivity of the new carers

and progress in the first year of placement. The authors were concerned to examine whether the experience of "preferential rejection" was related to poor outcome and if so, what might be the processes involved. Conclusions are tentative but suggest that practitioners should be alert to the possibility that some children who have siblings but are alone in the care system are more vulnerable to continuing difficulties in the first year of placement.

379 **Rushton A and Dance C (2004) 'The outcomes of late permanent placements: the adolescent years',** *Adoption & Fostering*, 28:1, pp. 49–58
Describes the most recent findings from the Maudsley Family Research Studies in which 133 children were placed with adoptive families (including some long-term foster placements) during middle childhood (5–11) and followed up to mid-adolescence (11–16). After a year, 92 per cent of the young people remained with their new families and six years later, 71 per cent of families were still together. Placement breakdown occurred at all points but on average at 34 months after placement. The reasons for placement endings were examined and differences between the disrupted and the "continuing but unhappy" placements were explored. In the continuing placements, the parents' views of their experiences fell into three groups: the happy throughout, the happy now but not always so, and the largely negative responses. Most of the parents in the last group were still being severely tested by developmental and behavioural problems including aggression and destructiveness.

380 Rushton A, Dance C, Quinton D and Mayes D (2001) Siblings in Late Permanent Placements. London: *BAAF*

A report of the findings of a significant study of siblings placed in new permanent placements in middle childhood (133 children with 72 new families; comparison group of siblings in the community). The study considered four key themes: the nature of sibling relationships, the decision-making process, evidence in relation to outcomes and post-placement support. The authors demonstrate the complexity of measuring outcomes in this area and indicate that it is difficult to design simple formulae to guide practice. The evidence in some research that the placement of children placed together acts as a protective factor needs to be considered carefully. Differential outcomes may reflect different individual needs.

381 Rushton A, Quinton D, Dance C and Mayes D (1997) 'Preparation for permanent placement: evaluating direct work with older children', *Adoption & Fostering*, 21:4, pp. 41–48

Part of a series of studies carried out from the Maudsley Hospital, south London. The purpose was to assess the quality and effectiveness of direct pre-placement work with children. Sample size: 61 children; interviews one month and one year after placement. No strong association found between social worker input and degree of problems at 12 months. Discusses the place of preparation, unforeseen life circumstances and varying social work practice/expertise.

382 Rushton A, Treseder J and Quinton D (1995) 'An eight-year prospective study of older boys placed in

permanent substitute families: a research note', *Journal of Child Psychology & Psychiatry*, 36:4, pp. 687–95

A small-scale prospective study examining the psycho-social development of a sample of boys placed in permanent families after the age of five years and followed up over an eight-year period. By eight years of age they had developed affectionate relationships within the adoptive family. However, overactive/restless behaviour and difficulty in relationship with peers appeared to be more persistent. Poorest outcomes were associated with high pre-placement adversity and low levels of positive parenting.

383 **Schofield G (2000) 'Parental responsibility and parenting: the needs of accommodated children in long-term foster-care,'** *Child and Family Law Quarterly*, 12:4, pp. 345–61

This article examines the position of the minority of children in long-term foster care who are accommodated at the request of their birth parent(s). Although there are inherently complex legal and emotional issues in long-term foster care, these are particularly evident in situations where the child is accommodated under section 20 of the Children Act 1989. The author describes a number of different scenarios in which the child is cared for by long-term foster carers but parental responsibility is retained by the birth parents, and identifies some of the practice dilemmas that may arise. This is particularly relevant to decisions in relation to contact.

384 **Schofield G (2002) Part of the Family: Pathways through foster care.** London: *BAAF*

Reports on the findings of a qualitative study based on

interviews with young adults who have grown up in long-term foster care. The author was able to identify a number of distinct pathways from the narratives of these young adults depending on a range of factors including their previous history and experience within the foster family. She approaches her analysis from a developmental perspective that includes an understanding of attachment but also recognises the significance of resilience and kinship networks. An important book which provides an excellent framework to guide practice.

385 **Schofield G, Beek M, Sargent K and Thoburn J, (2000) Growing Up in Foster Care.** London: *BAAF*
Discusses the first stage of a prospective, longitudinal study examining the needs of children in long-term foster care. The sample comprises children aged four to 12, making it an interesting study of middle childhood. The report of this first stage is largely descriptive and provides a vivid and detailed account of how long-term fostering is experienced from the perspective of children, foster and birth families. A further aim was to test whether attachment theory could provide a theoretical framework that would help practitioners to understand the complex patterns of behaviour observed. Provides useful illustrations for practitioners of how different attachment patterns impact the emotional life in the family.

386 **Selwyn J and Sturgess W (2002) 'Achieving permanence through adoption: following in US footsteps?',** *Adoption & Fostering*, 26:3, pp. 40–49
A comparison of permanency planning policies in the USA and the UK. The authors argue that the UK has been influenced by US policy but has been selective about the

US experience it has chosen to emulate. This includes the use of a range of permanency options, an emphasis on reducing delay and strategies based on targets. It is interesting to note that recent US legislation defines permanence as a 'stable and legally sanctioned relationship with caring, protective adults' (p. 43) and that, in some states, concurrent planning is mandatory.

387 **Simmonds J (2001) First Steps in becoming an Adoptive Parent: An evaluation of National Adoption Week 1999.** London: *BAAF*
Follows the experiences of a group of people who contacted BAAF following National Adoption Week 1999. It looks at their motivation and circumstances, the issues that concerned them and what happened next.

388 **Thoburn J (2002) Adoption and Permanence for Children who Cannot Live Safely with Birth Parents or Relatives, Quality Protects Research Briefings 5.** London: *Department of Health*
A brief overview of the research literature in relation to permanent placements. Disruption rates for children placed from care range from ten to 50 per cent depending on the age of the child and the definition of the sample. There is no significant difference in breakdown rates between children of minority ethnic origin and white children. Decisions in relation to siblings need to be made on a case-by-case basis. More research is needed in relation to the complex issues involved in contact decisions. The authors conclude with useful guidelines for practice. A fully referenced article is available online at www.rip.org.uk

389 **Thomas C and Beckford V with Lowe N and Murch M (1999) Adopted Children Speaking.** London: *BAAF*
This book reports the findings of a qualitative study that aimed to increase our understanding of children's views of the adoption process and the support they felt they needed. The sample comprised children who had lived with their adoptive families for an average period of five years. The children were able to speak with considerable openness about their wishes and feelings. Key themes that emerged included the need for sensitive preparation of children, the need for revision and updating of life story work and particularly the need to take into account children's wishes and feelings in the review of contact arrangements.

390 **Thompson S (1998) 'Perspectives on permanence: an attachment perspective',** *Representing Children,* 11:3, pp. 187–98
This article traces the development of the concept of permanency in the UK. Early ideas about permanence were strongly influenced by attachment theory, specifically an understanding of the child's need for a primary attachment figure. Theoretical and practice developments have broadened our understanding of children's needs. Empirical developments in relation to attachment theory have demonstrated the complex nature of attachment relationships, especially in the context of abuse and trauma. The importance of race and ethnicity, of children's need for identity and social as well as psychological parenting are well documented. Experience in practice has modified views about the reversibility of early trauma. Post-placement and post-adoption support services are therefore key components of any permanency policy.

391 **Treacher A and Katz I (eds.) (2000) The Dynamics of Adoption: Social and personal perspectives.** London: *Jessica Kingsley*

This collection of articles documents the experience of all those involved in the adoption process: adoptee, adoptive and birth parent and professional. The personal accounts provide detailed reflections on the experiences and demonstrate how fantasy and emotion are integral to the adoption process.

392 **Triseliotis J (2002) 'Long-term foster care or adoption? The evidence examined',** *Child & Family Social Work*, 7:1, pp. 23–33

A literature review comparing outcomes in long-term foster care and adoption on the basis of six key variables: stability, adjustment, sense of security and belonging, personal and social functioning, adult retrospective perceptions and substitute parents perspective. On the basis of the available evidence the author draws two main conclusions. Firstly, because of changes in practice within family placement, differences between the two groups are diminishing and in some groups evening out. Secondly, although there are some children for whom long-term fostering provides the most appropriate placement, adoption still provides 'higher levels of emotional security and a stronger sense of belonging' (p. 31).

393 **Triseliotis J, Shireman J and Hundleby M (1997) Adoption: Theory, policy and practice.** London: *Cassell*

Designed as an authoritative reference work in relation to adoption, this book provides a comprehensive overview of theory, policy and practice. The authors identify practice issues and outcome studies in relation to work with birth parents, adoptive parents and adopted children. Specific consideration is given to transracial, intercountry and single-parent adoptions. The book is addressed to audiences in both the UK and the USA, reflecting the background of the three authors.

394 **Ward H and Skuse T (2001) 'Performance targets and stability of placements for children long looked after away from home',** *Children & Society*, 15:5, pp. 333–46
Explores concerns that national performance indicators for children's services may not be adequately interpreted and used to improve service delivery for individual children. Data from a longitudinal study of 249 looked after children demonstrate that one target – improving placement stability – is more likely to be met if agencies can identify which children are frequently moved and why. While age and behavioural difficulties may have contributed to placement breakdown, the majority of the moves were planned transitions from one temporary placement to another. This suggests that the systems are not geared to meet the needs of children who cannot swiftly return home.

Infant adoption

Relevant literature is also to be found in the sections about birth family and books for children and adoptive parents.

395 **BAAF (2003) Adoption Planning for Babies: BAAF position statement.** London: *BAAF*
Sets out BAAF's position on adoption planning for infants and offers a number of recommendations on how to achieve the best possible outcome.

396 Castle J, Beckett C and Groothues C and the English and Romanian Adoptees (ERA) study team (2000) 'Infant adoption in England: policy and practice at placement', *Adoption & Fostering*, 24:4, pp. 45–56

Compares the impact of policies and practices of social services and voluntary adoption agencies on a sample of 52 adoptions of infants (research date: 1989). In the light of differences examined between contact, openness and post-placement support, the authors recommend that more co-operation between the sectors would result in mutual improvements. See also ref. 397.

397 Castle J, Beckett C, Groothues C and the English and Romanian Adoptees (ERA) study team (2000) 'Infant adoption in England: a longitudinal account of social and cognitive progress', *Adoption & Fostering*, 24:3, pp. 26–35

In many ways in-country infant adoptions are becoming a thing of the past. However, several factors arising from this study of social and cognitive progress in children adopted as babies may be equally salient for older-placed children, especially in middle childhood and early adolescence. From a sample of 52 children in the same number of families, placed before the age of six months, Castle *et al* looked at outcomes such as adoptive parents' marital and emotional adjustment, evaluation of the adoption and children's cognitive attainment in two phases – at age four and six years. Overall, the study confirmed earlier research to suggest that infant adoptions tend to lead to very good social and intellectual progress in children, as well as high parental satisfaction.

398 **Cousins W and Monteith M (2002) The Lives of Younger Looked After Children: Preliminary findings from the Multiple Placements Project.** Belfast: *Institute of Child Care Research, Queens University Belfast*

Presents the results of a study that involved a survey of social work files for looked after children under five years in Northern Ireland. The most stated placement option by the review forms was foster care. When it came to overall long-term plans, adoption was the commonly preferred option, followed by eventual return to the birth family.

399 **Cousins J and Morrison M with de Sousa S (2003) Right from the Start: Best practice in adoption planning for babies and other children.** London: *BAAF*

Examines how adoption practice has evolved in this area and offers a model of good practice in a modern context. Covers "relinquishing" birth mothers, birth fathers, the baby, adoptive parents, agencies, legal and medical issues, pre-birth planning, interventions after birth, formalising the plan and adoption support.

400 **Freundlich M (1998) 'Supply and demand: the forces shaping the future of infant adoption',** *Adoption Quarterly*, 2:1, pp. 13–46

Evaluates the impact for adoption policy and practice of changing patterns of availability of babies for adoption and adults seeking to adopt.

401 **Kemp S P and Bodonyi J M (2000) 'Infants who stay in foster care: child characteristics and permanency outcomes of legally free children first**

placed as infants', *Child & Family Social Work*, 5:2, pp. 95–106

This US study explored issues relating to children who remain in care for long periods, including length of stay, permanency outcomes and the effects of race and gender on the likelihood of these children achieving a permanent placement.

402 **Menard B J (1997) 'A birth father and adoption in the perinatal setting'**, *Social Work in Health Care*, 24:3/4, pp. 153–63

Examines emotional, legal and practice issues related to a birth father in adoption. The key issue can be the involvement of the birth father in the context of the birth mother's wishes and the planning with the adoptive parents. In this US discussion, there are debates about the birth father which challenge lawyers, adoption professionals and members of the adoption triad.

403 **Neil E (2000) 'The reasons why young children are placed for adoption: findings from a recently placed sample and a discussion of implications for subsequent identity development'**, *Child & Family Social Work*, 5:4, pp. 303–16

A report of the findings of a study of young children placed for adoption before four years of age. The aim was to examine the reasons for placement and consider the implications for identity development. The children fell broadly into three groups: relinquished infants, infants who had been placed at the request of their parent(s) but in complex circumstances, and infants placed as result of decisions by social services and the courts. The author argues that these very different biographical histories will present different challenges to adoptive parents as they help their children to understand the meaning of adoption.

404 Stone S (1994) 'Contact between adopters and birth parents: the Strathclyde experience', *Adoption & Fostering*, 18:2, pp. 36–38
Brief account of the impact on adopters of Strathclyde Social Work Department's requirement that all couples seeking to adopt a child under two years of age should be willing to meet with birth parents.

Contact

Many of the studies already listed consider the issues arising from contact between child and birth parents. Among those that deal at some length with the subject are: Fahlberg (1994 – ref. 120); Quinton *et al* (1998 – ref. 375); Hill (1999 – contributions especially by Waterhouse and Cleaver – ref. 132); Wheal (1999 – ref. 191) and Wilson, Sinclair *et al* (2004 – ref. 194). In this section, we bring together studies that are exclusively concerned with this issue.

405 Argent H (ed.) (1995) See You Soon: Contact with children looked after by local authorities. London: *BAAF*
Explores planning and managing appropriate contact from a variety of viewpoints, including a look at the history of contact arrangements, the legal framework, contact in the local authority setting and contact with children who have been abused.

406 **Argent H (ed.) (2002) Staying Connected: Managing contact arrangements in adoption.** London: *BAAF*
The principal contributors to this book are practitioners involved in day-to-day adoption services. They provide examples of innovative practice and try to answer questions of what works, what doesn't and why. Despite the diverse nature of contact arrangements there are some recurrent themes. Successful arrangements appear to be associated with clarity of purpose, flexible arrangements and built-in mechanisms for review.

407 **BAAF (1999) Contact in Permanent Placement: Guidance for local authorities in England and Wales and Scotland.** London: *BAAF*
Highlights factors to be taken into account in exploring whether a child's welfare would be promoted by planning some form of contact within the permanent placement, and the implications for agency policy and practice. Issue covered include assessment of the child's needs, attitudes of prospective carers, parents, birth relatives and significant others, and the views and experiences of current carers in relation to contact.

408 **Beek M (1994) 'The reality of face-to-face contact after adoption',** *Adoption & Fostering*, 18:2, pp. 39–43
Under what conditions might face-to-face meetings after adoption be successfully negotiated, and how might they affect adoptive relationships in the short and long term? Beek presents the findings of a small study which sought the views of adopters.

409 **Carter V, Magee S and Thoday R (1999) 'Adoption information exchange: evaluation of a letterbox system in a local authority',** *Adoption & Fostering*, 23:1, pp. 24–30

An evaluation of a letterbox system established to facilitate ongoing contact between birth and adoptive families on behalf of the adopted child. The adoption agency acts as an intermediary and provides a confidential process by which birth and adoptive families can share updating information. The majority of exchanges occurred annually and involved the exchange of letters, cards or photographs. The evaluation was based on a summary of the views of birth and adoptive family members and social work practitioners. Positive views were expressed by many participants. The evaluation did highlight some organisational issues and raised fundamental questions, such as how families who do not maintain the agreed arrangements should be followed up.

410 **Courtney A (2000) 'Loss and grief in adoption: the impact of contact',** *Adoption & Fostering*, 24:2, pp. 33–44.

This article describes a theoretical framework for understanding the adopted child's experience of loss. The author argues that in order to grieve the child needs to develop an internal working model of the birth parent based on memories, fantasy and information provided by carers, social workers and family members. Grieving involves not moving on but 'integrating this model into his or her everyday life by an ongoing process of re-negotiating the relationship' (p. 34). In developing this framework the author draws on ideas derived from attachment theory but also studies in relation to bereavement in children. The article concludes with some important implications for contact and openness.

411 **Fratter J (1996) Adoption with Contact: Implications for policy and practice.** London: *BAAF*
A report of the findings of a small-scale, qualitative study examining patterns of openness and contact in families adopting children with special needs. The study comprised interviews with adoptive parents, birth parents and adopted children. The findings lend cautious support to the move towards more openness in adoption, but the author stresses the importance of retaining a child-centred approach.

412 **Gair S (1999) 'Adoptive mothers' attitudes to contact: highlights from an Australian study',** *Adoption & Fostering*, 23:3, pp. 38–47
Explores coping positions or attitudes to contact taken by a sample of adoptive mothers in Queensland.

413 **Grotevant H D (2000) 'Openness in adoption: research with the adoptive kinship network',** *Adoption Quarterly*, 4:1, pp. 45–65
A brief overview of the current research literature regarding openness in adoption. The article includes discussion of the methodological issues involved in undertaking research in this area of practice. Open adoption is complex and involves the ongoing negotiation of appropriate boundaries between the birth and adoptive family but can work well if both birth and adoptive parents want this to happen.

414 **Logan J and Smith C (1999) 'Adoption and direct post-adoption contact',** *Adoption & Fostering*, 23:4, pp. 58–59

This research note provides a brief summary of the findings of a study in relation to direct contact. The aim was to consider this from the perspective of all those involved in the adoption triangle. Birth family members proved more difficult to contact than adoptive parents and children. The numbers interviewed were therefore substantially less than the other two groups. The majority of the children had been placed from care. Adoptive parents were largely supportive of contact arrangements. After some initial teething problems ongoing contact did not adversely affect the children's behaviour or the adopter's sense of entitlement. The study identified a number of contra-indications.

415 **Macaskill C (2002) Safe Contact? Children in permanent placement and contact with their birth relatives.** Lyme Regis: *Russell House Publishing*

Reports the findings of a study of children and young people in permanent foster care/adoption who maintained face-to-face contact with members of their birth family. Paradoxically, while many children had mixed feelings about the benefits of contact, the majority were still in favour of such arrangements continuing. Some children would have liked more contact, others less. The book includes a wealth of detail about contact arrangements that will be informative for practitioners and carers.

416 **McCartt Hess P and Ohman Proch K (1993) Contact: Managing visits to children.** London: *BAAF*

Handbook containing valuable guidance on good practice.

417 Miller Wrobel G M, Grotevant H D, Berge J, Mendehall T and McRoy R (2003) 'Contact in adoption: the experience of adoptive families in the USA', *Adoption & Fostering*, 27:1, pp. 57–67

A longitudinal study of openness in adoption. The children have been followed up at two stages, the second during adolescence. Although this is a study of infant placement, it provides an interesting theoretical framework for considering whether openness in adoption is of relevance to the placement of older children.

418 Mullender A and Kearn S (1997) "I'm Here Waiting": Birth relatives' views on Part II of the Adoption Contact Register for England and Wales. London: *BAAF*

The first research study to examine the views of birth relatives who have used Part II of the Adoption Contact Register for England and Wales. Through the responses of birth parents, siblings and other relatives, it explores the depth and complexity of the emotions of those involved and highlights the anomalies created by current legislation. Calls for major changes to create a more sensitive post-adoption system and recommends alterations in the law.

419 Neil E (1999) 'The sibling relationships of adopted children and patterns of contact after adoption', *Adoption & Fostering*, 23:1, pp. 59–60

This research note reports the interim findings of one part of a larger study in relation to contact after adoption. They refer specifically to the nature of sibling relationships in a cohort of young, recently placed adopted children. The study demonstrates the complex nature of sibling relationships. Sixty-eight per cent of the adopted children in the sample had full or half siblings. The mean number was three and the maximum ten. Siblings often live in many different locations, namely foster care, other adoptive families, with grandparents, birth parents, residential care, etc. Sixty-three per cent of the children with siblings had never lived with any of their brothers or sisters before they were adopted.

420 Neil E (2002) 'Contact after adoption: the role of agencies in making and supporting plans', *Adoption & Fostering*, 26:1, pp. 25–38

This article summarises the findings of a study examining contact after adoption. The study included interviews with adoptive parents where there were plans for face-to-face contact. The mean age of the children at placement was one year 11 months. It is important that agencies help adoptive parents to feel positively about contact arrangements. Evidence of ambivalence on the part of social workers led to infrequent meetings that were "controlled" rather than supported. A more successful model of agency involvement would include empowering birth and adoptive families to find their own comfort levels with contact and providing support where needed.

421 Neil E (2003) 'Accepting the reality of adoption: birth relatives' experience of face-to-face contact', *Adoption and Fostering*, 27:2, pp. 32–43

Reports the findings of a small-scale interview study of adoptive parents and birth relatives of children involved in face-to-face contact arrangements. The children were aged three years or under at the time of placement. The authors argue that the construct of "role ambiguity" provides useful insight into the particular nature of loss experienced by relatives whose children have been placed for adoption outside the birth family. The aim of the interviews was to assess how far birth relatives had been able to accept the reality of the role change arising from the child's placement for adoption. The findings indicated that the majority of relatives were able to do this and this in turn enabled adopters to be more sensitive to the inherent difficulties in contact situations. The author argues that practitioners with the experience of working with older children may underestimate the level of complexity in placements of younger children. However, moving to the point of some acceptance of the change in roles takes time. Anger and hostility in the early stages does not necessarily preclude positive experiences with contact at a later stage in the placement.

422 **Neil E, Beek M and Schofield G (2003) 'Thinking about and managing contact in permanent placements: the differences and similarities between adoptive parents and foster carers',** *Clinical Child Psychology and Psychiatry*, 8:3, pp. 401–18
Focuses on the issue of post-placement contact and discusses the qualities of foster carers and adopters that can best help children cope with issues of attachment, identity and loss when contact occurs.

423 **Quinton D, Rushton A, Dance C and Mayes D (1997) 'Contact between children placed away from home and their birth parents: research issues and evidence',** *Clinical Child Psychology and Psychiatry*, 2:3, pp. 393–413 (see ref. 426)

424 **Rajan P and Lister L (1998) 'Nottinghamshire's letterbox contact service',** *Adoption & Fostering*, 22:1, pp. 46–52

Describes a confidential service which aims to maintain links between adoptive parents and birth families once an adoption order has been granted.

425 **Ryburn M (1994) Open Adoption: Research, theory and practice.** Aldershot: *Ashgate*
This is an important book on open adoption. The first section identifies the legislation and its approach to openness and then reviews research on identity formation and identity in adoption, and goes on to examine the evidence in relation to contact and permanent placement. The second half of the book identifies the experiences of six parties who have experiences of open adoption in New Zealand and were part of a six-year follow-up study.

426 **Ryburn M (1998) 'In whose best interests? Post-adoption contact with the birth family',** *Child and Family Law Quarterly*, 10:1, pp. 53–70
This article and the one by Quinton *et al* (ref. 423) offer the reader two very different perspectives on the issue of contact. Quinton and colleagues provide a critical literature review in relation to short, long-term and adoptive placements. While not opposing the move towards openness in adoption, they argue for a more cautious approach until evidence of the benefits are more clearly established. Ryburn, however, interprets the evidence differently, arguing that there are indications of the benefits to all parties. A key issue, he suggests, is the capacity of even young children to maintain multiple attachments. Research in relation to contact and openness is complex and controversial. These articles provide useful summaries of available research, but also identify the key methodological and practice issues.

427 **Smith C and Logan J (2004) After Adoption: Direct contact and relationships.** London: *Routledge*
Reviews research evidence on contact arrangements between adopted children and their birth parents after the adoption placement, incorporating the views and feelings of children (including siblings), birth parents, grandparents and adoptive parents. Also considers the development of adoption policy and law in relation to this area. Altogether a balanced discussion on a very controversial subject.

428 **Sykes M R (2001) 'Adoption with contact: a study of adoptive parents and the impact of continuing contact with families of origin',** *Journal of Family Therapy*, 23:3, pp. 296–316
A small-scale, exploratory study examining adoptive parents' changing perceptions of openness. The author notes the subtle impact of complex, evolving relationships. Key issues for adoptive parents include a need to feel in control of contact arrangements. Surprisingly, this was associated more with direct than indirect contact. It could take up to three years for birth and adoptive families to reach a mutual accommodation. A developing sense of empathy for the birth mother might be developed at some emotional cost to the adoptive mother.

Birth family

This section contains a range of resources and studies that take special account of the experience of birth mothers and fathers. These include first-hand accounts and studies of the impact of relinquishing (or being required to relinquish) a child. Works related to search and reunion are listed separately.

429 **BAAF (1999) Child from the Past: Information for people who place their child for adoption in England and Wales.** London: *BAAF*
Information leaflet covering some of the concerns women may have about meeting an adult son or daughter who was adopted.

430 **Birthlink (2003)** www.birthlink.org.uk/index.html (accessed March 2004)
Birthlink operates the Scotland Adoption Contact Register, a computerised database to assist in linking adopted people, birth parents and birth siblings. The organisation provides information, counselling, support and assistance in the stages of searching and meeting. The site includes a list of resources, among them a reading list and details of relevant videos.

431 **Bouchier P, Lambert L and Triseliotis J (1991) Parting with a Child for Adoption: The mother's perspective.** London: *BAAF*
A major study of the personal and social circumstances, motivation, attitudes and current adjustment of mothers who relinquished children for adoption. The study provides a demographic profile of 46 mothers who had relinquished their children for adoption at least eight years previously (most during the 1960s and 1970s), accounts of their pregnancy and confinement, the reasons for and experience of parting from their child, the long-term effects on them and their expectations of future contact. (Most wished for some form of contact, reporting that they thought about their children 'most days' or 'most weeks'.) These mothers received little counselling or support at the time of relinquishment and the consequences of this decision would stay with them

throughout their lives. Concludes with messages for practice, including the need for counselling and support for mothers who have given up their children in the past or who are considering doing so now, and for the periodic release of non-identifying information about the child's progress and a move towards more open adoptions.

432 Brodzinsky D M, Schechter M D and Hening R M (1992) Being Adopted: The lifelong search for self. New York: *Bantam Doubleday Dell*

A readable account of the adoptees' growing understanding of adoption at different life stages, from childhood to maturity.

433 Charlton L, Crank M, Kansara K and Oliver C (1998) Still Screaming: Birth parents compulsorily separated from their children. Manchester: *After Adoption*

Gives voice to parents whose children have been adopted against their wishes. Two projects are described: Parents Without Children and Before Adoption. Records the experiences of parents and makes recommendations for good practice; information, counselling, advocacy and mediation would make a significant difference but are currently not readily available.

434 Clapton G (1997) 'Birth fathers, the adoption process and fatherhood', *Adoption & Fostering*, 21:1, pp. 29–36

A great deal of research has been carried out on birth mothers and the intense grief and sense of loss they feel on giving up their children for adoption. Much less is known about the experiences of birth fathers. Clapton surveys existing research, mainly in the USA and

Australia. Based on this and his own work, charting and interpreting the experiences of some 25 men, he goes on to ask some key questions about the nature of fatherhood and considers the implications for current policies and practice.

435 Clapton G (2002) Birth Fathers and their Adoption Experiences. London: *Jessica Kingsley*
Clapton's work is based on the experiences of 30 birth fathers separated from their children at birth. It discusses different notions of fatherhood, such as biological paternity, social fatherhood, sperm donorship and the "father figure", and considers issues such as the decision to give up a child for adoption, the child's desire to find his or her birth parents, and the facilitation of contact in later life. Potential readership would be parents, adopted adults and professional staff and includes suggestions for helpful practice.

436 Clapton G (ed.) (2003) Relatively Unknown. Edinburgh: *Birthlink*
Over 60 first-hand accounts from those who have used the Adoption Contact for Scotland.

437 Coleman K and Jenkins E (1998), Elephants Never Forget: Relationships between birth parents and adoptees. North Carolina: *Signature Publications*
This book, written by birth mothers who have experienced both relinquishment and reunion, addresses the processes, problems, sorrows and joys of reunion between birth parents and adoptees. Drawing on the experiences of about 40 birth parents, it emphasises that they never forget the children they gave up for adoption and, although sensitive to the needs of new families, may

be deterred by bureaucratic procedures, lack of information and fear of the consequences.

438 **Howe D, Sawbridge P and Hinings D (1992) Half a Million Women: Mothers who lose their children by adoption.** London: *Penguin*
A key work about the experiences of women who have relinquished their children for adoption. Woven into a sensitive account of the experiences of mothers, the book provides analyses of societal, medical, legal and psychological issues.

439 **Jackson J (2000) 'Developing a post-adoption groupwork service for non-consenting birth mothers',** *Adoption & Fostering*, 24:4, pp. 32–39
An account of groupwork offered by Support After Adoption for birth mothers whose children have been in care and then adopted. The service described began in 1998 in Nottingham and is now being extended to the Mansfield area. Outlines the background informing the development of this service, including links with other agencies working in this way, the options considered and chosen, and the aims and value base of the service finally offered. Describes the composition and process of the group as it developed and the themes that emerged. Finally, offers workers' and participants' evaluations of what these birth mothers gained from the group, highlights some of the learning outcomes for Support After Adoption and considers ways in which the team hopes to take this work forward.

440 **Kay J (1991) The Adoption Papers.** Tarset: *Bloodaxe Books*

A collection of poems dramatising the perspectives of adoptee, adoptive mother and birth mother.

441 **Mander R (1995) The Care of the Mother Grieving a Baby Relinquished for Adoption.** Aldershot: *Avebury*

Analyses the consequences of relinquishing a child for adoption using Kubler-Ross's framework for understanding grief and the dying process. Emphasises the chances of better outcomes for women who have had support during the grieving process along with the finding that the sense of loss never goes away.

442 **Mason K and Selman P (1996) Parents without Children: An evaluation and research report.** Newcastle: *Newcastle University*

Research and evaluation of the Parents Without Children project, set up as part of the Durham Diocesan Adoption Agency. See also refs. 433 and 443.

443 **Mason K and Selman P (1997) 'Birth parents' experiences of contested adoption',** *Adoption & Fostering*, 21:1, pp. 21–28

In recent years a growing proportion of adoption orders have been made without the consent of the birth mother, yet the needs of these "non-relinquishing" parents have received little attention. Mason and Selman present findings from research evaluating birth parents' experiences of contesting the adoption of their child(ren) which was carried out as part of a wider evaluation of Parents Without Children, an innovative project offering support for non-relinquishing birth parents.

444 **Trinder L (2000) 'The rights and wrongs of post-adoption intermediary services for birth relatives',** *Adoption Quarterly*, 24:3, pp. 19–25
Examines the ethics of post-adoption intermediary services on behalf of the birth relatives of adults who were adopted as children. Intermediary services can be seen as an attempt to equalise the rights to search of birth relatives and adopted people. They also reflect wider beliefs about the importance of genealogical information and openness. By their nature, however, intermediary services dispense with the informed consent of those who are contacted, may cause upset or harm and potential breach of confidentiality and privacy. This article argues that the rights of minorities must be respected and upheld. The Adoption Contact Register is put forward as a better alternative.

445 **Verrier N (1993) The Primal Wound: Understanding the adopted child.** Baltimore: *Gateway Press Inc.*
A powerful exploration of the deep wound left by separation of mother and child.

446 **Walby C and Symons B (1990), Who Am I? Identity, adoption and human fertilisation.** London: *BAAF*
Examines issues of identity based on studies of people who have been adopted. Enlarges the area of discussion by then considering families created as a result of sperm or embryo donation. Refers to policy and legislative frameworks as at 1990.

447 **Wells S (1993) 'Post-traumatic stress disorder in birth mothers',** *Adoption & Fostering*, 17:2 pp. 30–32
Based on her research as a birth mother, Wells presents extracts from her presentation at the world conference of

the International Society for Traumatic Stress Studies in Amsterdam (April 1993) which for the first time featured adoption on the agenda.

448 **Wells S (1993) 'What do birth mothers want?',** *Adoption & Fostering*, 17:4, pp. 22–26.
Starting from a survey of 262 birth mothers, Sue Wells argues strongly for a change in the adoption law. She concludes that the survey indicated that the stress resulting from relinquishment is profound and long lasting, that most people are unable to resolve their grief, that the decision about relinquishment was seldom a free choice (whatever its legal status) and that over half felt a clean break was not a good solution.

449 **Wells S (1994) Within Me, Without Me: Adoption – an open and shut case?** London: *Scarlet Press*
Collection of personal stories by mothers who have given their children up for adoption. Based on research spanning 40 years. Includes sections on "clean breaks", reunion, semi-open adoption and open adoption.

450 **Winkler R and van Keppel M (1984) Relinquishing Mothers in Adoptions: Their long-term adjustment.** Melbourne: *Institute of Family Studies*
An influential study of 213 mothers in Australia who relinquished their children for adoption, drawing attention to the enduring after-effects and service shortcomings. The study includes a comparision with the effects of perinatal death. Many of its recommendations for practice and policy are evident in later adoption law across many countries.

Search and reunion

451 **Feast J and Philpot T (2003) Searching Questions: Identity, origins and adoption.** London: *BAAF*
Based on a study of why some adopted people embark on a search for information or reunion with birth family members and others do not (see ref. 455), this book and video highlight the issues for all concerned. Illustrated by the real-life experiences of searchers and non-searchers alike, the package provides a greater understanding of the complexities and feelings likely to be encountered.

452 **Feast J, Marwood M, Seabrook S and Webb E (1998) Preparing for Reunion: Experiences from the adoption circle (2nd edition). London: The Children's Society**
Narratives of adopted people, adoptive parents and birth parents exploring the process of searching, preparation and reunion. Written in an accessible style and relevant particularly for all members of "the adoption triangle".

453 **General Register Office (2003) Adoption Contact Register.** www.gro.gov.uk/gro/content/adoptions (accessed September 2004)
Information about the Adoption Contact Register set up in 1991 to provide a safe and confidential way for birth parents and other relatives to assure an adopted person that contact would be welcome.

454 **Howe D and Feast J (2001) 'The long-term outcome of reunions between adult adopted people and their birth mothers',** *British Journal of Social Work*, 31:3, pp. 268–351
The authors investigated the experience of contact and

reunion of 48 adults. Although over half of adopted people were still in contact with their birth mother eight years or more following reunion, the number still in touch with their adoptive mother was higher still. Results are discussed in terms of the search for identity, parent–child relationships, genetic relatedness and the role of nurture.

455 **Howe D and Feast J (2003) Adoption, Search and Reunion: The long-term experiences of adopted adults.** London: *BAAF*
Based on a study of the experiences of 500 adopted people, this book (previously published by The Children's Society and now updated with a new introduction) looks at all possible influences on their decisions to seek or not to seek out their birth relatives. Extensive quotations from adopted people help to create a compelling narrative that tackles fundamental issues of identity, origins and relationships.

456 **Kirton D, Feast J and Howe D (2000) 'Searching, reunion and transracial adoption',** *Adoption & Fostering*, 24:3, pp. 6–18
Reports on findings from qualitative interviews with transracially adopted adults.

457 **March K (1995) The Stranger who Bore Me: Adoptee–birth mother relationships.** Toronto: *University of Toronto Press*
Canadian study of 60 adoptees' attempts to reunite with their birth mothers. Begins with a literature review (to 1995) and an account of the adoptees and how they made sense of their identity. Later chapters describe the search process and outcomes, the numbers who were rejected

after reunion, the numbers whose birth mothers had died and the 52 per cent who retained contact afterwards. Analyses the various patterns involved.

458 McMillan R and Irving G (1997) Heart of Reunion: Some experiences of reunion in Scotland. Ilford: *Barnardo's*
This study of 45 adoptees in Scotland who were reunited with their birth families describes both parties' expectations, their experiences and the impact of reunion on their lives.

459 National Archives of Scotland (undated) Adoption Records Fact Sheet
http://www.nas.gov.uk/miniframe/fact_sheet/adoption.pdf (accessed February 2004)
Government guidance about Scottish adoption records.

460 National Organisation for the Counselling of Adoptees and Parents (NORCAP) (1998) Searching for Family Connections. Wheatley, Oxon: *NORCAP*
A detailed step-by-step guide to searching birth records, from the experience of those who have been through it themselves. Aimed at adopted people but also recommended for counsellors.

461 Roche H and Perlesz A (2000) 'A legitimate choice and voice: the experience of adult adoptees who have chosen not to search for their biological families', *Adoption & Fostering*, 24:2, pp. 8–19
Presents the findings of an Australian pilot project that examined the reasons of those who decide not to search for their biological parents. These included loyalty to their adoptive parents, willingness to be found as opposed to

finding or searching, the role of current family and friends and a sense of belonging to a spiritual dimension.

462 Scottish Record Office (2003) Tracing your Scottish Ancestors: The official guide (3rd edition). Edinburgh: *Mercat Press*
Reference work about tracing families.

463 Smith J and Wallace R (2000) 'Providing a birth relative intermediary service: the non-searching adopted person's perspectives', *Adoption & Fostering*, 24:4, pp. 18–28
Examines the main messages and implications from a piece of research conducted by The Children's Society, focusing particularly on the views and experiences of non-searching adopted people who have been contacted on behalf of a birth relative.

464 Stafford G (2001) Where to Find Adoption Records: A guide for counsellors, adopted people and birth relatives. London: *BAAF*
This reference book is an invaluable starting point for adopted people wishing to find out more about their origins and birth relatives seeking news of their child who has been adopted. It shows how to trace missing adoption records and provides guidance on possible sources of information in England, Wales, Scotland, Northern Ireland, Eire and abroad. Includes details of records held by current and previous voluntary agencies, mother and baby homes and shelters, and social services and social work departments, as well as information on searching and a resource list.

465 **Trinder L, Feast J and Howe D (2004) The Adoption Reunion Handbook.** Chichester: *John Wiley & Sons*
Based on a large-scale research study, the authors have drawn on the real-life experiences of adopted people who have searched for and had a reunion with birth relatives. The result is a comprehensive step-by-step guide for anyone considering such a search, from 'how to begin' to 'how to set up a reunion' and 'rejection and reunion breakdown'. A very useful Appendix provides details of resources and other information on search and reunion in the UK, Ireland, Australia, New Zealand, Canada and the USA.

466 **Tugendhat J (1992) The Adoption Triangle: Searching and uniting.** London: *Bloomsbury*
Based on qualitative research, describes the effects of adoption for all parties. Useful material for birth parents, adoptive parents and adopted people. Includes topics such as tracing and reunion.

Support services for adoptive families

See also refs. 039, 046, 120, 122, 170, 171, 475, 476, 730, 793–796, 798–800, 813, 817, 823, 826–837.

467 **Argent H (ed.) (2003) Models of Adoption Support: What works and what doesn't.** London: *BAAF*
A collection of contributions drawing on the expertise of people with personal experience of adoption, volunteers and a range of professional staff from different disciplines including health and education. The majority of chapters are descriptions of innovative practice that suggest creative possibilities of how support services might be provided.

468 **Barth R P and Miller J M (2000) 'Building effective post-adoption services: what is the empirical foundation?',** *Family Relations*, 46:4, pp. 447–55
The authors start from the viewpoint that disappointment and disruption in adoption may be reduced by the provision of post-adoption services. However, their review indicates that while adoptive parents request a variety of services, few demonstration projects have been done to evaluate their effectiveness. The article recognises the dominant position of attachment theory in post-adoption services and identifies alternative approaches that may have a better fit with the needs and preferences identified by families. Argues for various service adaptations that would improve effectiveness and usability.

469 **Kluger M P, Alexander G and Curtis P A (eds.) (2000) What Works in Child Welfare.** Washington, DC: *Child Welfare League of America*
An anthology of research evidence, predominantly from the United States, written in an accessible style for both lay people and professionals. The book describes practice and clinical interventions considered to be effective in work with children and families at high risk of neglect and abuse. Of particular relevance are chapters in relation to permanency planning and open adoption.

470 **Lowe N, Murch M, Borkowski M, Weaver A, Beckford V and Thomas C (1999) Supporting Adoption: Reframing the approach.** London: *BAAF*
This book reports the findings of a study which was set up to review support services available to adoptive families during the critical period when the child moves from care to live with their new family. The study is

concerned with children from five years during the period from placement until 12 months after the adoption order is made. It is in three parts, examining the views of agency staff, adoptive parents and adopted children. The aim is to consider the levels of support available to children and families from a range of different disciplines during the adoption process.

The findings, described as descriptive and exploratory, examine a number of interesting theoretical constructs. An understanding of the theory underlying "status change" and "critical transitions" may be helpful in providing insight into the adoption process. The authors argue that a "contract service" model of adoption practice perhaps more fully meets the needs of children in placement. They conclude with a number of challenging recommendations for adoption policy and practice.

471 **Pallett C, Scott S, Blackeby K, Yule W and Weissman R (2002) 'Fostering changes: a cognitive-behavioural approach to help foster carers manage children',** *Adoption & Fostering*, 26:1, pp. 39–48
A description of a training programme for foster carers based on cognitive-behavioural methods that provides a model that could be used or adapted by staff within family placement teams. There was some improvement in hyperactivity and conduct problems but this did not reach levels of significance.

472 **Phillips R and McWilliam E (eds.) (1996) After Adoption: Working with adoptive families.** London: *BAAF*
This book is described as the first publication to focus solely on the needs of adoptive families for post-adoption

support. Recent changes in adoption legislation have confirmed the need for comprehensive support packages for adoptive families. Although there have been theoretical and practice developments since 1996, this collection gives a sense of the wide range of services needed by families, e.g. therapeutic services, respite care and educational support. Contributions about open and transracial adoption provide sensitive accounts of the support needs in these particular aspects of adoption practice.

473 **Rushton A and Dance C (2002) Adoption Support Services for Families in Difficulty: A literature review and UK survey.** London: *BAAF*
The first part reviews the literature on the need for adoption support and on the development and effectiveness of services. The main aim is to consider the needs of late-placed children adopted from care. Following recent Department of Health guidelines, the authors use the term "adoption support" rather than "post-placement" or "post-adoption" services. The second part of the book reports the findings of a study of the views of local authority and adoption agency staff. Although examples of good social work practice are evident, the development of services is patchy and inconsistent, with little systematic audit of need. Access for adoptive families to universal services, e.g. within education and specialist mental health settings, is important but these services need to be delivered in a way that recognises the additional dimension adoption brings.

474 **Swaine J and Gilson J (1998) 'Meeting the needs of adoptive parents under stress: a group work approach',** *Adoption & Fostering*, 22:2, pp. 44–53
Written by two practitioners, this article describes a time-

limited support group established to meet the needs of adoptive parents under stress. In planning the group the workers drew on ideas from gestalt psychotherapy. The aim was to provide an emotional space for adoptive parents to consider their own feelings, needs and parenting strategies. The family was viewed from a systemic perspective to avoid pathologising the child or blaming the child, parent or other family members.

Books for children, parents and carers

These are a selection of writings designed for children, birth parents or adoptive parents. Much of the interest arises from first-hand accounts. Some of the literature is prepared with one or other group in mind, but a significant number are of interest to all parties. Reference should also be made to the equivalent section of Chapter 2 and to the section in Chapter 6 about therapeutic interventions. Relevant publications from earlier in chapters include Heptinstall *et al* (2001 – ref. 353), Howe (1996 – ref. 357) and Treacher and Katz (2000 – ref. 391).

475 Archer C (1999a) First Steps in Parenting the Child who Hurts: Tiddlers and toddlers (2nd edition).
London: *Jessica Kingsley*
Primarily aimed at adoptive parents, but of considerable use to foster carers of young children, this book offers practical, sensitive guidance though the areas of separation, loss and trauma in early childhood. It reassures parents/carers that no problem faced as a result of a child's early experiences is too insignificant or undeserving of a solution. Archer sets out purposefully to encourage confidence and thereby to enable enjoyment of parenting the young person, on the basis that this is

the book she herself, as an adoptive parent, would have welcomed 20 years ago.

476 Archer C (1999b), Next Steps in Parenting the Child who Hurts: Tykes and teens. London: *Jessica Kingsley*

This volume follows on from the *First Steps* book above and continues the challenging journey through childhood and into adolescence. In essence, it is a book about love and the ability to express it towards the adopted child, despite persistent and often extreme tests of that love. The author explains the effects of early emotional trauma and reviews specific sensitive situations that commonly arise, emphasising that only the parent will know what action is right for their own particular family and set of circumstances.

477 BAAF (1999) Child from the Past (England and Wales). London: *BAAF*

See ref. 429.

478 BAAF (2003) If You are Adopted. London: *BAAF*

Provides basic guidance for people who have been adopted about tracing birth parents, the processes and emotions involved.

479 Byrne S and Chambers L (1997) Belonging Doesn't Mean Forgetting: Nathan's story. London: *BAAF*

A story about a little boy who is adopted. Four-year-old Nathan has just started school. His birth mother finds it hard to be a good mother and wants someone else to look after him, so Nathan goes to live with another family where he stays.

480 **Byrne S and Chambers L (1997) Hoping for the Best: Jack's Story.** London: *BAAF*
The first in BAAF's "My Story" series for children, this book focuses on an adoption that did not work out.

481 **Byrne S and Chambers L (1999) Joining Together: Jo's story.** London: *BAAF*
This book focuses on a step-parent adoption.

482 **Byrne S and Chambers L (1997) Living with a New Family: Nadia and Rashid's story.** London: *BAAF*
After the death of their father and after a period with foster carers, Nadia (10) and Rashid (7), a brother and sister, are adopted by Ayesha and Azeez. Another story to be used flexibly and creatively with children.

483 **Foxon J (2001) Nutmeg Gets Adopted.** London: *BAAF*
This children's book – first in the series (see refs. 271 and 272) – tells the story of Nutmeg, a little squirrel, and his younger sister and brother who go to live with a new family after their birth mother realises she cannot keep them safe. The story offers a practical way of helping children explore and understand some of the very painful memories that they will have of their early life. A comprehensive set of practice guidelines is included.

484 **Foxon J (2002) Nutmeg Gets Cross.** London: *BAAF*
See re. 271.

485 **Foxon J (2003) Nutmeg Gets a Letter.** London: *BAAF*
See ref. 272.

486 Hughes D (1994) What can a counsellor do? A personal account of counselling by a mother who parted with her child for adoption. London: *Post Adoption Centre*

Personal account of a mother's journey and the counselling she received.

487 Kahn H (2002) Tia's Wishes. London: *BAAF*

See ref. 274.

488 Kahn H (2003) Tyler's Wishes. London: *BAAF*

See ref. 275.

489 Keck G and Kupecky R (1995) Adopting the Hurt Child. Colorado Springs: *Pinon Press*

A work of particular relevance for adoptive parents, but also for social workers, mental health professionals and others who provide services for children and parents. Based on an attachment model of development, the book offers clear practical advice as well as a description and critique of welfare practice. See also ref. 568.

490 Lidster A (1995) Chester and Daisy Move On. London: *BAAF*

A story of two bear cubs who have to leave their parents and live with a foster bear family. Soon they learn they are to be adopted. The story encourages children to compare their own stories with that of Chester and Daisy. Work pages are provided for the children to write about their own experiences. Designed for use with children aged 4–10.

491 **Lord J (2002) Adopting a Child: A guide for people interested in adoption.** London: *BAAF*
Guide for potential adopters which describes the range of children for whom adoption is sought and the differences between adoption and fostering. Explains the legal and approval processes, as well as some guidance on the practicalities and costs. Includes information about intercountry adoption and adoption of step-children.

492 **Morris A (1999) The Adoption Experience: Families who give children a second chance.** London: *Jessica Kingsley*
Narrative accounts from adopters that focus in turn on the different stages of becoming an adoptive parent, from initial intentions to the adult tracing their birth parents. Includes smaller contributions from birth parents and from people who were themselves adopted.

493 **Morrison M (2004) Talking About Adoption to your Adopted Child (3rd edition).** London: *BAAF*
Covers the issues involved in discussing origins with an adopted child. Includes discussions relevant to children of all ages, children with disabilities and children who come from a different country or are of a different race or ethnic background. There is information on tracing birth parents, details of useful organisations and a list of useful books.

494 **Salter A N (2004) The Adopters' Handbook: Information, resources and services for adoptive parents.** London: *BAAF*
Information intended to reflect and promote the active engagement of adoptive parents in the social "service" which is adoption. Provides a context both for the

"human" process of bringing a child into a pre-existing family and meeting the specific needs of the child, and for the complex state service aspects of adoption. Adopting a child is a life process in which adults commit themselves to bringing a child into their home, to nurture them and, most importantly, to meet their specific needs. Yet adoption is also a service provided by local authorities or by an adoption agency. Adopters are active participants in that service and it is important to know as much as possible about the process of adoption and wider issues that may affect adoptive parents.

495 Shah S (2003) Adoption: What it is and what it means – a guide for children and young people. London: *BAAF*
A colourful illustrated guide to adoption services designed for children and for routine use by adoption agencies, conforming to the requirements of the National Minimum Standards for Adoption (2003). A similar guide exists about fostering (see ref. 282).

496 Sparks K (1995) Why Adoption? Experiences to share for teenagers and their adoptive parents. London: *BAAF/Thomas Coram Foundation*
Drawing on her experiences and those of her adoptive parents, and comparing these with other adopters, Kulwinder Sparks provides valuable insights into the experience of adoption from a young person's perspective.

497 van Gulden H and Bartels-Rabb L M (1995) Real Parents, Real Children: Parenting the adopted child. New York: *Crossroad Publishing*
'Are they real brothers and sisters?', 'Do you know who

your real mum is?' Contrary to the pejorative way many people use the term "real", adoptive parents and their adopted children are one another's *real* family. Making that family work and nurturing all of its members to be healthy individuals in rewarding relationships with one another is what this book is all about. The authors take parents and professionals through the stages of child development, explaining what adopted children at each stage commonly think and feel about adoption and how parents can respond.

4 Selected schemes and care arrangements

Fostering and adoption arrangements are made in many different ways and for a wide variety of purposes. This chapter focuses on six key areas: short-term placements, specialist and professional foster care schemes, kinship care, transnational arrangements, independent fostering providers and private fostering.

Short-term care is often, though not exclusively, associated with the use of family placement in the context of family support. Studies under this heading examine the views of the child and their carers, the factors associated with length of stay in foster care and provision for teenagers.

Among the topics examined in works on specialist foster care are the use of fostering as an alternative to secure accommodation in Scotland and a US project providing focused care in relation to youth offending or young people with mental health issues.

The importance of kinship care (care by family and friends) for children in need is becoming more widely recognised, with the government setting out to encourage its use and to resolve some of the difficulties and paradoxes involved. This section refers to research, practice guidance and policy documents.

Transnational arrangements require a specific understanding of international perspectives on the part of practitioners, lawyers and policy makers. Issues featured under this heading include intercountry adoption, the family placement of unaccompanied asylum seekers and refugee children and certain patterns in private fostering (see below).

Independent fostering providers (IFPs) are on the increase. This section lists key works that examine the extent of their use and the characteristics of the services provided.

The chapter concludes with a small selection of literature about private fostering.

Short-term placements

Some works directly relevant to short-term foster care are also listed in Chapter 2. The provision of respite/shared care for disabled children is cross-referenced to works related to disabled children in Chapter 5 (refs. 688–745).

498 Aldgate J and Bradley M (1999) Supporting Families through Short-term Fostering. London: *The Stationery Office*

The authors argue that, from being largely associated with disabled children, the use of short-term fostering in family support should be more formally recognised in general family support and interagency working under the Children Act 1989. The study presents the views of birth parents, children and carers and examines the professional implications for child protection and family support under the Assessment Framework.

499 Benedict M and White R B (1991) 'Factors associated with foster care length of stay', *Child Welfare*, 70:1, pp. 45–58

See ref. 102.

500 Bradley M and Aldgate J (1994/1999) 'Short-term family based care for children in need', in Hill M (1999) ***Signposts in Fostering*****,** London: *BAAF.*
Originally published in *Adoption & Fostering*, 18:4, pp. 24–29

Report of the Department of Health-funded study of short-term breaks for children in need. The study collated the views of children, parents and carers, and evaluated (short- and long-term) effectiveness. The authors conclude that the work is intensive, complex and demanding, often underestimated by those not directly involved. See also ref. 498.

501 **de Smet J (1995) A Qualitative Study of Planning Processes in Short-term Foster Care.** Hove: *East Sussex Social Services Department*
Practitioner-based research which arose from the concerns of a particular fostering and adoption team. The immediate reference is to East Sussex, but much of the material gathered and the model of enquiry is of general relevance.

502 **Dutt R (1998) 'Knowing when to move on',** *Community Care*, 20 August, p. 24
The author finds that African-Caribbean and Asian short-term foster carers are better at helping children to move on because they are more sensitive to issues of culture, religion, language and "race".

503 **McConkey R and Adams L (2000) 'Matching short-break services for children with learning disabilities to family needs and preferences',** *Child: Care, Health and Development*, 26:5, pp. 429–44
Reports initially a census in one health and social services board area of all the short breaks which families of a disabled child had taken in a 12-month period. The subsequent analysis gives profiles of the recipients of six types of short-term breaks: hospital-based overnight care, overnight stays in a residential home, domiciliary

service in the family home, breaks provided in another family home, residential holidays and breaks provided through leisure schemes organised after school or during holidays. A second study entailed interviews with families about their usage and preferences for each type of service.

504 **Pinderhughes E E (1998) 'Short-term placement outcomes for children adopted after age five',** *Children and Youth Services Review*, 20:3, pp. 223–49
US study which examines the effects of early short-term placements on children who are later adopted.

505 **Platts H, Hughes J, Lenehan C, Morris S and Flynn M (1996) We Miss Her When She Goes Away: Respite services for children with learning disabilities and additional health needs.** Manchester: *National Development Team*
Based on a series of visits and interviews, the report identifies the service elements most valued by children and their families, and suggests ways for service planners, purchasers and providers to provide choice, reliability and flexibily in local respite services. Includes summary of relevant legislation as at 1996.

506 **Sellick C (1996) 'Short-term foster care', in Hill M and Aldgate J (eds.) Child Welfare Services: Developments in law, policy, practice and research.** London: *Jessica Kingsley*
Shows how short-term foster care is a crucial service for families under stress. Sellick analyses the complexity of foster carers' roles, arguing that they need to be valued and supported, personally and financially.

507 **Sexty C (1997) Local Authorities and Short-term Break Care for Families Affected by HIV/AIDS in London,** London: *National Foster Care Association*
Summarises the findings from research on local authority practice in London in relation to care services for children and families affected by HIV/AIDS.

508 **Stalker K (ed.) (1996) Developments in Short-term Care: Breaks and opportunities, Research Highlights in Social Work 25.** London: *Jessica Kingsley*
This book reviews the findings of research into short-term care for a range of user groups, including disabled children, adults with learning disabilities, children in need and people with dementia. Particular attention is paid to the views of those in direct receipt of services. The issues of costings and quality are also examined.

509 **Stone J (1991) 'The tangled web of short-term foster care: unravelling the strands',** *Adoption & Fostering*, 15:3, pp. 4–9
Use of short-term placements has increased significantly. This article reports on a study that considered reasons for placement, length of placement, the possibility of drift to long-term placement and provision for teenagers.

510 **Stone J (1995) Making Positive Moves: Developing short-term fostering services,** London: *BAAF*
This book provides an account of the context and development of short-term foster care historically and since the Children Act 1989 and then moves on to a study of 183 children in short-term foster placements. The study identified four groups experiencing short-term foster care: (1) babies or young children whose plan was for

permanency; (2) children aged 0–9 requiring short placements of up to three months; (3) children aged 0–9 requiring long-term placements; and (4) young people aged 10+. Each group required a different service response.

Specialist fostering schemes

Much of the literature about specialist fostering is contained within general publications, for example in studies of *What Works* and reports such as Hayden *et al* (1999 – ref. 129); Waterhouse (1997 – ref. 189) and Clark *et al* (refs. 109–111). We list here some of the publications that are specific to specialist schemes or that set out to promote innovative models of practice.

511 Ainsworth F and Maluccio A (2003) 'Towards new models of professional foster care', *Adoption & Fostering*, 27:4, pp. 46–50
Ainsworth and Maluccio argue that foster care for children and young people is in crisis in Australia, the UK and the USA, as elsewhere. They recommend new models of foster care for consideration: (1) "Family for Family", which involves the recruitment of a foster family for a birth family; and (2) "Circle of Friends", which is designed for children and young people whose behaviours exhaust traditional foster carers. If developed further, these models, like those of Walker *et al* (2002ab – refs. 525 and 526) and Chamberlain (2003 – ref. 514), would add to the diversity of foster care services and make for a greater range of possible placements.

512 Audit Commission/Social Services Inspectorate/National Assembly for Wales

(undated). Making Ends Meet: Good practice. http://www.joint-reviews.gov.uk/money/children/4-323.html (accessed 10 January 2004)
An account of Dudley's professional fostering system, which is described as providing greater placement stability (4 per cent of children with three or more moves compared with 12 per cent national average) and provides a career route for foster carers.

513 **Chamberlain P (1998) Blueprints for Violence Prevention, Book 8: Multi-dimensional treatment foster care.** Colorado: *University of Colorado Centre for Study and Prevention of Violence*
See ref. 514 below.

514 **Chamberlain P (2003) Treating Chronic Juvenile Delinquents: Advances made through the Oregon Multi-Dimensional Treatment Foster Care Model.** Washington, DC: *American Psychological Association*
Describes and reports the effectiveness of a scheme for specialised community foster care, with improved outcomes both in terms of youth offending, integration in the community and mental health. Involves intensive support of foster carers, close liaison with education and training of social workers, foster carers and, if appropriate, birth families in the same approach to behaviour management.

515 **Curtis P A, Alexander A and Lunghofer L (2001) 'A literature review comparing the outcomes of residential group care and therapeutic foster care',** *Child and Adolescent Social Work Journal*, 18:5, pp. 377–92
Among the findings of this study in relation to treatment

foster care: most of the services at the time of the study were provided by private non-profit organisations; the majority of children in therapeutic foster care homes complete their course of treatment without a placement disruption, demonstrate improvement in social/psychological adjustment and behaviour, and are discharged to less restrictive settings. Also ref. 115.

516 **Hill M, Nutter R, Giltinan D, Hudson J and Galaway B (1993) 'A comparative study of specialist fostering in the UK and North America',** *Adoption & Fostering*, 17:2, pp. 17–22
Study of 230 agencies in the UK and North America. About 50 had specialist fostering schemes. Among the findings is the evaluation that 44 per cent of UK and 47 per cent of North American placements 'achieved their goals'.

517 **Hutchinson B, Asquith J and Simmonds J (2003) '"Skills Protect": towards a professional foster care service',** *Adoption & Fostering*, 27:3, pp. 8–13
The authors call for the professionalisation of foster care.

518 **Knorth E J, van den Bergh P M and Verheij P (eds.) (2002) Professionalisation and Participation in Child and Youth Care.** Aldershot: *Ashgate*
Brings together international research and recent findings about the professional quality of child and youth care and the participant quality of child care. Examines the tensions and possible antagonisms between childcare workers and children, young people, parents and foster carers participating as partners in care planning.

519 **Landy S and Munro S (1998) 'Shared parenting: assessing the success of a foster parent**

programme aimed at family reunification', *Child Abuse and Neglect*, 22, pp. 305–18
Evaluates a model of family support in which workers work with parents as well as providing substitute care for children. Found to be clearly advantageous in some situations, but least successful where there were especially grave or abusive problems.

520 **Miedema B and Nason-Clark N (1997) 'Foster care redesign: the dilemma contemporary foster families face'**, *Community Alternatives*, 9:2, pp. 15–28
Describes foster care in the West as being in a period of transition, based on new inclusive fostering models and the re-conceptualisation of foster care by child welfare agencies. Foster care is moving away from its traditional framework as an activity purely based on "love for the child" to the training of people to become professional foster parents. This transition from altruistic to professional care is complex and at times problematic. Based on data collected from 275 foster mothers in New Brunswick, a province in eastern Canada, the authors examine some of the complexity and contradictions that arise as child welfare agencies rethink the purpose of fostering and the role of foster carers.

521 **Sale A U (2004) 'A special breed'**, *Community Care*, 27 May, pp. 32–34.
Reports on the specialist services that provide foster carers for children from non-conventional backgrounds, e.g. trafficked children and children with HIV/Aids.

522 **Sellick C and Howell D (2003) Innovative, Tried and Tested: A review of good practice in fostering,** London: *Social Care Institute for Excellence*
Describes innovative initiatives in fostering, placing them in the context of findings from research studies. Researchers made targeted contact with fostering agencies and other organisations, requesting examples of good and innovative fostering practice. These practice examples were then "filtered" by researchers in relation to: (i) their relevance in respect of six pre-determined, key areas; and (ii) the research evidence about what is known to be effective.

523 **Szymanski L S and Seppala H T (1995) 'Specialized family care for children with developmental disabilities: the Finnish experience',** *Child Welfare*, 74:2, pp. 367–81
Describes features of Finland's specialised family care for children with disabilities, including training of foster parents and the preservation of relationships with biological families whenever possible. Includes a case study of a 12-year-old-child with learning difficulties and autism.

524 **Testa M F and Rolock N (1999). 'Professional foster care: a future worth pursuing?'** *Child Welfare*, 78:1, pp. 108–124.
A research study of the outcomes achieved by professional and specialised family foster care programme models in Illinois. Using five criteria, the authors compare the specialised programmes' results with the results from kinship care and non-relative foster care programmes. Findings are about both efficacy in different situations and cost-effectiveness.

525 **Walker M, Hill M and Triseliotis J (2002a) Testing the Limits of Foster Care: Fostering as an alternative to secure accommodation.** London: *BAAF*
Examines the Community Alternative Placement Scheme (CAPS) in Scotland, a project for young people presenting difficulties that would normally make family placement unsuitable. Using a comparison group of young people who were in secure accommodation, the study found that some benefited from the scheme approach while others were better suited to residential care. Research participants consisted of young people, carers, staff and other stakeholders.

526 **Walker M, Hill M and Triseliotis J (2002b) Fostering and Secure Care: An evaluation of the Community Alternative Placement Scheme (CAPS).** www.scotland.gov.uk/library5/education/ic72-00.asp (accessed June 2004)
Online summary of the findings of the independent evaluation of the innovative CAPS project (above) which provided family placements for young people who would otherwise enter or remain in secure care. This website (one of the "Interchange" series) describes the project and the evaluation of process and outcome, and discusses the implications for policy and practice. See also ref. 525.

527 **Walsh M and Reid M (2003) 'Lessons in care',** *Care and Health*, 3 December, pp. 37–38
Reports on the work of SACCS, a specialist provider of therapeutic care for traumatised and damaged children. SACCS began as a specialist in trauma recovery for sexually abused children placed in residential settings and plans to open a college offering training in therapeutic work for residential care staff.

Kinship care

The following publications discuss the extent to which kinship care is used, mainly in Europe and the USA, its outcomes, the question of financial equity, legal issues, carer assessment and policy implications.

528 **Argent H (2004) Related by Adoption: A handbook for grandparents and other relatives.** London: *BAAF*
Introduces grandparents-to-be and other relatives to information about adoption and how they can help guide children through the potentially confusing maze of 'values, standards and behaviours' they are likely to encounter on joining a new family.

529 **Broad B (1999) 'Kinship care: enabling and supporting child placements with relatives and friends', in BAAF (ed.), Assessment, Preparation and Support,** London: *BAAF*
Reports on research aimed at identifying the number and type of child placements with relatives and friends in the London Borough of Wandsworth for a specified period: January 1992–December 1996.

530 **Broad B (ed.) (2001) Kinship Care: The placement choice for children and young people.** Lyme Regis: *Russell House Publishing*
Collection of 16 papers that provide a guide to and critique of policy and practice in relation to kinship care. Includes overviews of research as well as guides to legal issues and training.

531 **Broad B, Hayes R and Rushforth C (2001) Kith and Kin: Kinship care for vulnerable young people.** London: *National Children's Bureau/Joseph Rowntree Foundation*

This research examined 50 kinship care placements (22 young people, 13 carers and 25 social workers). The reasons young people had been placed in kinship care included child abuse, inability of their previous carers to cope and the young person's own problematic behaviour. Nearly three-quarters of carers were over 50, half were grandparents and their ethnicity matched the young people. Advantages included maintaining links with siblings and friends, sustaining racial and cultural heritage and not being looked after by strangers. The main disadvantages were seen as limitations to freedom, financial hardship and lack of access to help available to care leavers. The authors argue that priority should be given to kinship care. Summary available online at www.jrf.org.uk/knowledge/findings/socialpolicy/d11.asp (accessed March 2004)

532 **Ehrle J and Geen R (2001) 'Kin and non-kin foster care: findings from a national survey'**, *Children and Youth Services Review*, 24:1/2, pp. 15–35

A US study using nationwide data. Findings suggested that children in the "kin" arrangements faced greater hardships than those in non-kin care. They more often lived in poor families and experienced food insecurity. They were more likely to live with a non-married care-giver who was not working and did not have a high school degree. In addition, fewer kin than expected received services to overcome these hardships. The article also draws attention to the vulnerability of large numbers of children living away from their parents who were not monitored by a child welfare agency.

533 **Flynn R (2002) 'Kinship foster care',** *Child & Family Social Work*, 7:3, pp. 311–21
A substantive research review of law, policy, practice and outcomes of kinship care in the UK from the past 20 years. Identifies training issues.

534 **Geen R and Berrick J D (2002) 'Kinship care: an evolving service delivery option',** *Children and Youth Services Review*, 24:1/2, pp. 1–14
This is the lead article to the journal's second special issue on kinship care, which provides an overview of the extensive US research and debate on the subject. Other articles include research studies of its prevalence, of caregiver/teacher educational assessments (Shore *et al*), analytical reviews and policy studies. Later editions of this US journal return regularly to the subject.

535 **Gleeson J P (ed.) (1999) Kinship Care: Improving practice through research.** Washington, D C: *Child Welfare League of America*
A review of the implications of (largely US) research on the growth and effects of kinship care.

536 **Greef R (ed.) (1999) Fostering Kinship: An international perspective on kinship foster care,** Aldershot: *Ashgate*
This book provides an international perspective on the policy dimension, social work role and race, gender and welfare in relation to kinship care. Although drawing from examples in Poland, the Netherlands, Belgium, Ireland, the USA and New Zealand, the book is primarily

concerned with identifying clear policy and good practice in kinship foster care.

537 **Hunt J (2003) Family and Friends Carers, Scoping Paper.** London: *Department of Health*
This informative discussion paper sets out a description of kinship care policy and practice. It considers the issues that arise and how such care is assessed and supported, setting out options for change and development. The paper recognises that there are many arrangements between family and friends who do not come to the notice of social services. The issues considered include assessment standards when relatives are being assessed as foster carers, payment and equity for caring for a family member, training and attitude development among professionals and the possible need for specialist support and structures.

538 **Laws S and Broad B (2001) Looking After Children Within the Extended Family: Carers' views.** Leicester: *De Montfort University, Centre for Social Action*
Reports research funded by the London Borough of Wandsworth as part of the Quality Protects programme. This research arose out of a programme of work on kinship care. The authors studied the number of cases involving an extended family member or friend, how the placements came about, their status and legal framework, and the views of carers, including the value they placed on the continuity of cultural background. Includes policy and practice recommendations.

539 **Naughton D and Fay K L (2003) 'Of kin and culture: US children and international kinship care placements',** *Adoption & Fostering*, 27:4, pp. 30–37

Naughton and Fay consider the situation of children whose families enter the USA through voluntary or forced migration, some of whom will inevitably be placed in foster care, for instance when parents die, are incarcerated or abandon or neglect their offspring. When evaluating placement decisions for these children, child welfare workers usually overlook the resources of grandparents and other close kin outside the country although they often have the ability and motivation to provide care for vulnerable relative children. Through case description and summary of domestic laws and international conventions, the authors identify challenges to cross-border placements and make recommendations for further research and consideration.

540 **O'Brien V (2000) 'Relative care – a different type of foster care: implications for practice', in Kelly G and Gilligan R (eds.), Issues in Foster Care,** London: *Jessica Kingsley*

O'Brien explores the differences and similarities between traditional foster care and foster care with relatives and sets out a number of reasons for the increase in use of kinship foster care in recent years. The shift from residential care to foster care, demographic trends and less suspicion of wider family dynamics have all played their part, as has the recognition that relatives and friends are often willing to take a group of siblings to keep them together.

541 **Philpot T and Broad B (2003) Family Problems, Family Solutions: Kinship care for children in need: an agenda for change.** Leicester: *De Montfort University*

An 18-page summary of UK and US evidence of kinship carers' and children's views about the impact of kinship care. Discusses issues of broader kinship care policy, and financial and support matters. Offers a suggested programme of reform to promote a more strategic approach to assessing and supporting kinship care placements.

542 **Pitcher D (2002) 'Placements with grandparents: the issues for grandparents who care for their grandchildren',** *Adoption & Fostering*, 26:1 pp. 6–14

Examines the experience of 33 grandparents who undertook the care of their grandchildren as a result of abuse or neglect. Many felt isolated from families and friends, with little support from social services, in need of advice and greater financial support. Also highlights the positive experiences of both grandparents and grandchildren and the special quality of these placements.

543 **Posner G J (2001) 'The extended family in care cases: fallback or centre stage?,** *Family Law,* 31, pp. 384–86

Considers the position of relatives in cases where there is no reasonable prospect of the child being successfully rehabilitated with either parent.

544 **Richards A (2003) 'Second time around for grandparents',** *Family Law*, 33, pp. 749–55

Reports a survey by the Family Rights Group which describes the experiences of grandparents caring for their grandchildren and analyses their reasons for taking a caring role, what help they need as carers and whether existing support services meet their needs and those of their grandchildren.

545 **Richards A and Tapsfield R (2003) Funding Family and Friends Care: The way forward.** London: *Family Rights Group*
Considers the needs of children living with a grandparent, other relative or friend who is responsible for their upbringing, and who would otherwise be looked after by a local authority. Discusses the financial implications and calls for family and friends care to be recognised as a distinct care arrangement supported by its own policy, guidance and regulations. Also calls for carers to receive financial help in the form of a state benefit.

546 **Strijker J, Zandberg G T and van der Meulen B F (2003) 'Kinship foster care and foster care in the Netherlands',** *Children and Youth Services Review*, 25:11, pp. 843–62
Presents the findings of a Dutch study of 136 placements. Reviews the primarily US empirical findings to date and sets out hypotheses based on US research about the differences between network and non-network foster care. In testing these, the study did not find statistical differences which support the US views but found that, when scaled for sample size, the results are quite similar.

547 **Sykes J and Sinclair I, Gibbs I and Wilson K (2002) 'Kinship and stranger foster care: how do they compare?',** *Adoption & Fostering*, 26:2, pp. 38–48
Part of a larger quantitative study on fostering. Sykes *et al* found differential use of kinship care in the seven local

authorities under scrutiny. Kinship carers had a similar demographic profile to other foster carers but tended to be more disadvantaged. The former faced particular difficulty over contact with birth families; they may help to unlock other family support and receive little training and little relief or assistance.

548 Talbot C and Williams M (2003) 'Kinship care', *Family Law*, 33, pp. 502–07
Considers the legal context in relation to research findings, contact issues, international experience, permanence and adoption, and outcomes for children.

549 Waterhouse S (1999) 'The use of kinship placements in court proceedings', *Seen and Heard*, 9:4, pp. 27–36
Waterhouse presents the results of an analysis of data held by two guardian ad litem panels (Northamptonshire and Oxfordshire) on children who are placed with kinship carers at the end of care proceedings. In total, 275 applications were identified, involving 465 children.

550 Waterhouse S and Brocklesbury E (1999) 'Placement choice for children: giving more priority to kinship placements', in Greef R (ed.), Fostering Kinship: An international perspective on kinship foster care, Aldershot: *Ashgate*
Marks the growth in kinship care and examines the reasons, some pragmatic and some child centred, that account for it. Documents the patterns, e.g. 50 per cent were single carers, and discusses the particular support networks required.

551 **Wheal A (1999) 'Family and friends who are carers', in Wheal A (ed.) The RHP Companion to Foster Care.** Lyme Regis: *Russell House Publishing*
Writing as a "network carer" herself, Ann Wheal initially puts forward a view as to the desirable framework for such care. She analyses the current situation as at 1998, provides an overview of research, and describes a small study providing information on a variety of issues, including the motivation of carers, their training needs and policy issues.

Transnational arrangements

This section refers to intercountry adoptions, asylum seekers' children, unaccompanied asylum seekers and refugees, and child trafficking. Law and guidance about intercountry adoption is listed in Chapter 1. Further works, in particular those by Rutter and O'Connor, refer to studies of the outcomes of adoptions from Romanian orphanages (see Chapter 6). In addition, the literature on private fostering (e.g. Olusanya and Hodes, 2000 – ref. 600) and on kinship care, is also sometimes concerned with international dimensions of family placement.

552 **Argent H (1996) 'Children in need: unaccompanied refugees',** *Adoption & Fostering*, 20:1, pp. 24–29
Discussion of the problems facing refugee children, based on an interview with Louise Williamson, former Director of the Children's Division of the Refugee Council.

553 **Ayotte W (1998) Supporting Unaccompanied Children in the Asylum Process.** London: *Save the Children*

Provides background information about work with asylum-seeking young people, identifying key practice and making recommendations.

554 **Ayotte W (2000) Separated Children Coming to Western Europe: Why they travel and how they arrive.** London: *Save the Children*

Analyses the reasons for the presence in Western Europe of children separated from their family, the means of their journey and how they survive. The report is based on documentary research and interviews with children and professionals. It makes recommendations relating to asylum, children's rights, trade, aid and foreign policy, trafficking, family reunification and training for professionals.

555 **Ayotte W and Williamson L (2001) Separated Children in the UK: An overview of the current situation.** London: *Save the Children/British Refugee Council*

Using the Statement of Good Practice of the Separated Children in Europe Programme as a measure, this report examines what happens to unaccompanied children once they arrive in the UK: how they are treated by the immigration system, what sort of legal representation they receive, what welfare advice they can access, how they are looked after by social services, where they are accommodated and other issues. Identifies where practice in the UK is strong in comparison with other countries and also difficulties, such as high levels of racism, inadequate care, trafficking, detention and family tracing and reunification.

556 **BAAF Health Screening of Children Adopted from Abroad, Practice Note 46.** London: *BAAF*
Provides simple recommendations for further health assessment of children adopted from abroad on arrival in the UK. Also points the medical practitioner towards further sources of information.

557 **Bann C and Tennant R (2002) Unaccompanied Asylum-seeking Children, Highlight Series 190.** London: *National Children's Bureau*
Two-page summary covering arrival in the UK, local authority services, health needs, youth services, education, accommodation and legal support.

558 **Beckett C, Bredenkamp D, Castle J the English and Romanian Adoptees (ERA) study team (1999) 'The role of social workers in intercountry adoption: an analysis of the experience of adopters from Romania',** *Adoption & Fostering*, 23:4, pp.15–25
Presents findings from a research study which shed light on the difficulties encountered in England, and which showed some evidence that those applicants approved by specialist local authority social workers had a more sustained sense of the importance for the child of issues concerning their background and identity.

559 **Brazier M (1999) 'Can you buy children?',** *Child and Family Law Quarterly*, 11:4, pp. 345–54
Examines the ethical, legal and social issues surrounding the payment of money to obtain a child. Written about surrogacy but relevant to intercountry adoption.

560 **Dennis J (2001) Where are the Children? A mapping exercise on numbers of unaccompanied asylum-seeking children in the UK: September 2000–March 2001.** London: *BAAF/Refugee Council*
Gives statistics for children by nationality and by known location in the UK, with a view to providing local authorities and other service providers with the necessary information for resource allocation.

561 **Department of Health/Social Services Inspectorate (1995) Unaccompanied Asylum-seeking Children: A training pack.** London: *DH*
Compiled to accompany the Department of Health's publication, *Unaccompanied Asylum-seeking Children: A practice guide*, included in this pack. Covers the social and historical contexts that have compelled various groups to seek asylum, the refugee experience, the legal framework, cross-cultural communication and social care difficulties and responses.

562 **Gilbert J (ed.) (2001) Unaccompanied Refugee Children: Have the lessons been learnt? (revised edition).** London: *Jewish Council for Racial Equality*
Twenty-page overview of the history of the Kinder-transport and the situation of unaccompanied child refugees today. Provides an anthology of readings and case studies and makes suggestions for discussion and further research. Briefly presents findings from a recent study into social attitudes. Offers suggestions for practical action and outlines a model school assembly to introduce children to the concepts of asylum and refugees. Includes a list of useful resources and organisations.

563 **Greenfield J (1995) 'Intercountry adoption: a comparison between France and England',** *Adoption & Fostering*, 19:2, pp. 31–36
Compares procedures for intercountry adoption in England and France as at 1995.

564 **Haugard J, Wojslawowicz J and Palmer M (2000a) 'International adoption: children predominantly from Asia and South America',** *Adoption Quarterly*, 3:2, pp. 83–93
Reviews the research evidence about outcomes of intercountry adoptions of Chinese and other children.

565 **Haugard J, Wojslawowicz J and Palmer M (2000b) 'International adoption: children predominantly from Romania',** *Adoption Quarterly*, 3:2, pp. 73–83
Reviews the research evidence about outcomes for the intercountry adoption of Romanian children.

566 **Hodes M (2000) 'Psychologically distressed refugee children in the United Kingdom',** *Child Psychology & Psychiatry Review*, 5:2, pp. 57–68
Forty per cent of refugees who enter the UK are under the age of 18 and many are unaccompanied children. Key issues are the prevalence of psychiatric disorders, resilience and protective factors, treatment options and the need for multi-agency support and help from specialist mental health services, including links with schools and social services. Illustrated with case studies.

567 **Hübinette T (2004) 'Adopted Koreans and the development of identity in the "third space"',** *Adoption & Fostering*, 28:1, pp. 16–24
Examines Western views on international adoption and

the Korean perspective, which is reflected in that country's view of international adoption as a national trauma and a painful reminder of the country's dependency on the West.

568 **Keck G and Kupecky R (1998) Adopting the Hurt Child.** Colorado Springs: *Pinon Press*
Chapter 6 of this work about attachment issues and adopting older children is specific to intercountry adoptions. The authors consider the specific requirements to provide families for children rather than vice versa and look at some of the common attachment implications, including the difficulty of establishing a clear picture of trauma and attachment experiences before adoption and of maintaining continuity for the child's identity in respect of culture and family. Presents a picture of the issues (and suggestions about ways forward) which is accessible to parents as well as professionals.

569 **Kidane S (2001a) I Did Not Choose to Come Here.** London: *BAAF*
Selam Kidane is Refugee Project Consultant at BAAF. This report is based on interviews with 33 refugee children from eight countries including Afghanistan, Rwanda, Ethiopia, Eritrea, Somalia and Yugoslavia. Recounts and highlights their experiences of being an asylum-seeking child and what they would like to see changed.

570 **Kidane S (2001b) Food, Shelter and Half a Chance: Assessing the needs of unaccompanied asylum-seeking and refugee children.** London: *BAAF*
A practice guide for professionals working with unaccompanied asylum-seeking and refugee children. Examines their special needs and the importance of

appropriate care arrangements and placement choices. Discusses the Looking After Children materials and provisions of the Children [Leaving Care] Act 2000. Raises a number of good practice issues and provides references and suggestions for further reading.

571 Kidane S and Amerena P (2004) Fostering Unaccompanied Asylum-seeking and Refugee Children: A training course for foster carers. London: *BAAF*

At the time of writing, there were nearly 10,000 unaccompanied asylum-seeking and refugee children in the UK. These children have survived the consequences of conflict and persecution: trauma, injury, pain, loss and separation. Once in the UK, local authorities have a duty to look after these vulnerable children to the same standards as any other looked after child. An increasing number are being placed in foster care. This course provides an introduction to the issues involved in caring for such children. It covers such topics as where refugees come from and why, understanding their experiences, feelings and needs, meeting their practical needs, preparation for leaving care and caring for the carers. Includes resource lists and a CD-ROM of handouts for use in the training.

572 Kirton D (2000) 'Intercountry adoption in the UK: towards an ethical foreign policy?', in Selman P (ed.), Intercountry Adoption: Developments, trends and perspectives. London: *BAAF*

Analyses some of the ethical issues surrounding intercountry adoption. Argues that the way forward resides as much in cultural norms as in the treatment of individual cases.

573 **Kohli R (ed.) (2003) 'Child and family social work with asylum seekers and refugees', Special Issue.** *Child & Family Social Work*, 8:3
Editorial introducing this special issue on working with asylum seekers and refugees. Other contributions include articles about children's rights and social work with asylum seekers and responses to unaccompanied children (in Norway, Ireland and the UK). Book reviews further focus on transnational issues. Also see ref. 536.

574 **Mather M and Kerac M (2002) 'Caring for the health of children brought into the UK from abroad',** *Adoption & Fostering*, 26:4, pp. 44–54
Mather and Kerac discuss the limitation of Department of Health guidance and identify the range of health problems which frequently go unrecognised in intercountry adopted children. Although the same problems apply to refugee and asylum-seeking children, these already traumatised young people carry the double burden of the problems they arrive with and the difficulties that arise once they are in the UK. The authors provide practical suggestions for making health care, for this group in particular, ethical, humane and acceptable.

575 **Mitchell F (2003) 'The social services response to unaccompanied children in England',** *Child & Family Social Work*, 8:3, pp. 179–89
Offers a critical appraisal of the evidence concerning three broad issues that have emerged from the research literature: the referral and assessment process, the use of the child welfare legislative framework and the provision of placements and other support offered to unaccompanied children. Concludes that the evidence base is relatively weak as much of the research has focused on

mapping the problem and raising awareness of the difficulties such children face, whereas little is known about the nature and context of the social work response and what models of care are appropriate.

576 Naughton D and Fay K L (2003), 'Of kin and culture: US children and international kinship care placements', *Adoption & Fostering*, 27:4, pp. 30–37
See ref. 539.

577 Russell S (1999) Most Vulnerable of All: The treatment of unaccompanied refugee children in the UK. London: *Amnesty International*
Outlines the position of unaccompanied refugee children who arrive in Britain seeking protection, with reference to the United Nations Convention on the Rights of the Child.

578 Rutter M, O'Connor T G, Beckett C and the English and Romanian Adoptees (ERA) study team (2000) 'Recovery and deficit following early profound deprivation', in Selman P (ed.), see below
A report of the work of the English and Romanian Adoptees Study Team. Concludes with a brief review of the implications of the study for the practice of intercountry adoption. See Selman (below) and other works by these same authors, listed in Chapter 6, for further details of their findings.

579 Selman P (ed.) (2000) Intercountry Adoption: Developments, trends and perspectives. London: *BAAF*
A wide-ranging description and analysis of the issues in intercountry adoption. This authoritative collection

provides an overview of the development of intercountry adoption to 2000. Contains a substantial section on research into outcomes (including work by Rutter *et al*, as above), accounts of intercountry adoption specific to the UK, worldwide perspectives and personal accounts from the viewpoints of all participants in the process. Makes recommendations for improved practice.

580 Sjögren J S (1996) 'A ghost in my own country', *Adoption & Fostering*, 20:2, pp. 32–35
Ji Sun Sjögren was born in Korea and brought up in Belgium where she was adopted by her Swiss mother and Swedish father at the age of two. She visited her native Korea for the first time at the age of 26. She describes what it can feel like to be caught between two worlds and speaks for the right of every child to know her or his origin and to be the rightful owner of a birth certificate.

581 Somerset C (2004) Cause for Concern? London social services and child trafficking. London: *ECPAT UK*
Research by ECPAT UK on London social services awareness of the level of child trafficking in the UK and their response to trafficked children. Examines ways of identifying children in exploitative situations and discusses preventive work. Provides good practice guidelines on interagency protocol and dealing with asylum-seeking children.

582 Stanley K (2001) Cold Comfort: Young separated refugees in England. London: *Save the Children*
Based on interviews with 125 young unaccompanied asylum seekers and 125 professionals who work with

them. Focuses on their needs in the areas of social services, education, health, immigration, social integration and housing, highlighting the gaps in provision and examples of good practice.

583 **Stone R (2000) Children First and Foremost: Meeting the needs of unaccompanied, asylum-seeking children.** Ilford: *Barnardo's*
Reports on the findings of a survey of provision to unaccompanied children seeking asylum who are in need, the majority of whom are between 16 and 17 years of age. The most significant problem experienced by local authorities in delivering services is the lack of appropriate accommodation and placements.

584 **Triseliotis J (1991) 'Intercountry adoption: a brief overview of the research evidence',** *Adoption & Fostering*, 15:4, pp. 46–52
Reviews metholodogical and statistical information from previous studies, examines background issues and reviews outcome studies of children's functioning and adjustment and racial and ethnic identification.

585 **Triseliotis J (2000) 'Intercountry adoption: global trade or global gift?',** *Adoption & Fostering*, 24:2, pp. 45–54
Triseliotis argues that a significant part of intercountry adoption lacks legal, moral or professional legitimacy, often amounting to a quest for children rather than a service to meet their needs.

586 **Verhulst F (2000) 'The development of internationally adopted children', in Selman P (ed.)** ref. 579
Study of the behavioural development of 2,148 adoptees,

mainly from Asia, aged 10–14 at the time of the study, which took place over three years. Findings showed increasing levels of problems in behaviour as the children grew older, contrasting with other studies (principally of intraracially adopted children). Their analysis indicated that this increasing problem level was as marked in European intercountry adoptions as in "transracial" adoptions, concluding that it may be more to do with an increasing sense of "lack of connectedness" as adolescents grew older.

587 **Warren C (1999) Intercountry Adoption: A social work perspective, Social Work Monographs 171.** Norwich: *University of East Anglia*
Includes a summary of research findings about the outcomes of intercountry adoption.

Independent fostering providers (IFPs)

In the last decade there has been a notable increase in the number of independent fostering providers (formerly known as agencies). Literature about Care Standards is relevant to their work, as are studies about supply and demand of family placement (both in Chapter 1). A limited number of broader reviews of fostering (e.g. Triseliotis *et al*, 1995 – ref. 185; Wilson *et al*, 2004 – ref. 194) pay specific attention to IFPs. They are used for providing planned long-term placements, for specialist services and also for foster care that must be integrated with educational or health provision.

588 **Collier F (1999) 'Independent agencies', in Wheal A (ed.) The RHP Companion to Foster Care.** Lyme Regis: *Russell House Publishing*

Provides a brief overview of the situation in relation to IFPs as at 1999. Although the paper is not presented as a formal statement from BAAF, the author clearly presents the organisation's overview of a number of the issues raised by the development of such agencies and their correlation with various government reports.

589 **Lord J (1998) Working with Independent Fostering Agencies: Guidance for local authorities in England and Wales.** London: *BAAF*
Discusses the issues which local authorities need to consider before placing looked after children through independent foster care agencies. Intended as a practice guide.

590 **Sellick C (1999) 'Independent fostering agencies: providing high-quality services to children and carers?',** *Adoption & Fostering*, 22: 4, pp. 7–14
Sellick reviews the relevant practice and research literature on the expanding independent fostering sector. He concludes that they are likely to continue to grow as they have established a model of a largely satisfied workforce and developed their services to the point that they have become providers of specialist therapeutic placements. He also suggests that if local authorities consider them in this light, IFP fees will appear less excessive and that they can begin to complement the local authorities' other provision.

591 **Sellick C (2002) 'The aims and principles of independent fostering agencies: a view from the inside',** *Adoption & Fostering*, 26:1, pp. 56–63
Attitudes within the wider child placement public sector towards the place of IFPs remain largely negative,

especially when expressed by local authority senior managers. These are considered alongside some other views that have emerged from the findings of relevant research, based on examination of the mission statements of 55 IFPs included in a national survey of the services, costs, staff, foster carers and children and young people in such placements.

592 **Sellick C and Connolly J (2001) National Survey of Independent Fostering Agencies,** Norwich: *University of East Anglia*

This national survey demonstrates the major expansion of independent fostering agencies since 1993. Reports on the shift towards meeting the needs of children who require a comprehensive range of educational, health and emotional support in addition to a specialist fostering service. Also indicates how social work practice is influenced by changing patterns of provision.

593 **Sellick C and Connolly J (2002) 'Independent fostering agencies uncovered: the findings of a national study',** *Child & Family Social Work*, 7:2, pp. 107–20

This article presents the findings of a survey of IFPs in England, Scotland and Wales. Information was gathered about their operational arrangements, services, fees, staffing, foster carers and the children and young people in placement. The information is supplemented by an earlier evaluation of one large English agency and by reference to the available relevant literature. The expansion of IFPs has been generally greeted with hostility by local authority managers because of what is perceived as the loss of foster carers to the independent sector, the costs of the IFPs and their position outside the public welfare sector. The authors question the validity of these views following an examination of the status of the agencies, the background of their foster carers and the circumstances surrounding the placements of the children and young people.

Private fostering

594 **Batty D (ed.) (1995) Caring for Other People's Children: A guide for private foster carers.** London: *BAAF*
Outlines the law in relation to private fostering and gives practical advice on the particular dietary and healthcare needs (including skin and hair care) of children from different ethnic, cultural and religious traditions, particularly those from West Africa.

595 **Bostock L (2003) Effectiveness of Child-minding Registration and its Implications for Private Fostering, Position Paper 1.** London: *Social Care Institute for Excellence*
Available online at
www.scie.org.uk/publications/positionpapers/pp01.pdf (accessed September 2004)

596 **Bostock L (2004) 'By private arrangement? Safeguarding the welfare of private foster children',** *Children & Society*, 18:1, pp. 66–73
A comprehensive assessment of arrangements for the regulation of private foster care. Reviews research into the registration of childminders and considers whether such a system should be developed for private foster care.

597 **Department of Health (2001) Private Fostering: A cause for concern.** London: *DH*

This seven-page booklet suggests causes for concern around private fostering, outlines the rules governing the practice, the responsibilities of agencies, and sources of information and support for private foster carers. Includes a list of organisations and a useful bibliography.

598 **Holman B (2002) The Unknown Fostering: A study of private fostering.** Lyme Regis: *Russell House Publishing*

This book begins with a history of private fostering from 1850 to 2000. The second section is concerned with interviews of private foster children, private foster carers and professionals. Ends with a discussion of current dilemmas and possible ways forward.

599 **Holman B (2003) 'Private fostering: old problems, new urgency',** *Adoption & Fostering*, 27:1, pp. 8–18

Traces the development of private fostering in the last 50 years and then analyses what is known about it at present. Many different groupings are involved, including West African and Chinese children and foreign language students under 16. Evidence suggests that satisfactory care can be provided but some children are vulnerable to abuse. Black foster children may not have their racial and cultural needs met in white foster homes. Local authorities possess considerable duties and powers concerning private fostering but few apply them. Outlines some suggestions as to how private foster children can be properly safeguarded.

600 **Olusanya B and Hodes D (2000) 'West African children in private foster care in City and Hackney',** *Child: Care, Health and Development*, 26:4, pp. 337–42

A study of private fostering among African families living in Britain. Six hundred randomly selected families with a child born between June 1988 and May 1991, resident in one health authority, were sent a questionnaire, and families with children in foster care were asked additional questions about their experiences. Two-hundred-and-six (34 per cent) of the questionnaires were analysed. Seventy-six per cent of the respondents were from Nigeria, 65 per cent had already heard about private fostering and 29 (14 per cent) had sent one of their children to private foster care. Only one family felt that foster care was a suitable option; the remainder would have preferred alternative facilities such as nursery placement. Of the 29 children in foster care, nine parents said their children were unhappy and five rated the foster parents as "bad". Most children were visited fortnightly, some more frequently and only two never visited. Private fostering in this group of children was found to be less common than in earlier studies.

601 **Philpot T (2001) A Very Private Practice: A report into private fostering.** London: *BAAF*

Philpot exposes the weaknesses of the present private fostering system by revealing why so little is known about privately fostered children, their parents and the carers themselves and how easy it is for these children, largely of West African origin, to remain hidden from public scrutiny. Illustrated with moving stories of children who, in the most extreme cases, have been exposed to neglect, danger or abuse, this campaigning report indicates how good practice can make a difference to better protecting children in private foster care and proposes a comprehensive programme for reform.

602 **Philpot T (2003) 'Private eye',** *Young Minds Magazine*, 67, pp. 29
Explains why action is urgently needed for children living with private foster carers. The government has proposed central monitoring and minimum standards but Philpot argues that compulsory registration is needed.

603 **Rickford F (1995) 'Hidden from view',** *Health Visitor*, 68:12, pp. 485–86
A health visitor's perspective on the cultural and emotional shock, leading to lasting damage, which can be occasioned by the private fostering of children (particularly from Africa) with families in the UK 'beyond the reach of statutory health and social services'.

604 **Save the Children (1997) Private Fostering: Development of policy and practice in three local authorities; a report of a study undertaken by the African Family Advisory Service.** London: *Save the Children*
A 42-page study of policy and practice towards private foster care in three local authorities which have significant numbers of children of West African origin. The report identified some possible ways forward in achieving an appropriate balance between family autonomy and the protection of children.

605 **Social Services Inspectorate (1994) Signposts: Findings from a national inspection of private fostering.** London: *DH*

606 **Social Services Inspectorate (2002) By Private Arrangement: Inspection of arrangements for supervising children in private foster care.** London: *DH*

607 **Sunmonu Y (2003) Cherish.** London: *Mango Publishing*
This moving, sometimes funny first novel charts the conflicts of a Nigerian girl privately fostered by a white family in the UK.

608 **Wolthuis A and Blaak M (2002) 'Children for sale in Europe: facts about trafficking in children for sexual purposes',** *International Children's Rights Monitor*, 15:2, pp. 28–30
The majority of known cases of trafficking in children for sexual purposes concern 15–18-year-old girls, but there are also cases of boys and younger children aged from ten to 14. There are very few reports of very young children being trafficked for sex. The authors recommend: that the children involved be treated as victims and not offenders; more research to find coherent and effective ways to tackle trafficking; that the police and immigration authorities establish mechanisms to enable them to exchange information and co-ordinate responses; and that special structures be developed to protect unaccompanied asylum seekers.

609 **Woollard C and Clarke B (1999) 'Private fostering', in Wheal A (ed.) The RHP Companion to Foster Care.** Lyme Regis: *Russell House Publishing*

Following a case study from one of the authors who is a health visitor, this chapter analyses the political, policy, philosophical, ethical and individual issues involved in "private" fostering (a term which they suggest has a number of misleading implications).

610 Yaya B (1996) 'Finding substitute carers for unaccompanied refugee children: the European dimension', *Social Work in Europe*, 3:3, pp. 49–51
Looks at the problems associated with finding foster placements for unaccompanied refugee children.

5 Race, ethnicity, gender, sexuality, disability and family placement

This is the first time that the BAAF family placement bibliography has included a separate chapter dealing with issues of race, ethnicity, gender, sexuality and disability. Previous editions have featured relevant works focusing on race, ethnicity and disability within broader sections, and, for some people, there is an argument for doing so rather than listing them separately. However, the literature on questions of race and disability has been growing; in addition, there is now a significant body of work related to sexuality, especially the debate concerning foster care and adoption by lesbians and gay men. We wanted to recognise these debates, as well to highlight the importance of such issues to family placement.

By far the largest section in this chapter is that dealing with questions of race and ethnicity, and this in turn is dominated by the debate over transracial placement. There is now a growing literature on the issue of lesbians and gay men as foster carers and adopters, although questions of gender are still rarely addressed. The section on disability reflects the tendency to focus on the placement of disabled children; there is little published work which considers disabled people as carers.

There are, however, two important points to remember when consulting this literature. First, it is limited in terms of quantity and, at times, quality. It is therefore unwise to make broad claims about complex questions such as "racial identity" and family placement on the basis of work which has a number of methodological, ethical and epistemological limitations. Nevertheless, many people do make such generalisations, as Paul Gilroy reminds us when he notes that 'quantifying and assessing the racial or ethnic self is a more hazardous and evasive operation than professional commentators in general, and social workers in particular, like to admit' (Gilroy, 1994, p.xi – introduction to ref. 623 below). Indeed, whether there is a 'racial self' at all, much less whether it can be assessed or quantified, is a complex debate rather than an agreed idea, but this has not prevented some of the literature on transracial placement from determining racial identification from limited quantitative data.

The second point, following on from this, is that issues of race, gender, sexuality and disability within family placement are ethical and political questions which cannot, and perhaps should not, be decided on the basis of the research "evidence" alone. For example, much of the research literature reviewed here is really too thin or too limited to support either a for or against "same-race placement" position, and it is important to recognise that both are ethical and political standpoints. What is usually missing from the literature is any discussion of what such complex concepts as "same-race" actually mean, or perhaps how they are constructed and used within the debate itself.

Another example of the political and ethical nature of these questions is foster care and adoption by lesbians and gay men. Most of the literature deals with the experiences of lesbian and gay carers and, while there is a body of work that considers children who live with gay parents, there is no research study as yet which has looked at children who have been placed with lesbian or gay foster carers and adopters. Nevertheless, this does not prevent some commentators from opposing all forms of gay parenting, including foster care and adoption. This section reviews one UK example from a Christian right-wing organisation (Morgan, 2002 – ref. 674), but also refers to a counter-argument which challenges Morgan's account of the research "evidence" (Hicks, 2003 – ref. 667). The point that

Hicks makes is that all claims about lesbian and gay foster care and adoption are moral and political positions which cannot, and should not, be determined from a supposedly "objective" reading of the research.

Race and ethnicity

611 Almas T (1992) 'After recruitment: putting the preparation and training of Asian carers on the agenda', *Adoption & Fostering*, 16:3, pp. 25–29

This article, by a UK practitioner, argues that exclusive emphasis on the recruitment of black and Asian adoptive and foster carers has resulted in neglect of their training needs. The author supports separate initial training courses for Asian applicants since this can address language and cultural barriers. He suggests that Asian applicants need to talk about same-race placement, how to work with birth parents who may be from the same community, what is expected of them and how to maintain confidentiality. He argues that Asian applicants may not have considered the issue of sexual abuse. This may be best addressed in separate groups for male and female applicants, since for cultural reasons Asian applicants will feel more relaxed in single-sex environments.

612 BAAF Recruiting Black Families, Practice Note 18. London: *BAAF*

A helpful guide to strategies for recruiting black families, based on the experiences of agencies that have had success in this area.

613 **Bagley C (1993) 'Transracial adoption in Britain: a follow-up study, with policy considerations',** *Child Welfare*, 72:3, pp. 285–99

Longitudinal British research study of 27 black/mixed-race and 25 white children adopted by white parents. A range of quantitative measures was used to determine that all the children showed excellent outcomes for social adjustment and identity issues. However, the black adoptees lived in primarily white environments and few white adopters had black contacts or were able to transmit any sense of black heritage to their children. The author argues that there is no evidence that transracial adoption is harmful and that it should be considered for black children who cannot be placed inracially.

614 **Barn R (1993) Black Children in the Public Care System.** London: *BAAF/Batsford*

UK-based research study of the care careers of black children within an inner-city social services department. Using a combination of data, both quantitative and qualitative, the study found that black children were over-represented within the care system and that professionals held more negative attitudes about black families. Black children were more likely than white children to be placed in foster care rather than residential homes, and transracial placements had been phased out within the borough under study. Black children were less likely to return home on trial than white, but they had greater contact with their birth families. Barn argued that black children and families received a poor social work service in which ideas about black families as deficient were present.

615 **Barn R (ed.) (1999) Working with Black Children and Adolescents in Need.** London: *BAAF*

This edited collection contributes to social work theory on communicating and working with black children "in need". The chapters are all by black contributors and cover racial "identity", direct work and communication issues, anti-racist practice and preparing young people for independence. The contributions by Michael Mallows, Sally Baffour and Sue Jardine deal with racial identity groupwork with transracially adopted young people, a black adopter's account of the adoption process and a story of growing up and dealing with racial identity by an adult of Chinese descent who was transracially adopted.

616 **Barn R (2000) 'Race, ethnicity and transracial adoption', in Treacher A and Katz I (eds.), The Dynamics of Adoption: Social and personal perspectives.** London: *Jessica Kingsley*

An introduction to, and overview of, the main debates on transracial adoption in the UK since the 1960s. Barn also reviews some of the major research studies, such as Gill and Jackson (1983 – ref. 624) and Tizard and Phoenix (2001 – ref. 650). She recommends efforts to recruit more black adopters and suggests that black children in care are more vulnerable without the support of the black family or community, but she also states that these children's security and stability should take precedence over political standpoints.

617 **Barn R, Sinclair R and Ferdinand D (1997) Acting on Principle: An examination of race and ethnicity in social services provision for children and families.** London: *BAAF*

This UK-based research is a study of issues of race and

ethnicity in the case histories of 196 children looked after by three local authorities. Building upon Barn (1993 – ref. 614), the authors combined data from case files, interviews with a sub-sample and analysis of agency policies. The majority of children of African, Caribbean and Asian descent were placed in families that reflected their ethnic and cultural backgrounds, and there was no evidence that black children were languishing in care due to poor placement opportunities. However, about 40 per cent of the mixed parentage and all other minority ethnic children (such as those of Chinese descent) were placed transracially, and such placements were also used for short-term care. The report recommends better ethnic monitoring, clear policies on race issues, better staff training and more resources for working with black families and communities.

618 **Brooks D and Barth R P (1999) 'Adult transracial and inracial adoptees: effects of race, gender, adoptive family structure, and placement history on adjustment outcomes',** *American Journal of Orthopsychiatry*, 69:1, pp. 87–99

US longitudinal research study of adoption outcomes among a group of children adopted by white parents. An original sample of 737 adoptive families was surveyed in 1977, with a second-wave follow-up of 372 of the original sample in 1980, and a third wave of 224 in 1993. The survey used mainly quantitative measures to determine such outcomes as educational performance, social adjustment, functioning and ethnoracial discrimination and identity. The adoptees appeared remarkably similar and were well adjusted, with females typically exhibiting fewer difficulties. White and African-American males exhibited the most problems. No significant differences were found for ethnoracial scores and none of the adoptees had a weak racial identity. The authors suggest their findings support transracial adoption and note that, of their sample, it was the white male adoptees who had the most adjustment problems. For a critical response to this study, see Rushton and Minnis (2000 – ref. 642).

619 Carter-Black J (2002) 'Transracial adoption and foster care placement: worker perception and attitude', *Child Welfare*, 81:2, pp. 337–70

US ethnographic research study of the views and opinions of nine female and one male black child welfare worker on transracial adoption and foster care. The author conducted open-ended, semi-structured face-to-face interviews and found that the workers emphasised meeting children's needs as paramount. They saw transracial placements as far from ideal, noting that some white carers disregarded the importance of race. However, they also said that successful transracial placement was possible and preferable to drift and delay within the care system. The author notes that her respondents disagreed with the arguments made by Hayes (1993), as they argued that children from minority ethnic backgrounds have a right to develop a distinct ethnic identity and awareness of their cultural heritage.

620 Charles M, Rashid S and Thoburn J (1992) 'The placement of black children with permanent new families', *Adoption & Fostering*, 16:3, pp. 13–19

Large UK-based research survey of children placed for adoption. Using case file data and interviews with agency workers, the authors argue that black children of mixed racial heritage are over-represented among their cohort of adoptees. Of the black and other minority ethnic children studied (n = 241), 68 per cent were transracially placed. Placement breakdown was highest among children aged between 12 and 14 years at placement, and children of mixed parentage were also more likely to experience placement breakdown than either black or white children.

621 **de Haymes M V and Simon S (2003) 'Transracial adoption: families' identity issues and needed support services',** *Child Welfare*, 82:2, pp. 251–72
US research study considering the views and concerns of transracial adoptive families. The authors carried out 20 qualitative interviews with children aged 8–14 years and their adoptive parents. The children lived in predominantly white communities and argued that their parents didn't always recognise racism or talk about "race" issues. The adopters didn't always feel supported by professionals and noted a lack of resources when they did seek to address their child's racial and cultural heritage. The article ends with a list of suggested resources and supports for transracial adoptive families.

622 **Flynn R (2002) Short Breaks: Providing better access and more choice for black disabled children and their parents.** Bristol: *Policy Press*
A review funded by the Joseph Rowntree Foundation to identify good and innovative practice from the literature and frontline work in the area of short breaks for children who are from black minority ethnic groups. Includes analysis of the definitions and debates around "short break", "black" and "ethnic minority". Having identified some of the patterns (and barriers to access), the study makes recommendations about "what works", acknowledging barriers, providing adequate resources

for short breaks, asking children what they want, ensuring diversity, and so on. These are translated into messages specifically for central and local government and for short-break providers.

623 **Gaber I and Aldridge J (eds.) (1994) In the Best Interests of the Child: Culture, identity and transracial adoption.** London: *Free Association Books*
A collection of articles that considers the debate on transracial adoption. The book was edited by members of the campaigning group 'Children First in Transracial Fostering and Adoption' which believes that finding the right ethnic match for children is important, but that this should not be pursued to the point where children suffer prolonged delays within the care system. Therefore, although the book presents a detailed discussion of the transracial placement debate, it supports transracial adoption as a viable placement for black children. Paul Gilroy's brief foreword critiques the essentialist ideas about racial groupings and identities that have featured on both sides of the transracial debate, and Gaber's chapter reviews the history of transracial adoption in the UK. Other chapters discuss questions of racial politics and identity, attachment, law and the US perspective.

624 **Gill O and Jackson B (1983) Adoption and Race: Black, Asian and mixed race children in white families.** London: *Batsford/BAAF*
One of the most frequently cited UK research examples, Gill and Jackson's is a follow-up study looking at adoption outcomes in 44 families, 36 of whom had adopted transracially and eight of whom had at least one black adopter. These placements were originally made in the 1960s. On a range of measures (family and peer

relationships, education, self-esteem, behaviour), the children functioned well, though they lived in predominantly white worlds with few black friends. Parents did not pay much attention to their children's racial backgrounds but explained that they didn't want to make their child feel 'different'. The children perceived themselves as 'coloured' or 'brown' (the term "black" was not generally used) and had little pride in their racial backgrounds. Most famously, Gill and Jackson reported that these children 'perceived themselves to be "white" in all but skin colour' (p. 81). The authors advocated black families for black children where possible, but did not support the view that transracial adoption is necessarily damaging.

625 **Griffith E E and Silverman I L (1995) 'Transracial adoptions and the continuing debate on the racial identity of families', in Harris H W, Blue H C and Griffith E E H (eds.), Racial and Ethnic Identity: Psychological development and creative expression.** New York: *Routledge*

A review chapter looking at US statistics, research evidence, law and arguments for and against transracial adoption. The authors point out that black children are over-represented in the care system and that they may wait twice as long as white children for adoptive placements. They state that longitudinal outcome data show that transracial adoption can be successful, and argue that a "colour-blind" approach to adoption makes sense in most cases, especially if this prevents black children from drifting within the care system.

626 **Hawkins-Leon C G and Bradley C (2002) 'Race and transracial adoption: the answer is neither simply black or white, nor right or wrong',** *Catholic University Law Review*, 51:4, pp. 1227, 1276–85

An overview of transracial adoption debates in the US. The authors note that research studies show that 46 per cent of children in US foster care are African-American (three to four times the figure for the population as a whole), and that these children spend longer in foster care than their white counterparts. Following an historical overview of transracial adoption in the US, they review US law and the arguments for and against transracial adoption. They argue that existing studies of transracial adoption are limited and that African-American children do not get their racial and cultural needs met by transracial placements.

627 **Hayes P (1993) 'Transracial adoption: politics and ideology',** *Child Welfare*, 72:3, pp. 301–10

Discusses the discourse surrounding transracial adoption. The author examines the form and content of the transracial adoption debate, pointing out certain assumptions that are made within it. The piece is interesting because it challenges the monolithic view of "black community" relied upon by some opponents of transracial adoption, but Hayes ultimately espouses humanistic values which are individualistic and downplay the importance of issues of 'race' and ethnicity.

628 **Hollingsworth L D (1998) 'Promoting same-race adoption for children of color',** *Social Work*, 43:2, pp. 104–16

An overview of US transracial adoption history and of the arguments for and against it. The author suggests that transracial adoption is a simplistic solution to the problems facing black children and argues instead for increasing the pool of available black families as well as tackling the complicated issues which lead to the over-representation of black children within the care system.

629 **Ince L (1998) Making it Alone: A study of the care experiences of young black people.** London: *BAAF*
Ince's research is a qualitative in-depth study of ten black young people's experiences of long-term care in two English local authorities. Interviews were carried out with the young people and with two social work professionals, and were supported by case file data. Ince argues that transracial placements (by which she means placement of black children in white foster or adoptive families or in all-white residential homes) exposed most of the young people to overt and covert racism and discrimination. Those who remained within the extended family and the black community had a stronger perception of their black identity, and those in foster care fared better than those in residential homes.

630 **Kapp S A, McDonald T P and Diamond K L (2001) 'The path to adoption for children of colour',** *Child Abuse & Neglect*, 25:2, pp. 215–29
US research survey of 1,550 Kansas children referred for adoption. African-American children were over-represented in the referrals (32 per cent). In addition, their adoption decisions and placements took longer than those of either white or other minority ethnic children.

631 **Katz I (1996) The Construction of Racial Identity in Children of Mixed Parentage: Mixed metaphors.** London: *Jessica Kingsley*

A UK research study of children with white mothers and black fathers. Qualitative data were generated through direct observations and semi-structured interviews with 14 families. Katz argues that racial issues were always present within the family dynamics and were affected by relationships and feelings. The families had differing ideas about 'race' but all wanted their children to have a positive "mixed" identity. Those children who were verbal described themselves as "mixed" in various ways, but Katz notes that this did not indicate "mixed up". Katz uses these findings to challenge same-race family placement arguments because, he suggests, these tend to homogenise the interests of black children, rely upon unexamined ideas about race and ethnicity, and do not acknowledge changes in adoption and racial identities among children since the 1960s.

632 **Keller T E, Wetherbee K, Le Prohn N S *et al* (2001) 'Competencies and problem behaviours of children in family foster care: variations by kinship placement status and race',** *Children and Youth Services Review*, 23:12, pp. 915–40

US research study, based in Seattle, Washington, of behaviour and social competence of 240 foster children, 28 per cent of whom were in kinship placements and 72 per cent in non-kinship foster care. Quantitative data on child behaviour were generated from caregiving adult responses. Black children were far more likely than whites to be in kinship, rather than foster care (72 per cent of all African-American children were in kinship care but only 11 per cent of whites). In addition, children in kinship care were functioning better and black children showed less problem behaviours than their white counterparts.

633 **Kirton D (1999) 'Perspectives on "race" and adoption: the views of student social workers',** *British Journal of Social Work*, 29:5, pp. 779–96

Research study examining levels of support among UK social work students for "same-race" and transracial adoption. The study uses quantitative data from questionnaires returned by 835 students. There was a wide range of views with an overall "soft" support for same-race placements. Minority ethnic students were more supportive of same-race adoption than white counterparts, as were those who intended to pursue a social work child care career. The students raised a number of issues and questions about this topic and did not display "politically correct" answers.

634 **Kirton D (2000) "Race", Ethnicity and Adoption.** Buckingham: *Open University Press*

This book gives an overview of race, ethnicity and adoption in Britain. Kirton examines different paradigmatic approaches to the question of race and adoptive placements. He notes a liberal paradigm that tends to play down the relevance of race, a black radical paradigm that highlights the role of racism but tends to adopt a rather simplistic view of a "positive black identity", and the post-modern challenge to the traditional for/against transracial placement debate. This challenge asks some difficult questions about the fixed views of "race" and "culture" operated by both sides of the debate, but Kirton argues that there is still a great need to recruit more black adoptive families given that many children are still transracially placed.

635 Macey M (1996) 'In the best interests of the child? Race and ethnic matching in adoption and fostering', *Representing Children*, 9:2, pp. 83–98

A review of UK and US debates and research on issues of transracial adoption. The author challenges the conceptual inadequacies and essentialist views of race and identity found on both sides of the argument about transracial adoption, and suggests that research finds that transracially adopted children do not develop psychological, identity or adjustment problems or negative attitudes about black people. Taking into account the large numbers of black and mixed parentage children in need of adoptive homes, the author argues that transracial adoption is necessary and positive in some cases.

636 McRoy R G (1994) 'Attachment and racial identity issues: implications for child placement decision-making', *Journal of Multicultural Social Work*, 3:3, pp. 59–74

This article reviews US research evidence on issues of attachment and racial identity formation in family placement of black children. The author argues that quality of care is crucial in the formation of attachments and that this, along with the formation of a positive racial identity, depends upon skilled carers. A colour-blind approach to issues of race is not helpful, and the author advocates placements that optimise the match between the racial heritage of the child and carers.

637 McRoy R G, Oglesby Z and Grape H (1997) 'Achieving same-race adoptive placements for African-American children: culturally sensitive practice approaches', *Child Welfare*, 76:1, pp. 85–104

Overview article that considers working towards same-race adoption in the USA. The authors review the Multi-ethnic Placement Act which became US law in 1994 and which stipulates that a placement cannot be denied solely on the basis of race, but also suggests that cultural, ethnic and racial background should be considered. The authors also discuss various US projects designed to increase the numbers of adopters from ethnic minorities, and outline recommendations for improved social work practice in this area. They support a same-race placement policy.

638 Moffatt P G and Thoburn J (2001) 'Outcomes of permanent family placement for children of minority ethnic origin', *Child & Family Social Work*, 6:1, pp. 13–21

Quantitative research study of the outcomes for 297 UK children of minority ethnic origin in permanent family placements. Both parents of 42 per cent of the children were of minority ethnic origin and 58 per cent of the children had mixed parentage. Children of middle age-range or with problem behaviours were more likely to have placement breakdowns. There was no effect on placement success due to the child's ethnic origin, whether the placement was classed as foster care or adoption, or whether birth family contact was maintained. Overall, 72 per cent of placements were successful (that is, were not found to have broken down).

639 Prevatt-Goldstein B (2000) 'Ethnicity in placement', Special Issue. *Adoption & Fostering*, 24:1

Includes articles on the strengths of black families, responding to "Irish invisibility", meeting the placements of Jewish children and a research review on trans-national placements.

640 **Prevatt-Goldstein B and Spencer M (2000) "Race" and Ethnicity: A consideration of issues for black, minority ethnic and white children in family placement.** London: *BAAF*

This guide offers general practice guidelines relating to race and ethnicity, recognising that needs arising from racial origin, culture, religion and language influence all the other needs of the child and must be met alongside them. The placement of black children and white children, agency guidelines and matching where there are diverse ethnicities are examined, together with some practice dilemmas.

641 **Rushton A and Minnis H (1997) 'Transracial family placements',** *Journal of Child Psychology & Psychiatry*, 38:2, pp. 147–59

A literature review of research on transracial family placement in the UK and USA since the 1970s. This article gives an overview and discussion of findings from some of the main research examples, but also raises some important methodological concerns. The authors urge caution in generalising from specific findings on transracial placements and suggest that much more research, including detailed qualitative studies, is needed in this area. Despite the suggestion that over 70 per cent of transracial placements have successful outcomes, the authors remind us that the social context is still a racist one. For this reason, they suggest that ethnically matched placements will be in the best interests of the child and community in most instances.

642 **Rushton A and Minnis H (2000) 'Research review: transracial placements',** *Adoption & Fostering*, 24:1, pp. 53–58

A critical review of the study by Brooks and Barth (1999). Rushton and Minnis argue that their study has significant methodological limitations, such as sample attrition, bias, basing measures of adjustment and racial identity on parental accounts and trying to measure complex ideas such as "ethnoracial identification" quantitatively. They conclude that, although transracial placements show generally favourable outcomes, the methodological problems preclude definitive conclusions. It is suggested that more in-depth, qualitative research on this issue is needed.

643 **Seaberg J R and Harrigan M P (1999) 'Foster families' functioning, experiences and views: variations by race',** *Children and Youth Services Review*, 21:1, pp. 31–55

US research study that used postal survey by questionnaire. Respondents were foster mothers (n = 271), of whom half were white, 43.7 per cent African-American and 0.8 per cent other. African-American women were more motivated by love and a desire to help children than white women, who were more likely to indicate self-motivations to foster. The black women had generally been fostering for longer and had fostered more children than the white women. Black women were also more sympathetic towards birth parents, as white women expressed more anger in this respect. However, white women were far more likely to seek and gain professional support than their black counterparts. On many other measures there were more similarities than differences between the groups.

644 **Silverman A R (1993) 'Outcomes of transracial adoption',** *The Future of Children*, 3:1, pp. 104–18

A review piece looking at a range of US research into outcomes of transracial adoption carried out in the 1970s and 80s. The author argues that the research supports transracial adoption as a viable option, with adoptees exhibiting good self-esteem and adjustment. Problems in pre-adoptive history and delays in permanent placement account for far more of the adoptees' post-placement difficulties than does racial antagonism. Most transracial adoptees evaluate their background and appearance positively and do not deny their racial identification.

645 Simon R J and Roorda R (2000) In their own Voices: Transracial adoptees tell their stories. New York: *Columbia University Press*

Following an introduction that summarises the historical background to the debates about transracial adoption, this book presents the transcripts of interviews with 24 adults (one of whom is a co-author). Twenty-three were aged between 22 and 31 (one man was 57). All identify themselves as black or mixed race and were adopted by white families. The book concludes with a brief summary and analysis based on the interviews.

646 Small J (1986) 'Transracial placements: conflicts and contradictions', in Ahmed S, Cheetham J and Small J (eds.), Social Work with Black Children and their Families. London: *Batsford/BAAF*

This article by a UK practitioner is seen as a "classic" statement of the same-race placement position. Small argues that, historically, transracial placement was about meeting the needs of white carers but that it resulted in racial identity confusion for black children. He cites Gill and Jackson (1983) as evidence of this and argues that they should not have supported transracial placements on the basis of their findings. He argues that black children need to develop a "black psychic image" and that this cannot be done if they are cut off from other black people and role models. Although Small does not discuss the specifics of a black identity, he does provide a set of guidelines for the selection and preparation of white carers where transracial placement is the only option.

647 Small J (1991) 'Ethnic and racial identity in adoption within the United Kingdom', *Adoption & Fostering*, 15:4, pp. 61–68

A follow-up article to Small (1986) which argues against the "colour-blind" approach to the placement of black children. After reviewing relevant UK research, including Gill and Jackson (1983), Small proposes that transracial placement jeopardises the identity needs of black children. He reviews a number of factors that affect racial and ethnic identity and goes on to argue in favour of recognising the strengths of black families and the need to recruit more black foster carers and adopters.

648 Smith P M and Berridge D (1993) Ethnicity and Childcare Placements. London: *National Children's Bureau*

Overview of the main issues of ethnicity and family placement. The authors review arguments for and against ethnic matching in placements before going on to discuss some of the major British and US research studies. They conclude that research does not support transracial placements and that there is no evidence available from transracially placed adults (although this may now be superseded by studies such as refs. 618 and 649.

649 **Thoburn J, Norford L and Rashid S P (2000) Permanent Family Placement for Children of Minority Ethnic Origin.** London: *Jessica Kingsley*

A major UK-based research study of 297 placements of children of minority ethnic origin with 268 families between 1979 and 1987. Seventy-one per cent were placed with white carers. The authors used case file data and interviews with the children and families. About 82 per cent of placements did not break down, but only 72 per cent were successful in most respects. Disruption rates did not differ according to ethnicity of children or carers. In the final chapter, the authors review their own findings and argue that some transracially placed children did suffer stress from being separated from their ethnic and cultural heritage. They also note that some white families were able to successfully parent black and other minority ethnic children. While acknowledging the complexity of racial identities, the authors support the general principle of placing children with parents who can meet their needs and who are of a similar cultural and ethnic background.

650 **Tizard B and Phoenix A (2001) Black, White or Mixed Race? Race and racism in the lives of young people of mixed parentage (revised edition).** London: *Routledge*

This UK research project looked at the racial identities of young people of mixed parentage living with their biological parents. Tizard and Phoenix interviewed 58 young people from 32 different schools. Just under half of the sample thought of or described themselves as "black", and preferred terms like "mixed race", "brown", "mixed", "coloured" and "half-caste". Sixty per cent had a very positive sense of racial identity, but most had what the authors term 'multiple' racial identities. Tizard and Phoenix challenge the assumption that mixed race children "should" have a black identity or that, without a black parent, their racial identities will be damaged. The authors do not suggest that "race" issues are irrelevant to foster care and adoption, but they do state that children's development may be more affected issues such as parental class.

651 Zeitlin H (2002) 'Adoption of children from minority groups', in Dwivedi K N and Varma V P (eds.), Meeting the Needs of Ethnic Minority Children (2nd edition). London: *Jessica Kingsley*

This overview and discussion of adoption suggests that "same-race placement" is actually an extremely complex idea since there is no such thing as a single "black race" or "black culture". Problematically, however, some of the research that opposes transracial placement suggests that there is because it relies on rather simplistic views of "race", "culture" and "identity". The author suggests that matching children's race and culture with parents is ideal, but a cultural match alone is better than leaving children to face undue delays within the care system.

Intercountry adoption

References specifically to intercountry adoption are listed in Chapter 4, along with other works relating to transnational issues in family placement.

Gender and sexuality

652 **Alexander C J (2001) 'Developmental attachment and gay and lesbian adoptions',** *Journal of Gay & Lesbian Social Services*, 13:3, pp. 93–97

Brief research note that emphasises the need to promote secure attachments for all adopted children. The author is concerned that the attachment and psychological problems exhibited by many adopted children are sometimes interpreted as the effects of parental sexuality for children adopted by lesbians or gay men. He emphasises that research shows that children with gay parents develop normally, and that lesbian and gay carers are often particularly sensitive about having their parenting skills being negatively judged on the basis of their sexuality.

653 **Barrett H and Tasker F (2001) 'Growing up with a gay parent: views of 101 gay fathers on their sons' and daughters' experiences',** *Educational & Child Psychology*, 18:1, pp. 62–77

Research report on preliminary findings from the UK-based Gay and Bisexual Parenting Study. Data were produced from questionnaires returned by 101 gay or bisexual fathers, seven of whom were fostering and two of whom had adopted. Generally, older children were more likely than younger ones to know about their father's sexuality and the parents rated daughters as slightly more positive about this than sons. Most children were rated as having experienced few difficulties relating to their father's sexuality, but the parents raised tensions due to having to keep this a family secret, being teased or bullied and feeling different as potential problem areas.

654 **Brodzinsky D M, Patterson C J and Vaziri M (2002) 'Adoption agency perspectives on lesbian and gay prospective parents: a national study',** *Adoption Quarterly*, 5:3, pp. 5–23

The first ever US national survey of adoption agency perspectives on lesbian and gay carers. The authors surveyed 214 agency directors via questionnaire and report that seven respondents incorrectly assumed that lesbians and gay men were prohibited by law from adoption, while another 29 were unsure about the legal position in their state. Sixty-three per cent of agencies did accept lesbian and gay applications, but public and special needs agencies were more likely to do so than Christian fundamentalist, Catholic, private or infant/toddler agencies. Known lesbian or gay adoptions accounted for 1.6 per cent of all placements made and 37.7 per cent of the agencies had made at least one such placement (figures which are likely to be an underestimate). Fifteen per cent had rejected gay or lesbian applicants.

655 **Brooks D and Goldberg S (2001) 'Gay and lesbian adoptive and foster care placements: can they meet the needs of waiting children?',** *Social Wor*k, 46:2, pp. 147–57

US-based qualitative study of social work responses to the topic of lesbian and gay adoptive and foster care placements. Their study involved semi-structured interviews with ten social work staff involved in foster care and adoption services, as well as a focus group discussion with 11 gay and lesbian adoptive and foster parents. They found a prevailing assumption within the child welfare system that gay men and lesbians are unfit to raise fostered and adopted children, and an over-scrutiny of sexuality at the expense of other important factors. Staff, however, praised existing gay/lesbian carers for their strengths and willingness to consider special needs children. Overall there was a lack of explicit agency policies on this issue and the authors felt that respondents tended to play down the unique challenges that gay or lesbian placements present. They suggest that social work must address these challenges because gay and lesbian applicants do face issues specific to their sexuality.

656 **Children of Lesbians & Gays Everywhere.** USA: www.colage.org/
Web-based resource and support for children and young people with lesbian, gay, bisexual or transgendered parents. Includes pages for children, parents, researchers and the media. Lists events/activities (but these are US-based), and offers a penpal service for children.

657 **Cosis Brown H (1991) 'Competent child-focused practice: working with lesbian and gay carers',** *Adoption & Fostering*, 15:2, pp. 11–17
A discussion paper that considers how social workers might address working with gay and lesbian foster care and adoption applicants. Brown argues that children's needs can be met by gay or lesbian carers who have been fully and adequately assessed and suggests that social workers need to draw upon knowledge, values and skills. She argues that existing research demonstrates that sexuality itself is not a determinant of the ability to parent children; what is important is the quality of the relationship. Brown goes on to list five key areas specific to lesbians and gay men, which she thinks should be discussed in any assessment.

658 **Cosis Brown H (1992) 'Gender, sex and sexuality in the assessment of prospective carers',** *Adoption & Fostering*, 16:2, pp. 31–34

This article looks at how issues of gender, sex and sexuality might be addressed in any fostering or adoption assessment. Brown argues that these should be addressed for all applicants, not just lesbians and gay men. She proposes that any assessment should look at how households organise roles and how they view gender issues, how applicants view sex, how they have organised their sexual lives and how they would talk to and deal with sexual issues raised by children placed. Brown emphasises that good carers will have clear ideas about sexual boundaries and be able to reinforce these with children who may have been abused in the past. Finally, she lists a series of pointers to help practitioners think about these issues.

659 **Finn J L (1994) 'Contested caring: women's roles in foster family care',** AFFILIA: *Journal of Women & Social Work*, 9:4, pp. 382–400

An overview article that highlights gender issues and the oppression of women which is reproduced within the foster care system. The author argues that the subordinate status of women within the home and within society must be challenged, and this includes confronting the little value, economic or cultural, placed upon the caring work done by women as foster carers. The author also argues that the "bad birth mother/good foster mother" dichotomy must be opposed along with the view that middle-class nuclear families are preferable for all children needing care.

660 Gailey C W (1998) 'Making kinship in the wake of history: gendered violence and older child adoption', *Identities: Global Studies in Culture & Power*, 5:2, pp. 249–92

This US-based study draws upon qualitative data from interviews with 109 adoptive parents, five social workers, five birth mothers, three female relatives and participant observations of adoption services. The author argues that children placed for adoption have frequently been subject to forms of gendered violence. She found that, prior to adoption, all the children had been violated, witnessed violence, been verbally abused or had been subject to many changes of placement, and that girls in particular had experiences of sexual assault. However, most adoptive parents were not given training to deal with these issues and some avoided discussing such topics with their adopted children 'unless absolutely necessary'. The author argues that carers need support groups and professional help to deal with gendered violence; otherwise it will be perpetuated or reproduced.

661 Gilligan R (2000) 'Men as foster carers: a neglected resource?', *Adoption & Fostering*, 24:2, pp. 63–69

Gilligan, who has been a foster carer himself, set out to highlight questions about the role and experiences of men as foster carers in fostering couples. The sparse literature relevant to the topic is reviewed; some of the therapeutic and practical reasons for the significance of the man's role in foster care are considered; findings from a small exploratory study of male foster carers and their role are presented; and certain policy implications arising are discussed.

662 Golombok S (2000) Parenting: What really counts? London: *Routledge*

This book considers a number of debates within parenting, including whether children need more than one parent, whether fathers are necessary and whether genetic ties matter. Chapter 4 deals with questions of sexuality and summarises the author's research, which was a UK-based longitudinal study of the outcomes in children with lesbian mothers. In most respects, the children of lesbians developed in similar ways to those of heterosexual mothers and their gender, sexual identity, peer relationships and social and psychological adjustment were not adversely affected. Golombok argues that all the research demonstrates that sexuality does not adversely affect parenting or child development in any way; what matters in all families is the quality of relationships between children and their carers.

663 Golombok S (2002) 'Adoption by lesbian couples: Is it in the best interests of the child?', *British Medical Journal*, 324:751, pp. 1407–08. Available online at www.bmj.bmjjournals.com/cgi/content/full/324/7351/1407

A brief summary of the author's longitudinal study of UK children brought up by lesbian parents. As young adults, they did not differ from their counterparts from heterosexual families in terms of quality of family relationships, psychological adjustment, peer relationships or sexual identity. Such points are used to support adoption by lesbians.

664 Hicks S (1996) 'The "last resort"?: Lesbian and gay experiences of the social work assessment process in fostering and adoption', *Practice*, 8:2, pp. 15–24

UK research study reporting on qualitative interviews with 11 lesbians and gay men who had been assessed as potential foster carers or adopters. The respondents reported discriminatory attitudes about sexuality from social workers, that they had to educate their social workers about lesbian and gay issues, or that they had to raise the issue of sexuality in the assessment themselves. Applicants were frequently asked about "gender role models" and were confused about why social workers deemed it appropriate for them to care for boys or girls only. Some had faced outright rejection by agencies when they "came out" as lesbian or gay. The author argues against using lesbian or gay carers as a "last resort", pointing out that discrimination on the basis of sexuality alone is unjust.

665 **Hicks S (1997) 'Taking the risk? Assessing lesbian and gay carers', in Kemshall H and Pritchard J (eds.), Good Practice in Risk Assessment and Risk Management 2: Protection, rights and responsibilities.** London: *Jessica Kingsley*

This book chapter considers the supposed "risks" that lesbians and gay men allegedly pose to children. The author argues that such ideas actually betray a desire to uphold traditional gender roles and heteronormativity. In addition, he points out that existing research shows that the children of lesbians and gay men do not experience such problems with their development. After reporting on the views of lesbian and gay carers who had been assessed for foster care or adoption (ref. 664), the author argues for an assessment approach which does assess sexuality alongside all other areas necessary to any childcare assessment, but in addition acknowledges that it is lesbians and gay men who experience oppression within a heteronormative social welfare system. Finally, Hicks lists some pointers for assessment practice.

666 Hicks S (2000) '"Good lesbian, bad lesbian . . .": regulating heterosexuality in fostering and adoption assessments', *Child & Family Social Work*, 5:2, pp. 157–68

Hicks reports on a UK-based research study which generated qualitative data from interviews with 30 local authority fostering and adoption social workers. He uses queer and feminist theories to argue that lesbian applicants assessed by the respondents challenged the discourse of "compulsory gender and heterosexuality" which structures fostering and adoption as a whole. This discourse relies upon assumptions that heterosexuals make the best carers for children, especially in the areas of gender and sexual identity role models. Ideas about "the lesbian" in social work assessments are analysed to show how she was constructed as a "threat", as "militant/feminist" and even sometimes as an "automatically safe carer", to make the point that social work assessments are productive of versions of the category "lesbian".

667 Hicks S (2003) 'The Christian Right and homophobic discourse: a response to "evidence" that lesbian and gay parenting damages children', *Sociological Research Online*, 8:4 at www.socresonline.org.uk/8/4/hicks.html

This short article responds to claims by Christian right-wing organisations and by Morgan (2002 – ref. 674) that gay parenting, including fostering and adoption, actually damages children. The author uses examples to dispute the claims by the Christian writers that children of gay parents suffer gender and sexual identity confusion, and demonstrates that these authors actually present a version of homosexuality as diseased and dangerous. Challenging the supposed "objectivity" of the Christian writers' work, the author argues that they actually present an anti-gay moral position and construct what he terms a Christian homophobic discourse.

668 **Hicks S and McDermott J (eds.) (1999) Lesbian and Gay Fostering and Adoption: Extraordinary yet ordinary.** London: *Jessica Kingsley*
This UK book collects together a series of 17 personal accounts by lesbians and gay men who have fostered or adopted children, 27 adults caring for 40 children or young people in all. The contributors are diverse in terms of age, ethnicity, gender and class and include single carers as well as couples. In addition, the editors provide an extended essay that pulls out key themes emerging from the accounts. This will be of great interest to other lesbians and gay men as well as anyone working in the field of foster care and adoption, especially social workers carrying out such assessments. The essay also considers issues of research, UK policy and law in this field.

669 **Inch L J (1999) 'Aspects of foster fathering',** *Child Adolescent Social Work Journal*, 16:5, pp. 393–412
Empirical study of the experiences of men as foster carers, highlighting the experience of becoming a foster carer, attachment and loss, attitudes to the birth family and the dynamics of contact between birth family and foster/adoptive family. See also ref. 661.

670 **James S E (2000) 'Lesbian and gay adoptions: an introduction to emerging clinical and ethical issues',** *Lesbian & Gay Psychology Review*, 1, pp. 4–10

US overview article that looks at practice and ethical issues involved in lesbian and gay adoptions. The author discusses ways in which practitioners can help lesbian and gay applicants to deal with problems with legality of such adoptions, with conflicting values that may emerge within the adoption system on this issue and with preparing parents to deal with potential discrimination for themselves and for potential adopted children. Ethical dilemmas, such as having to hide sexuality at certain points yet having to be honest with children, may also emerge. The author also writes about the need to provide adequate support to lesbian and gay adopters.

671 **Mallon G P (1999) Let's Get this Straight: A gay- and lesbian-affirming approach to child welfare.** New York: *Columbia University Press*

US text that deals with gay and lesbian issues within child welfare practice. It contains a chapter on gay men and lesbians as adoptive and foster parents, as well as one which considers gay/lesbian children/youth and their placement needs. Using case studies, the author reviews gay/lesbian foster care and adoption in the USA and lists a number of issues specific to lesbian or gay carers that agencies should consider. He also considers the specific needs of gay and lesbian young people who require out-of-home placements, and the range of emotional, physical and sexual violence/harassment that such children experience.

672 **Mallon G P (2000) 'Gay men and lesbians as adoptive parents',** *Journal of Gay & Lesbian Social Services*, 11:4, pp. 1–22

Review article that also uses case studies. The author reviews relevant research showing that children of lesbians and gay men develop in similar ways to those of heterosexuals. He points out that many agencies seem to adopt 'less said the better' or 'don't ask, don't tell' policies on gay and lesbian adoptions and argues that explicit policies should be developed. Mallon outlines a number of points for professionals to consider when developing such policies and suggests several areas that they should use in making assessments of applicant suitability. Finally, he outlines the negative consequences of inaction on this issue of policy.

673 **McCann D and Tasker F (2000) 'Lesbian and gay parents as foster carers and adoptive parents', in Treacher A and Katz I (eds.), The Dynamics of Adoption: Social and personal perspectives.** London: *Jessica Kingsley*

This chapter presents an overview of lesbian and gay foster care and adoption. The authors discuss why lesbians and gay men might choose foster care or adoption as routes to parenthood, before outlining relevant UK law in this area. They go on to examine issues involved in the assessment of lesbian/gay applicants, using the case study of Jenny and Susan's adoption application. The authors then review relevant research to show that lesbians and gay men make effective parents and that their children do not "suffer" as a consequence of their sexuality. They discuss the case of Peter's placement with David and Martin, and the way in which the couple dealt with homophobic insults used by Peter in anger when he was an adolescent.

674 **Morgan P (2002) Children as Trophies? Examining the evidence on same-sex parenting.** Newcastle-upon-Tyne: *The Christian Institute*

This book, published by the UK Christian Institute, argues against all forms of lesbian and gay parenting including foster care and adoption. The author presents a highly partisan account of research findings to claim that such children are damaged. The book takes a particular Christian moral stance that sees only heterosexual relationships as valid and criticises most research into lesbian/gay parenting on methodological grounds. These points are challenged by Hicks (2003 – ref. 667) who also points out that Morgan presents a view of lesbians and gay men as diseased and dangerous to children. For this reason, the claim that this book is an "objective" assessment of research evidence is highly questionable.

675 **Perrin E C (2002) 'Technical report: co-parent or second-parent adoption by same-sex parents',** *Pediatrics*, 109:2, pp. 341–44. Available online at www.pediatrics.aapublications.org/cgi/content/full/109/341

Brief paper that reviews research on lesbian and gay parenting in the context of adoption. Although some of the research has methodological limitations, there is no evidence of systematic differences between gay and non-gay parents in emotional health, parenting skills and attitudes towards parenting. No data have pointed to risks to the children and, in some cases, they benefit from living arrangements where same-sex couples may share child care and household tasks more equally than heterosexuals.

676 **Pink Parents UK** www.pinkparents.org.uk
UK-based website for lesbian, gay or bisexual parents and their children. Services include information for parents and children, a national magazine, information for professionals, events listings (UK-based), publications and information for researchers/students.

677 **Polikoff N D (1997) 'Resisting "Don't ask, don't tell" in the licensing of lesbian and gay foster parents: why openness will benefit lesbian and gay youth',** *Hastings Law Journal*, 48:6, pp. 1183–93
Brief US paper that argues that lesbian and gay foster parents should be used openly by agencies and that their sexuality should be open rather than implicit or hidden. Polikoff argues that this is especially the case when trying to place young lesbians and gay men, but she supports the approval of lesbian/gay foster carers across all types of placement.

678 **Positive Parenting Campaign**
www.positiveparentingcampaign.freeservers.com
UK website of the Positive Parenting Campaign which promotes and supports all aspects of lesbian and gay foster care and adoption. The group offers training, advice and support, and lists other relevant contacts, including UK support groups for lesbians and gay men interested or involved in foster care and adoption.

679 **Reilly T (1996) 'Gay and lesbian adoptions: a theoretical examination of policy-making and organisational decision-making',** *Journal of Sociology & Social Welfare*, 23:4, pp. 99–115
This article examines why so few US states and child welfare agencies have any policy on gay and lesbian

adoption. A survey of 50 states showed that most have ambiguous policies on this topic. The author suggests that this might be because drafting a policy might actually highlight a practice that would provoke public controversy. Agencies prefer to use lesbian and gay adopters without acknowledging this in policy, or this policy issue is not addressed because it is associated with troublesome problems and work that agencies prefer not to resource. The author argues that lack of formal policy supporting gay or lesbian adoptions is bad practice.

680 **Ricketts W (1991) Lesbians and Gay Men as Foster Parents.** Portland: *National Child Welfare Resource Centre, University of Southern Maine*
Pioneering US study that examines lesbian and gay foster care. Ricketts argues that lesbians and gay men are an untapped resource for providing foster care and that agencies must make efforts to recruit them and discuss questions of sexuality openly. After examining the influence of homophobic ideas on US social welfare practice, the author challenges common concerns about lesbian/gay parents through research evidence. He then discusses a case study of gay foster parents in Boston and relevant US law, and makes the case that lesbians and gay men should not be excluded from consideration as foster carers on the basis of their sexuality.

681 **Ricketts W and Achtenberg R (1990) 'Adoption and foster parenting for lesbians and gay men: creating new traditions in family',** *Marriage & Family Review* 14:3/4, pp. 83–118. **Simultaneously published in Bozett F W and Sussman M B (eds.), Homosexuality and Family Relations.** New York: *Harrington Park Press*

This overview examines the ways in which lesbian/gay foster care and adoption are creating "new" family forms. As more lesbian and gay applicants are being open about their sexuality, they are nevertheless open to discrimination from courts, childcare agencies and other professionals. The authors use a number of case studies to illustrate the skills and abilities that lesbian/gay carers bring and conclude that professionals need more training to work with such applicants. They also suggest that professionals consult research on lesbian and gay parenting that does not support discrimination on the basis of sexuality.

682 **Romaine M (2003) Assessing Lesbian and Gay Foster Carers and Adopters, BAAF Practice Note 44.** London: *BAAF*

Practice note for social workers who are assessing foster care or adoption applications by lesbians and gay men. The note reviews a range of research studies, as well as relevant UK legislation/policy, to argue that such assessments should proceed on the basis of equality. Having discussed the point that sexuality is in no way a determinant of the ability to parent, the author considers a number of issues that assessors should think about when working with lesbian or gay applicants (including parenting capacity, stability of relationships, child development outcomes and dealing with prejudice).

683 **Ryan S D (2000) 'Examining social workers' placement recommendations of children with gay and lesbian adoptive parents',** *Families in Society: The Journal of Contemporary Human Services*, 81:5, pp. 517–28

A research paper that reviews US social workers' placement considerations in relation to gay and lesbian adoption. The author surveyed 80 agency representatives using a questionnaire. African-American and white workers were more homophobic than Hispanic, Native American, Asian and other groups, as were men rather than women and Christians rather than others. Training on sexuality issues had a significant effect on reducing homophobic attitudes among workers.

684 **Saffron L (2001) It's a Family Affair: The complete lesbian parenting book.** London: *Diva Books*
UK guide for lesbians considering parenting. Part 3 deals with adoption and foster care and explains the processes involved for any potential lesbian applicants. Through case studies the main issues are highlighted but, although it is important to deal with problems and potential discrimination, some may find these overly negative.

685 **Sullivan A (ed.) (1995a) Issues in Gay and Lesbian Adoption: Proceedings of the 4th annual Peirce-Warwick Adoption Symposium.** Washington, DC: *Child Welfare League of America*
This US conference report points out the need for professional training on dealing with lesbian and gay adopters and also the requirement for explicit policy development. Chapters provide an overview of the debates, a consideration of US law and a detailed literature review of existing research relating to gay/lesbian parents and their children.

686 **Sullivan A (1995b) 'Policy issues in gay and lesbian adoption',** *Adoption & Fostering*, 19:4, pp. 21–25
Short summary paper taken from Sullivan (1995a) that looks at the development of agency policy on lesbian and

gay adoption. The author argues that agencies ought to develop clear policies in this area because adoption has become more inclusive, there are agencies already making placements with gay or lesbian adopters and there is a need to tackle institutional and staff prejudice. She provides a list of pointers for agencies considering such policies.

687 Sullivan T R and Baques A (1999) 'Familism and the adoption option for gay and lesbian parents', *Journal of Gay & Lesbian Social Services*, 10:1, pp. 79–94
This Canadian review paper includes two case studies. The author argues that homophobic ideas result in a narrow heterosexual definition of "family" within adoption services, but uses the case studies to show how lesbian and gay adoptions can be successful.

Disability

688 Abbott D, Morris J and Ward L (2000) Disabled Children and Residential Schools: A study of local authority policy and practice. Bristol: *Norah Fry Research Centre*
This and the following report (Abbott *et al*, 2001) are significant for examining the issues around the placement of children away from home without their participation in decision making and without social services authorities taking proper responsibility under childcare legislation. These issues are central to the experience of many disabled people (see refs. 704 and 725) and affect respite care as well as residential care. The study pointed out that children may be living in

residential schools because of a lack of individually tailored family placement including short-break services. In addition, placements may have been made for implicit child protection reasons but without child protection services and planning, as would have occurred if family or residential placement procedures were followed. Researchers also discovered a lack of awareness and clarity with regard to agencies' responsibilities to disabled children. The first stage of the research study (this report) examined the policies and practices of 21 education and social services authorities. The follow-on research (below) looked at four authorities in more detail, speaking to a wide range of education and social services professionals, interviewing 34 parents and 32 children. The research involved a reference group of young disabled people.

689 **Abbott D, Morris J and Ward L (2001) The Best Place to Be? Policy, practice and the experiences of residential school placements for disabled children.** York: *York Publishing Services/Joseph Rowntree Foundation*

See above, ref. 688.

690 **Argent H (1998a) 'Who wants George? Recruiting alternative families for children with disabilities',** *Adoption & Fostering*, 22:1, pp. 40–45

Based upon Argent and Kerrane (1997 – ref. 692), this article uses the case study of George, a 12-year-old disabled boy, to highlight the characteristics of those applicants who make good foster or adoptive carers for disabled children. Such carers generally have flexible attitudes, are able to cope with prejudice, do not keep family secrets and have a good social support network.

Argent argues that the specific needs of disabled children requiring placement should be highlighted in publicity designed to find families for them.

691 **Argent H (1998b) Whatever Happened to Adam? Stories of disabled people who were adopted or fostered.** London: *BAAF*
Presents accounts by 20 disabled people and the families who fostered or adopted them. At the time of publication, the disabled people were all 20 years old or over and the book looks back over their lives. The carers and the disabled people talk about the process of fostering or adoption, childhood, adolescence and moving into adulthood. Although the author used a framework for interviewing the families, they were encouraged to speak about their experiences in their own way. Therefore, Argent asserts that the book does not represent a systematic enquiry into placement outcomes. Especially useful to prospective foster carers or adopters of disabled children, but also for all those working in this field.

692 **Argent H and Kerrane A (1997) Taking Extra Care: Respite, shared and permanent care for children with disabilities.** London: *BAAF*
Practice guide that looks at all aspects of a comprehensive social work service for disabled children, including respite, shared and permanent forms of care. The authors argue for a flexible range of services and the guide reviews good practice in the following areas: key UK legislation, assessing children's needs, recruiting substitute families, training and assessing carers, introducing disabled children to their new carers, supporting placements, residential care, working with disabled children in placement, working with birth parents and

dealing with problems and disruptions. Alongside this runs a diary and commentary by a practitioner who set up and developed a local authority service for disabled children.

693 **Audit Commission (2003) Services for Disabled Children: A review of services for disabled children and their families.** London: *Audit Commission for Local Authorities and the National Health Service in England & Wales.* www.audit-commission.gov.uk/Products/NATIONAL-REPORT/EE944EBA-B414-4D76-903E-A4CAOE304989/Disabled-report-pdf
This report could be useful for all those working to meet the needs of disabled children as it addresses the range of services required, how to include disabled children in everyday life, how to address those children's changing needs and the role of professionals. The report is based on qualitative data from interviews with 240 disabled children, siblings, parents and a disabled young person's group. Case Study 4 reports on the Nottinghamshire County short-breaks service.

694 **BAAF (1996) The Placement of Children with Disabilities, Practice Note 34.** London: *BAAF*
Outlines a ranges of issues to consider when preparing to place disabled children in permanent care, including preparation of carers, children and their birth families. Introductions, the role of the medical adviser and post-placement support are also addressed.

695 **Baldwin S and Carlisle J (1994) Social Support for Disabled Children and their Families.** London: *HMSO*
A literature review of support and services available to disabled children and their families. Includes 280

references on topics such as living with disability, need for support (this includes home-based as well as family-based respite care) and allocation of resources.

696 **Ball M (1998) Disabled Children: Directions for their future care.** London: *Department of Health*
The message picked out from this report by the Welsh Health Evidence Bulletins about Healthy Living (28 June 1999, Chapter 6) is that respite care provides health gain for parents and children. This DH guide to good practice was based on a series of seven regional seminars held by the Social Services Inspectorate in 1997. The seminars were designed to share findings from research and inspections on the support required by disabled children and their families. The report identifies direct work with children and families, and joint working between agencies as areas for improvement. Also presents case studies of good practice.

697 **Begum N, Hill M and Stevens A (1994) Reflections: The view of black disabled people on their lives and community care.** London: *CCETSW*
Collection of papers looking at issues affecting black disabled people in Britain. Includes discussion of social work training and concepts and the provision of education and social services for children in particular. Analyses different approaches to fostering and respite care.

698 **Beresford B (1994) Positively Parents: Caring for a severely disabled child.** London: *HMSO*
Reports the findings of a qualitative longitudinal study of parents caring for a severely disabled child that examined strategies used to cope with and adapt to daily

pressures and problems, including reference to the significance of respite care. Many of the issues about finance, housing, mobility problems, lack of holidays and contact with services and professionals are interlinked. For example, the deficits in provision of home-based and family-based respite care are seen to be related to the exceptional levels of poverty among these parents. The later report (Beresford, 1995, *Expert Opinions: A national survey of parents caring for a severely disabled child*, published in conjunction with the Joseph Rowntree Foundation) is now out of print.

699 **Beresford B (2002) 'Preventing the exclusion of disabled children', in McNeish D, Newman T and Roberts H (eds.) What Works for Children? Effective services for children & families.** Buckingham: *Open University Press*
This research report considers the ways in which disabled children are excluded from everyday life and social welfare/education services. In the past, for example, respite care was often a specialist, residential service, viewed as meeting the needs of parents rather than children. The author addresses a number of ways in which disabled children can be included in everyday activities or services as well as the decisions made about their lives.

700 **Beresford B, Sloper P, Baldwin S and Newman T (1996) What Works in Services for Families with a Disabled Child?** Ilford: *Barnardo's*
See ref. 699.

701 **Borland M, O'Hara G and Triseliotis J (1991) 'Placement outcomes for children with special needs',** *Adoption & Fostering*, 15:2, pp. 18–28
Scottish three-year research study of the placement outcomes of children with special needs placed in the early 1980s. The authors studied 40 (out of 194) placements that had disrupted and 60 that had not, through quantitative data generated from records and questionnaires completed by social workers and parents. Disruptions increased for older children and for those with behavioural problems, while placements of children with learning difficulties were relatively stable. Once a placement began to deteriorate, social work support was usually unable to prevent breakdown. Overall, 80 per cent of the placements studied achieved stability within three years and the disruption rate of 20 per cent is one of the lowest found in UK research studies.

702 **Chamba R, Ahmad W, Lawton D and Beresford B (1999) On the Edge: Minority ethnic families caring for a severely disabled child.** Bristol: *The Policy Press*
Over two-thirds of the parents in this study said they needed respite care, while only 25 per cent were receiving it. The report presents the findings of a national UK survey involving almost 600 parents that examined the needs and circumstances of minority ethnic families caring for a severely disabled child. It describes their living circumstances and experiences, and identifies their needs and the extent to which these are being met through formal and informal support systems. Comparisons are also made with the findings of an earlier survey looking at the experiences of white families; black families were even more disadvantaged than white families with a disabled child, known from

previous studies to be disproportionately suffering from low income, unsuitable housing, high unemployment and other indicators of stress.

703 **Chan J and Sigafoos J (2001) 'Does respite care reduce parental stress in families with developmentally disabled children?',** *Child and Youth Care Forum*, 30:5, pp. 253–63
A review of studies about respite care for children with learning disabilities examining the effects on parental stress. Reveals that respite care is associated with significant reductions in parental stress for the majority of parents who use it.

704 **Cocks A (2000) 'Respite care for disabled children: micro and macro reflections',** *Disability and Society*, 15:3, pp. 507–19
Considers issues of power and control in relation to disabled children and the provision of respite care in out-of-home settings. The author proposes that it is possible to identify broader social mechanisms through such micro-level explorations.

705 **Cowen P S and Reed D A (2002) 'Effects of respite care for children with developmental disabilities: evaluation of an intervention for at risk families',** *Public Health Nursing*, 19:4, pp. 272–83
This US research study used questionnaires to assess family functioning among 148 families who used respite care for their children (n = 256). About half of the families were living below the federal poverty level. Respite care resulted in lower stress and improved family functioning that also reduced the child maltreatment rate.

706 **Cox M E, Orme J G and Rhodes K W (2002) 'Willingness to foster special needs children and foster family utilisation',** *Children and Youth Services Review*, 24:5, pp. 293–317

US research study of 876 foster families that examined their willingness to foster special needs children (including not just disabled children but also those with behavioural issues, illness, drug or alcohol concerns, those who had been sexually abused and teenagers). Families who had been willing to consider special needs children had fostered more children overall, had taken children with more types of special needs, had more foster children living with them, had fostered for longer and were less likely to discontinue fostering than those who were not willing to consider special needs children.

707 **Davies D (2001) Study Specification for a Value for Money Project on NHS and Local Government Services for Disabled Children, Young People and their Families.** London: *Audit Commission*

708 **Department of Health, Social Services Inspectorate, (1998) Disabled Children: Directions for their future; (1998b) Removing Barriers for Disabled Children: Inspection of services to disabled children and their families.** London: *HMSO*

709 **Dobson B and Middleton S (1998) Paying to Care: The cost of childhood disability.** York: *York Publishing Services (for the Joseph Rowntree Foundation)*

Analysing the roles of parent in terms of "parent and carer", this report identifies the challenge for services as providing appropriate support for both aspects, including collaborative "short-break" care, whether home or placement based. Overall, the purpose of the report is to examine the impact of childhood disability on family life. It compares the minimum essential budget standards for children of differing ages and disabilities with actual incomes. The study used budget standards based on the priorities and experiences of nearly 300 parents of severely disabled children and concluded that the minimum cost of raising a child with a disability is around three times as much as for a child without a disability. Implications for service delivery and benefits provision are discussed. Although the study focuses fundamentally on finance, it demonstrates how all aspects of family life are interlinked.

710 **Erich S and Patrick L (1998) 'Factors contributing to family functioning of adoptive children with special needs: a long-term outcome analysis',** *Children and Youth Services Review*, 20:1/2, pp. 135–50
US research study of families in which a total of 145 children with special needs had been placed for adoption. The survey assessed family functioning and found that the majority of the families had moderate to high scores. Those families who received family therapy reported lower levels of functioning but had adopted children with greater difficulties. Where there were more children in the home, functioning was high and those families that did the best had parents who spent more time addressing family issues, solving problems and seeking support.

711 **Glidden L M (2000) 'Adopting children with developmental disabilities: a long-term perspective',** *Family Relations*, 49:4, pp. 397–405
US research study of 123 families who had adopted at

least one child with a developmental disability. The researcher used semi-structured interviews with parents at both five and ten years after the initial placement was made. Quantitative data on family functioning, stress and coping levels were generated, and the author found low depression scores, above-average adjustment and good levels of coping, even among families who subsequently adopted a further child. Social workers are reminded to be aware that single adopters sometimes face extra difficulties and to note that initial depression in adopters is a potential risk factor for increased depression on placement.

712 **Glidden L M and Johnson V E (1999) 'Twelve years later: adjustment in families who adopted children with developmental disabilities',** *Mental Retardation*, 37:1, pp. 16–24

In response to the limited long-term follow-up data on disabled children who were adopted, this US study used questionnaires with 18 families nine years after initial contact. Mothers and fathers completed the questionnaires and the researchers also spoke to mothers separately. The families showed good adjustment and none of the adoptions had disrupted, with 50 per cent having gone on to adopt at least one additional child. Parents also spoke of difficulties, adolescence being a period of significant rewards and problems for their disabled adoptees.

713 **Goodinge S (1998) Removing Barriers for Disabled Children: Inspection of services to disabled children and their families.** London: *Department of Health*

Summarises the findings of inspections carried out in

eight local authorities in England. The inspections examined services provided to disabled children and their families and focused on areas such as service values and principles, information provision and service development. Among its conclusions are that short-break services were 'almost universally regarded by parents as a critical service in supporting families within the community' (Section 4.21).

714 Groze V (1996) 'A one- and two-year follow-up study of adoptive families and special needs children', *Children and Youth Services Review*, 18, pp. 57–82

US research study of 133 families who adopted a special needs child. The study used a random sample and followed families over two years, generating quantitative data through survey methods. Results showed that, over time, parents became more convinced that children had been abused or mistreated prior to their adoption, and there was a general increase in use of professional services and support. Children's behaviour overall did not change much over the years, but the pressures of adolescence increased strain upon the families. Nevertheless 70 per cent of the families rated the adoptions as having a positive effect. The author argues for a comprehensive system of professional support for such families, including respite care.

715 Jones V, Lenehan C and Robinson C (2000) Stronger Links: A guide to good practice for children's family-based short-term care services. Bristol: *The Policy Press*

This second edition sets out good practice within the framework of the Children Act 1989. It covers all aspects of running a family-based short-term care service including recruitment, assessment of children, families and carers, reviews, monitoring placements and training and support. Includes material emphasising guidance about providing diverse and accessible services.

716 Kennedy M (1996) 'Sexual abuse and disabled children', in Morris J (ed.) Encounters with Strangers: Feminism and disability. London: *The Women's Press.*

Kennedy's review of abuse and disabled children (like other studies) highlights the greater vulnerability of disabled children owing to their exposure to multiple and extra-familial caregivers, family and institutional placements being a typical part of this pattern.

717 Leung P and Erich S (2002) 'Family functioning of adoptive children with special needs: implications of familial supports and child characteristics', *Children and Youth Services Review*, 24:11, pp. 799–816

This research examined family functioning among US families in which a total of 117 special needs children had been adopted. Children with lower behavioural problem scores lived in families with higher levels of functioning and this was enhanced by support from the adopter's partner, other adoptive parents, physicians and day care. However, families who sought support from relatives, schools and professionals (social workers and therapists) showed lower levels of functioning. This is because these families had children with greater problems and so sought additional help. It does not mean that professional help results in poorer family functioning.

718 **Lightburn A and Pine B A (1996) 'Supporting and enhancing the adoption of children with developmental disabilities',** *Children and Youth Services Review*, 18:1/2, pp. 139–62

A report of two US research studies on coping and adaptation in families who adopted disabled children. The total sample covered 114 adoptions in 52 families. Study 1 used qualitative methods (observation, interviews, diaries, field notes) to look at coping strategies and Study 2 used both quantitative (standard tests) and qualitative (interview) data to test family adaptation. All the families showed successful outcomes and none had disrupted. Adequate information about the child's history was vital to adopters, as was a range of post-placement supports (financial, community, professional help).

719 **Macadam M and Robinson C (1995) Balancing the Act: The impact of the Children Act 1989 on family link services for children with disabilities.** London: *National Children's Bureau*

The main aim was to assess the extent to which the Family Placement Regulations have been implemented by family link services, to evaluate the impact regulations have had and in particular to see whether they improved practice in placing children with disabilities. The study was carried out in two stages: initially, a postal survey was conducted with all family link services for children in England and Wales; the second stage involved a detailed study of six such services to see how they were operating under the Children Act. Recommendations are made.

720 **McConnell D, Llewellyn G and Ferronato L (2002) 'Disability and decision-making in Australian care proceedings',** *International Journal of Law, Policy and the Family*, 16:2, pp. 270–99

An Australian study, the method, conclusions and analysis of which have relevance for UK practitioners, researchers and policy makers. The authors conducted an interview and observational study of court process and decision-making accompanied by a record review in the Sydney children's court. Study findings highlight several reasons that help explain why parents with intellectual disability are over-represented in care and protection proceedings and why their children are more likely to be placed in out-of-home care. These reasons include beliefs about parental (in)capacity, the "diagnostic-prognostic rationality" of decision makers, the need for parent compliance in an adversarial system, lack of suitable support services and poorly resourced legal representatives. Implications for policy and for practice are discussed.

721 **McGlone K, Santos L, Kazama L, Fong R and Mueller C (2002) 'Psychological stress in adoptive parents of special needs children',** *Child Welfare*, 81:2, pp. 151–71

US research study that used both quantitative and qualitative methods to explore the nature and extent of parenting stress among 25 sets of adoptive parents of 35 children with special needs. More than half of the children had some notable health problems or developmental delays. Adoptive parents listed behaviour problems, medical concerns, children's untruthfulness or withdrawal from communication, family conflict and the extra workload involved as creating stresses. They also felt that social workers did not provide enough background information on the adopted children, that some placements seemed "rushed" and that they were not always consulted on decisions. The authors recommend that agencies attempt to anticipate, identify and support adopters' stresses.

722 **Marchant R and Page M (1993) Bridging the Gap: Child protection work with children with multiple disabilities.** London: *NSPCC*

A report examining the protection of children with multiple disabilities. Includes chapters on preventive work, conducting investigations and therapeutic work. Like other studies of this subject, it emphasises the additional vulnerability of disabled children because they are more likely to be exposed to multiple and extra-familial providers of intimate care. Although the regulatory framework is that in place in 1993, the book identifies the principles of preventive and intervention responsibilities at personal, organisational and policy levels which are valid within any welfare regime. Contains material applicable to social workers, carers and policy makers involved in the family placement of disabled children.

723 **Mencap (1999) Opening Doors to Short-term Breaks.** London: *Mencap*

A guide for carers of people with learning difficulties that aims to raise awareness of entitlements to short-term breaks and the right to have their needs assessed by social services.

724 **Morris J (1998) Still Missing? Vol 1: The experiences of disabled children and young people living away from their families; Vol 2: Disabled children and the Children Act.** London: *Who Cares? Trust*

This influential study reports the experiences of young disabled children away from home and examines how three social services departments were implementing the Children Act 1989 as it applies to disabled children. Contrary to the provisions of the Act, it was found that some children were spending time away from their families in forms of respite care without the knowledge or involvement of the social services authority. In addition, there was little evidence of the children's wishes and feelings being ascertained about placement. The majority of the children had communication difficulties, but there was also little evidence that social workers had training in communicating with them. The project had a reference group of disabled young people who had spent most of their childhood away from their families. This group pointed out that disabled children and young people need an independent advocate to find out what the disabled child needs and whose only responsibility is to support the child. Summary available online at the Joseph Rowntree website:
www.jrf.org.uk/knowledge/findings/socialcare/scr378.asp

725 **Morris J (1999) 'Disabled children, child protection systems and the Children Act 1989',** *Child Abuse Review*, 8:2, pp. 91–108

Includes comparisons of patterns of abuse suffered by disabled children with those experienced by a non-disabled group. The patterns were different, caused partly by the greater likelihood of medical intervention and children having personal care provided outside the home. Reports that Children Act regulations are less likely to be complied with when disabled children are in placement, arguing that this means that the levels of protection provided for in the Act are not given. See also refs. 688, 689, 716, 722 and 724.

726 **Mountney J (1991) Children with Disabilities in Foster Care: A survey by the National Foster Care Association.** London: *NFCA*

UK research survey by questionnaire of 74 foster care agencies on their approach to work with disabled children. Most had general rather than specialist teams. Twenty-three per cent of agencies did not know how many disabled children they had placed and 31 per cent did not know how many of their carers were approved for such children. There was a lack of specialist workers, targeted recruitment of carers or training on work with disabled children. Follow-up semi-structured interviews were carried out with representatives from five agencies and the report recommends a register of disabled children in foster care, better training for workers and carers, targeted recruitment of carers for disabled children and better support for their carers.

727 **National Foster Care Association (1991) Fostering Children with Disabilities: A guide for carers.** London: *NFCA*

A guide for foster carers offering information on different types of disability and sources of support. Discusses issues such as communication, play, education and moving into adulthood.

728 **National Foster Care Association (2000) Rights of Passage – Young disabled people: the transition from foster care to adult life: a study of young people with learning difficulties.** London: *NFCA*
Reports on a research project that considered how young disabled people in foster care could be best supported to move on into independence. Qualitative data were generated from case studies of six young people with learning difficulties (aged 17–21 years) who were in foster care on their 16th birthdays. A mixed picture of experiences is presented and the report recommends advocacy services to help young disabled people get their views across, assistance to access transport and leisure services, support for carers during and after the transition phase, funding to help maintain contact between the young people and their former carers, better sex education initiatives, help to access education and careers services, benefits and accommodation advice and the involvement of young disabled people in the planning and development of services for them. Foster carers are seen to offer a crucial source of support to young disabled people prior to and after they have moved on.

729 **Newitt B, Jones V and Robinson C (1997) Quality Counts: A review of quality assurance in family-based short-term care.** London: *Shared Care UK*
Looks at ways of consulting parents, carers and disabled service users about the quality of their local family-based, short-term care scheme.

730 **Oliver S (2000) Supporting the Adoptive Parents of Special Needs Children, Social Work Monographs 183.** Norwich: *University of East Anglia*
This monograph provides an overview and review of the

literature pertaining to the support needs of parents who adopt special needs children including those who are disabled. Oliver looks at the development of post-adoption support services in the UK and suggests that these have a crucial role to play in maintaining the adoptive placements of special needs children and preventing their breakdown. She argues for better resources to support the development of recruitment and preparation of carers, that the carers of special needs children require a full social and background history on their children and for an increase in post-adoption support services in the UK.

731 Preece D (2002) 'Consultation with children with autistic spectrum disorders about their experience of short-term residential care', *British Journal of Learning Disabilities*, 30:3, pp. 97–104

There are inherent difficulties in consulting with children who are diagnosed with autistic spectrum disorders (ASD). Case studies were undertaken investigating the impact of the characteristics of autism upon researchers' abilities to elicit children's opinions about their experience of short-term residential care. Preece identifies factors that maximised the children's input and the accuracy of the results.

732 Prewett B (1999) Short-term Break, Long-term Benefit: Family-based short-term care for disabled children and adults. Sheffield: *Joint Unit for Social Services Research*

Reports the findings of the third UK national survey conducted for Shared Care Network and includes discussion of family-based short-term schemes in operation and the views of service users, and makes recommendations for future practice.

733 **Prewett B (2000) Committed to Caring: The views of short-break carers for children, who are "hard to place".** York: *York Publishing Services (for the Joseph Rowntree Foundation)*
Children and young people who have complex healthcare needs or "challenging behaviour" and/or who come from minority ethnic families are often not provided with short-break services: they are categorised as "hard to place". This study investigated why short-break carers provided breaks for "hard-to-place" children and looked at their recruitment, assessment, training and support.

734 **Rhodes A, Lenehan C and Morrison J (1999) Promoting Partnership – Supporting disabled children who need invasive clinical procedures: a Barnardo's guide to good practice for family support services.** Ilford: *Barnado's*
Outlines ways in which health and social services can work together to manage the needs of disabled children requiring medication or additional support. Includes discussion of relevant legislation, insurance and responsibility as well as carrying out health assessments, drawing up healthcare plans and working with invasive clinical procedures.

735 **Robinson C (1991) Home and Away: Respite care in the community.** Birmingham: *Venture Press*
Practical guide to establishing and running a family-based respite care service.

736 **Robinson C and Jackson P (1999) Children's Hospices: A lifeline for families.** London: *National Children's Bureau*
One of the findings of this study was that the use of hospice care for children sometimes reflects the inability of other more appropriate family-based services to provide the needed quantity or quality of respite.

737 **Robinson C, Jackson P and Townsley R (2001) 'Short breaks for families caring for a disabled child with complex health needs',** *Child & Family Social Work*, 6:1, pp. 67–75
Reports on two UK studies, the first of which considered disabled children who were staying in hospices, and the second those who were being tube fed. Interviews were conducted with 77 families and some professionals. Both studies showed that almost a third of families used a link or shared care scheme. Parents were positive about this support but complained that they had to wait a long time to be allocated a link carer. The authors suggest that link foster care is poorly resourced and that payments are rarely sufficient to attract individuals to come forward and offer the commitment that the service requires.

738 **Robinson C and Stalker K (1993) 'Patterns of provision in respite care and the Children Act',** *British Journal of Social Work*, 23:1, pp. 45–63
Reports on findings of a three-year research study that examined patterns of respite care provision to disabled children within three English local authorities. Quantitative data were generated from questionnaires (filled in by a range of professional staff) and case records. Overall, the uptake rate for respite services for

children with severe learning difficulties was on average 37 per cent. Older children, those in low-income families and those from black, Asian and minority ethnic groups were all less likely to take up respite services and more likely to use health and institutional care. The authors argue that requirements to regulate and widen respite care services will also place increased pressure upon what is already a scarce resource.

739 **Rosenthal J A (1993) 'Outcomes of adoption of children with special needs',** *Adoption: The future of children*, 3:1, pp. 77–88
Reviews research on special needs adoption outcomes. Key predictors for the risk of disruption include placement of older children (risk of disruption increases with age), inadequate background information given to adopters, rigidity within the adoptive family patterns, poor support networks and children with a history of abuse or mental health issues. Children's behaviour problems are the single largest source of stress for adoptive families and about five per cent of adoptions of children with developmental disabilities and ten to 15 per cent of adoptions of children older than three years at placement end in disruption. The author notes that non-traditional and minority ethnic families cope well with disabled and special needs children, and that such adoptions should be better resourced and supported nationally and by agencies.

740 **Russell P (1992) The Children Act 1989 and Disability.** London: *National Children's Bureau*
This is the concise "Highlight" (no. 109 in the National Children Bureau's series) written by the person who

drafted the official guidance about the Children Act and children with disabilities.

741 **Russell P (1993) 'A challenge for child protection procedures', in Pritchard J, Good Practice in Child Protection: A manual for professionals.** London: *Jessica Kingsley*

Continues to be a useful resource for staff, carers and students concerned with the care of disabled children, including those in foster and respite care. Refers to the anticipatory concerns of parents about the safety of their children in link, foster and residential care, and to the dimensions of "system abuse". The author emphasises the importance of listening to "the whole child" and not attempting narrow child protection investigations as yet another part of the "assessment industry" into which disabled children may be drawn. Adequate support services such as link care may be an important preventive service in relation to families vulnerable to abuse and neglect. The chapter is an authoritative summary of the context (including statistics), preventive measures and interventions relevant to the abuse of disabled children. The overall message is that much greater vigilance is required about the safety and protection of disabled children than has traditionally been evident.

742 **Tarleton B (2003) 'Committed to caring: family-based short-break carers' views of their roles',** *Adoption & Fostering*, 27:1, pp. 36–46

See Prewett (2000). Reports on a study of 53 carers offering short-term breaks for children with high support needs.

743 **Tarleton B and Macaulay F (2002) Better for the Break? Short-break services for children and teenagers with autistic spectrum disorders and their families.** York: *Shared Care Network*
Presents the findings of a survey of short-break services for children and adolescents with autistic spectrum disorders and their families within the UK. Services surveyed included family-based short breaks, residential short breaks, domiciliary/outreach support, sitting services, befriending schemes, playschemes and clubs. A key message of the survey was confirmation of the lifelong need of families for high-quality services that targeted specific support needs appropriately.

744 **Wates M (2002a) 'Disability and adoption: how unexamined attitudes discriminate against disabled people as parents',** *Adoption & Fostering*, 26:2, pp. 49–56
One of the very few articles to focus on disabled people as potential adoptive parents. Wates argues that disabled people are under-represented among those who apply or are approved as adopters within the UK and points out that this is in part due to the reluctance of agencies to address and meet disabled parents' support needs. She writes that disabled applicants often have to educate their assessors during the application process, arguing that disability and parenting support requirements should not be a barrier to being considered as an adoptive parent.

745 **Wates M (2002b) Supporting Disabled Adults in their Parenting Role: A review and analysis of local authority policies and protocols.** York: *York Publishing Sevices*

There are particular issues around the support of parents with learning disability and judgements about their capability to care for their own children. This work is a brief review of local authority policies in relation to the support of learning disabled parents.

6 Attachment, therapeutic help and life story work

Themes of attachment, loss and trauma are integral to the placement of children in foster and adoptive care. Understanding the nature of loss is a key aspect of adoption work, whether with adopted children, adults, adoptive parents or birth family members. Abuse in its many forms and with its associated trauma is the principal reason for nearly two-thirds of care placements and no doubt a subsidiary reason for many more. Understanding the effects of trauma on the attachment capacities of children, especially when that trauma is caused by the potential attachment figure, is central to family placement practice, as is an appreciation of risk and resilience.

Attachment theory has recently been described as one of the dominant theories underpinning family placement practice (Schofield, 2001 – ref. 819). Although there are differences there are also overlapping themes in theories of attachment and theories of resilience. However, social workers have also been criticised for an oversimplified use of attachment theory and a tendency to give insufficient credence to other factors within the child's environment that may be affecting the child's behaviour and social/emotional development (Rushton and Mayes, 1997 – ref. 773). There are some problems with terminology and a need to be clear about the difference between insecure attachment and attachment disorder. For these various reasons it seemed important to include in this Bibliography details of recent theoretical, empirical and clinical developments within the field.

Particular emphasis has been given to recent empirical work within clinical settings. Developing evidence of the impact of some forms of depression and substance misuse on the attachment process is of particular relevance to childcare practitioners (ref. 752). Recent work in relation to disorganised attachment is also significant because of established links with maltreatment and externalising behaviour difficulties (see ref. 788).

The chapter begins with literature detailing recent theoretical and practice developments. This is followed by references with a strong empirical focus, including a final section listing publications related to life story work. It could be argued that the theoretical basis for life story work is broader than attachment theory. However, in assisting children and young people to develop a coherent narrative of their life story the links are clear.

It was not within the scope of this Bibliography to include a comprehensive list of references in relation to direct work with children. Readers are therefore advised to consult the publication lists of key national organisations, including BAAF, the Fostering Network, NSPCC, the National Children's Bureau, SCIE and Barnardo's.

Theoretical and empirical developments

746 Ayoub C, Fischer W and O'Connor E (2003) 'Analyzing development of working models for disrupted attachments: the case of hidden family violence', *Attachment and Human Development*, 5:2, pp. 97–119

Ayoub and colleagues draw on dynamic skills theory to explain how individuals modify their working models of attachment throughout the life span. The authors develop a framework to explain the impact of childhood trauma and violence. Behaviour that might be viewed by attachment theorists as "disorganised" is described as a "trauma dance". This they argue is a 'highly sophisticated adaptation to a traumatic environment' (p. 101). This framework is used to describe why children assessed as "disorganised" in infancy develop punitive caregiving strategies by six years of age.

747 **Belsky J and Pasco Fearon R M (2002) 'Early attachment security, subsequent maternal sensitivity and later child development: Does continuity in development depend upon continuity of caregiving?',** *Attachment and Human Development*, 4:3, pp. 361–87

This article reports the findings of an analysis of data collated as part of the NICHD Study of Early Child Care. The aim was to assess the prediction of attachment theorists that both past experience and current quality of caregiving would influence psychosocial development in young children. However, the findings suggest that better developmental outcomes were associated with early insecurity followed by subsequent sensitive care, in contrast to early security followed by subsequent insensitive care. The evidence also highlights the importance of contextual factors in the development of attachment security.

748 **Bolen R (2002) 'Child sexual abuse and attachment theory: Are we rushing headlong into another controversy?',** *Journal of Child Sexual Abuse*, 11:1 pp. 95–124

Reviews the literature examining the relationship between sexual abuse and attachment. The author considers a number of key hypotheses: for example, whether insecure attachment increases vulnerability to or is a consequence of sexual abuse. She concludes that the empirical evidence is limited. Attachment theory may, however, have the potential to provide insight into the dynamics of abusive relationships. It is important that "microsystem" factors are not considered in isolation from "macrosystem" factors and wider cultural influences on the manifestation of child sexual abuse.

749 **Briere J N (1992) Child Abuse Trauma: Theory and treatment of the lasting effects.** London: *Sage*
The author describes the psychological impact of abuse. He argues that the impact of abuse derives both from the abusive experience and the child's accommodation to that experience. Basing his work on an integration of clinical insights with empirical research, he suggests that psychological disturbance may include cognitive distortion, altered emotionality and impaired self-reference. An important work describing complex material in an accessible style.

750 **Cassidy J and Shaver P R (eds.) (1999) Handbook of Attachment: Theory, research and clinical applications.** New York: *Guilford Press*
Draws on contributions from leading researchers to provide a detailed and up-to-date analysis of recent theoretical and empirical developments in the field of attachment. The book begins with an overview of key theoretical constructs including an important analysis of the role of internal working models. The second section is written from a biological perspective and includes a chapter discussing the role of temperament. The next section addresses issues of measurement of attachment at different stages in the life cycles. This is followed by

further chapters considering the clinical implications for work with both children and adults. Contributions in relation to attachment and psychopathology in childhood and attachment disorganisation are of particular relevance to childcare practitioners. The final section includes an analysis of the application of attachment theory to childcare policy and practice.

751 **Cicchetti D and Carlson V (eds.) (1989) Child Maltreatment: Theory and research on the causes and consequences of child abuse and neglect.**
Cambridge: *Cambridge University Press*
An authoritative text providing a comprehensive overview by leading developmental researchers of the causes and consequences of child maltreatment. Of particular relevance are a number of contributions examining the impact of maltreatment on attachment. Crittenden and Ainsworth argue that the construct of anxious attachment is a 'critical variable which may help us to understand why maltreatment affects many areas of individual or family functioning' (p. 457). Aber *et al* assert that many of the problems maltreated children present are 'derivative of the central problem – an over-concern with security issues reflecting an expectation of unresponsive, unavailable and rejecting adults' (p. 614). This, they suggest, cannot be proven from current evidence but is a working hypothesis with important implications for practice.

752 **Cicchetti D, Toth S L and Lynch M (1995) 'Bowlby's dream come full circle: the application of attachment theory to risk and psychopathology',**
Advances in Clinical Child Psychology, 17, pp. 1–75
An important chapter examining theoretical and

empirical developments in attachment theory with specific reference to high-risk and clinical populations. Particular emphasis is given to a review of the literature in relation to attachment in maltreated children, children with oppositional disorders and children whose primary caregiver has experienced depression or substance misuse. The author considers the implications for practice and concludes with suggestions for further theory and research.

753 **Crittenden P M (1990) 'Internal representational models of attachment relationships',** *Infant Mental Health Journal*, 11:3, pp. 259–77

A theoretical article examining the construct of internal working models, a central tenet of attachment theory. The author emphasises the complex nature of internal working models as they operate within parent–child and adult–adult relationships. Particularly significant is the link made with an understanding of memory. She examines the development of procedural, semantic and episodic memory and describes the difficulties for children and adults when there is inconsistency between these different memory systems. The reader is challenged to think about how children integrate experiences from different relationships into their internal representations of attachment.

754 **Crittenden P M (1992a) 'Children's strategies for coping with adverse home environments: an interpretation using attachment theory',** *Child Abuse & Neglect*, 16, pp. 329–43

Reports the findings of a study comparing the coping strategies of four groups of young maltreated children with a group of young children who have received adequate care. The findings suggest that different types of adverse circumstances may affect the social development of children in different ways. The author argues that some behaviours (compulsive compliance/ avoidance), although adaptive in the short term, may affect the child's emotional development in the longer term. Specifically they may 'decrease the likelihood that the child would be able to recognise sensitive and tolerant individuals should they become available' (p. 341).

755 **Crittenden P M (1992b) 'Quality of attachment in the pre-school years',** *Development and Psychopathology*, 4, pp. 209–41

Crittenden describes the process and nature of attachment behaviour in pre-school children. She argues that consideration should be given to two further defended patterns, compulsive caregiving and compulsive compliance. She suggests that during the pre-school years coercive strategies may be evident in ambivalent children. Includes detailed consideration of the complex nature of disorganised attachment.

756 **Crittenden P M (1992c) 'Treatment of anxious attachment in infancy and early childhood',** *Development and Psychopathology*, 4, pp. 575–602

Crittenden draws on a number of different perspectives to develop a theoretical framework to understand the problems created for young children by the experience of anxious attachment. Particularly helpful is the way knowledge about the development of memory is linked to an understanding of the development of anxious attachment. Each of the memory systems (procedural, semantic and episodic) can be linked to different therapeutic interventions. A framework can therefore be developed for interventions with children at different ages and stages of development.

757 **de Wolff M S and van IJzendoorn M H (1997) 'Sensitivity and attachment: a meta-analysis on parental antecedents of infant attachment',** *Child Development*, 68:4, pp. 571–91

This article describes the findings of a meta-analysis examining the question of parental antecedents of attachment security. Sixty-six studies were included in the meta-analysis. The aim was to examine the validity of the previously held view that parental sensitivity was a key determinant of attachment security. The findings suggest that in normal settings sensitivity is an important but not exclusive condition of attachment security. Other aspects of parenting were also found to be significant. The authors argue that studies of attachment need to look at broader contextual issues, particularly when considering children living in stressful environments. It is important when considering siblings to take into account the influence of non-shared environmental factors.

758 **Dubner A E and Motta R W (1999) 'Sexually and physically abused foster care children and Post Traumatic Stress Disorder',** *Journal of Consulting and Clinical Psychology*, 67:3, pp. 367–73

A report of the findings of a study established to examine whether there is a link between child abuse and the development of symptoms of Post Traumatic Stress Disorder (PTSD). Three groups of children in foster care were compared. They comprised 50 children who had experienced sexual abuse, 50 children who had experienced physical abuse and 50 children where there was no record of abuse. The findings demonstrated a high level of PTSD symptoms in the abused children.

759 **Green J and Goldwyn R (2002) 'Attachment disorganisation and psychopathology: new findings in attachment research and their potential implications for developmental psychopathology in childhood',** *Journal of Child Psychology and Psychiatry*, 43:7, pp. 835–46

This critical literature review examines research in relation to disorganised attachment and considers the implications for research and clinical practice. Disorganised attachment has been linked to specific characteristics of parent–child relationships associated with high-risk populations. However, there is also some evidence of disorganised attachment in children with neuro-developmental vulnerability. Disorganised attachment appears to be a marker for difficulties in a number of areas of development including behaviour, the development of self-esteem and emotional regulation. The hypothesis that this derives from problems in the area of attachment alone needs to be tested against alternative explanations. Given that many children adopted from care have a history of maltreatment/trauma, an assessment of attachment representation may help to identify placements most at risk.

760 **Harris P L (1999) 'Individual differences in understanding emotion: the role of attachment status and psychological discourse',** *Attachment and Human Development*, 1:3, pp. 307–24

Reviews the research literature examining children's understanding of emotion. Emphasis is given to longitudinal studies that examine the development of emotional understanding over time. The evidence suggests there is considerable stability in how young children perceive and express emotions. The author offers two interpretations of this evidence. The first closely links the development of emotional understanding with the development of attachment; secure attachment is therefore seen as a critical step in this process. The second views quality of discourse within the family as the key mediating factor. Therefore, it is the quality of communication that is critical. The implication, if this is correct, is that insecurely attached children might increase their understanding of emotions with specific help. This could be provided by a therapist outside the family network.

761 Hodges J and Steele M *et al* (2000) 'Effects of abuse on attachment representations: narrative assessments of abused children', *Journal of Child Psychotherapy*, 26:3, pp. 433–55

This article describes how narrative techniques can be used to assess both the impact of abuse and the process of healing and recovery. Such techniques used initially as a clinical tool have been developed for research purposes. The aim is to assess the child's mental representation of adult figures. The rationale is that the impact of early abusive experiences is mediated at least in part through the child's attachment representations. The play narrative does not necessarily depict actual experience but how the child has made sense of that experience and the defensive strategies used. The techniques were utilised with a sample of children in the four to eight age group. The authors conclude with preliminary findings comparing children recently removed from abusive situations with those who have begun to settle with adoptive families.

762 **Hodges J, Steele M, Hillman S *et al* (2003) 'Changes in attachment representations over the first year of adoptive placement: narratives of maltreated children',** *Clinical Child Psychology and Psychiatry*, 8:3, pp. 347–63

Reports preliminary findings from the Thomas Coram Adoption Project. This is a prospective, longitudinal study of children placed for adoption after a history of adversity. The mean age of the children at placement was six years one month. The study follows the children through the first two years of placement. There is a comparison group of children placed for adoption before 12 months of age.

One of the aims of the study was to monitor, through the use of story stem techniques, changes in the child's internal working models of attachment. The story stem allows children to represent their experiences and expectations of adults in displaced form. At the first assessment the children displayed more avoidant and disorganised characteristics than the sample group. A year later, although positive adult characteristics had increased, negative ones did not significantly decrease. Therefore, while new and more positive representations were developing they did not automatically transform established patterns. Also see Kaniuk *et al* (2004 – ref. 723).

763 **Howe D (2001) 'Age at placement, adoption experience and adult adopted people's contact with their adoptive and birth mothers: an attachment perspective',** *Attachment and Human Development*, 3:2, pp. 222–37

Reports the findings of one aspect of a larger study comparing a group of adult adopted people who had initiated a search for one or more of their birth relatives (searchers) with those who had not (non-searchers). The data refer specifically to age at placement and current levels of contact with the adoptive or birth mother. Adults who had been placed at younger ages were more likely to evaluate their adoption experience positively and to maintain higher levels of contact than those placed later. Of those adults who had initiated contact with their birth mother, frequency of contact was again associated with earlier age at placement. These findings are discussed within an attachment framework.

764 Howe D, Brandon M, Hinings D and Schofield G (1999) Attachment Theory, Child Maltreatment and Family Support: A practice and assessment model.
Basingstoke: *Macmillan*
This book, written essentially for practitioners, aims to bridge the gap between theory and practice by presenting recent developments in attachment theory and considering the implications for practice. The authors address complex material in a helpful and accessible style. Especially helpful are chapters which focus on the four key infant attachment patterns and explain how these change through the life cycle. Attachment strategies associated with each pattern are therefore described as they affect behaviour in childhood, adolescence, adulthood and parenthood. An essential read for childcare practitioners needing to understand the complex nature of attachment patterns.

765 Kaniuk J, Steele M and Hodges J (2004) 'Report on a longitudinal research project exploring the development of attachments between older, hard-to-place children and their adopters over the first

two years of placement', *Adoption & Fostering*, 28:2, pp. 61–67

The study reported here explored the development of attachments between a group of 63 children aged four to eight years at placement, all of whom had a history of separations and neglect or abuse. The 63 children and their adopters (42 families) were followed up for two years after placement. They were compared with a group of 48 children who had been adopted as infants (under 12 months of age) but who were of similar age as the research sample at the time of the study. Measures used included measures of the children's attachments and psychological development and of the adopters' attachment status and experience as parents. Uniquely in the field of adoption this project has included measures of attachment that look below the surface to explore the inner worlds of both the children and the adopters. The children's schools were also contacted for a report on their progress. Also see Hodges *et al* (2003 – ref. 762).

766 Liotti G (1999) 'Disorganization of attachment as a model for understanding dissociative psychopathology', in Solomon J and George C (eds.), Attachment Disorganization. New York: *Guilford Press*

In this chapter the author presents a theoretical model linking early disorganisation of attachment as one route to the development of dissociative disorders in pre- and post-adolescence. Liotti includes a helpful description of disorganised attachment, including the conflicting thought processes for a child who experiences acute fear in the context of their primary attachment relationships. He examines how shifting thought processes (seeing the self as victim, rescuer or persecutor) prevent an integrated understanding of attachment experiences. Painful exclusion of attachment feelings may lead to overly aggressive or overly sexual behaviour in older children. This complex chapter provides considerable insight into the behaviour of children who have experienced early traumatic care and will be of interest to staff who wish to understand the concept of disorganised attachment in more depth.

767 Lyons-Ruth K (1996) 'Attachment relationships among children with aggressive behaviour problems: the role of disorganised early attachment patterns', *Journal of Consulting and Clinical Psychology*, 64:1, pp. 64–73

Reviews the literature examining the early attachment experiences of young children who display aggressive behaviour. The author argues that attachment theory extends our understanding of the factors that may contribute to the development of aggressive behaviour. The wider literature identifies the importance of parental hostile and rejecting behaviour in the developmental trajectory leading to aggressive behaviour in young children. However, Lyons-Ruth asserts that this aggressive behaviour is likely to be preceded by a disturbance in the attachment relationship characteristic of disorganised attachment. Attachment theory would suggest that underlying the behaviour patterns observed in these children is 'a disruption in the functioning of the child's primary attachment relationships which leave the child without an organised relationally oriented strategy for regulating felt security' (p. 17).

768 **Nelson K (1999) 'Event representations, narrative development and internal working models',** *Attachment and Human Development*, 1:3, pp. 239–52

Nelson reviews the similarities and differences between her theory of event representation and the more traditional view of attachment theory about how children develop interning working models of themselves and their attachment figures. She places particular emphasis on the development of language. Internal working models, she argues, may change not only in response to changes in the pattern of care giving but also as a result of the opportunity language provides for reflection and the development of shared narrative. An important task of parenting is to help a child develop an understanding of events and experiences through the development of narrative. Although the author does not make specific reference to adoption practice, the implications for life story work and telling are of some interest.

769 **O'Connor T G, Bredenkamp D and Rutter M (1999) 'Attachment disturbances and disorders in children exposed to early severe deprivation',** *Infant Mental Health Journal*, 20:1, pp. 10–29

This article reports significant findings from the English and Romanian Adoptees (ERA) study team. The study followed the progress of Romanian adoptees placed with families in the UK following a history of severe deprivation in an institutional setting. This is a longitudinal study based on a random sample stratified by age. The study includes a comparison group of infants placed within the UK.

The aim of the article was to examine the construct of attachment disorder drawing on empirical data from the study. At the time of assessment the children were four years of age. The authors conclude that inhibited and disinhibited attachment disorders are both distinguishable from more generalised behaviour difficulties. The critical causal factor appears not to be 'institutional social deprivation *per se* but the lack of a consistence and responsive caregiver – and the opportunity to form selective attachments' (p. 24).

770 **O'Connor T G, Rutter M and the English and Romanian Adoptees (ERA) study team (2000) 'Attachment disorder behavior following early severe deprivation: extension and longitudinal follow-up',** *Journal of American Academy of Child and Adolescent Psychiatry*, 39:6, pp. 703–12
This second article reports the findings when the children were six years of age. The findings indicate a close association between duration of deprivation and the severity of attachment disordered behaviour. Although there was a correlation with attentional and conduct problems, there appeared to be a distinct set of symptoms and behaviour. The findings offer some validation to the construct of attachment disorder.

771 **O'Connor T G and Zeanah C H (2003) 'Attachment disorders: assessment strategies and treatment approaches',** *Attachment and Human Development*, 5:3, pp. 223–44
This target article introduces the special edition of *Attachment and Human Development* in relation to attachment disorder. The authors begin with a critique of the basic construct and discusses limitations of the clinical definitions of inhibited and disinhibited attachment disorder. The relationship between disorganised attachment and attachment disorder is also discussed.

They argue that it may be helpful to consider a continuum of attachment disturbance. It would then be possible to differentiate secure attachment, "ordinary" forms of insecure attachment, disorganised attachment, secure-based distortions and finally disorders of non-attachment. The article includes a review of the current state of knowledge about assessment and treatment and describes this as "work in progress" given the limited research base in relation to both areas.

772 **Perry B D and Pollard R (1998) 'Homeostasis, stress, trauma and adaptation: a neuro-developmental view of childhood trauma',** *Child and Adolescent Psychiatric Clinics of North America*, 7:1, pp. 33–51

Perry and Pollard describe the impact of traumatic experiences on the development of young children considered from the perspective of developmental neuro-biology. They argue that because of the sensitivity of the brain in early childhood, traumatic experiences occurring during this period will influence subsequent social, emotional and cognitive development. While predictable and nurturing caregiving contribute to the development of resilience, early trauma may result in a tendency to experience hyper-arousal and dissociative experiences in response to stress. Caregivers need to understand that experiences that trigger previous memories associated with fear may lead to behaviours which, if misunderstood, appear oppositional. This may have application to arrangements for contact.

773 **Rushton A and Mayes D (1997) 'Forming fresh attachments in childhood: a research update',** *Child & Family Social Work*, 2:2, pp. 121–27

A brief review of the literature examining to what degree maltreated children are able to develop satisfactory relationships once placed with new families. The authors argue it is important not to 'carelessly ascribe to the attachment process behaviours which may derive from other aspects of the child's experience and development' (p. 121). Ten studies are reviewed. The evidence suggests that satisfactory relationships are developed for most late-placed children with their new parents. However, less is known about why instability can occur at later stages in the placement, particularly during adolescence. It is important that resources are targeted at those families most in need. Further refinement of methods to assess and monitor the development of attachment in late-placed children would be an important foundation for further research.

774 **Rushton A, Quinton D, Dance C and Mayes D (1998) 'Preparation for permanent placement: evaluating direct work with older children',** *Adoption & Fostering*, 21:4, pp. 41–48
See ref. 380.

775 **Rutter M (1995) 'Clinical implications of attachment concepts: retrospect and prospect',** *Journal of Child Psychology and Psychiatry*, 36:4, pp. 549–71
A critical review examining the core constructs of attachment theory 25 years after the publication of Bowlby's seminal work. The author identifies aspects of attachment theory which have received subsequent empirical support and comments on areas which have since proved not to be correct. He concludes that many of the major tenets of attachment have been broadly confirmed.

However, unanswered questions remain. He explores a "round baker's dozen" of issues that require further clarification. Examples include a lack of precision in understanding how internal working models work, concern to more fully understand attachment relationships beyond infancy and a need to comprehend how children integrate experiences from different attachment relationships.

776 Rutter M, Andersen-Wood L, Beckett C *et al* (1999) 'Quasi–autistic patterns following severe early global privation', *Journal of Child Psychology & Psychiatry*, 40:4, pp. 537–49

This article reports the findings of the ERA study team in relation to the evidence of quasi-autistic patterns of behaviour observed when the children were four and six years of age. Six per cent of the children showed autistic-like patterns of behaviour. A further six per cent showed milder, usually isolated autistic characteristics. There were no such features in the UK comparison group. The children with autistic features tended to show a greater degree of cognitive impairment and had experienced a longer duration of severe deprivation.

777 Schofield G (2002) 'The significance of a secure base: a psychosocial model of long-term foster care', *Child & Family Social Work*, 7:4, pp. 259–72

The author draws on data from a study examining the retrospective views of adults who have experienced long-term foster care. Based on the themes identified, the author develops a psychosocial model for social work practice in long-term foster care. The model was influenced by two of the dominant theoretical models underpinning family placement practice, viz attachment and resilience. A further influence was an understanding of how a sense of belonging and a sense of family were understood by the adults in the study. The author considers the implications for practice by considering a number of key themes viz the need to act, to think, to belong and to hope.

778 **Schore A N (2000) 'Attachment and the regulation of the right brain',** *Attachment and Human Development*, 2:1, pp. 23–47
This article provides a brief informative account of contemporary neuroscience research of specific relevance to attachment theory. The author describes the role of right brain processes that underpin a child's earliest attachment experience and are the store of information relating to internal working models. A further understanding of these processes, he argues, will have important implications for the design of therapeutic interventions.

779 **Schuengel C, Bakermans-Kranenburg M J and van IJzendoorn M H (1999) 'Frightening maternal behavior linking unresolved loss and disorganized infant attachment',** *Journal of Consulting and Clinical Psychology*, 67:1, pp. 54–63
Reports the findings of a significant study of disorganised attachment in a low-risk sample. It has been suggested that disorganised attachment develops in situations where the infant experiences fear in the context of their primary attachment relationships. The key mediating factor therefore is the behaviour of the parent which the child perceives as frightening. In low-risk samples disorganised attachment is associated with unresolved parental loss. The aim of this study was to test whether

in these circumstances there was evidence that frightening behaviour was the link. Secure mothers with unresolved loss displayed less frightening behaviour than insecure mothers. Unresolved loss in secure mothers did not predict disorganisation in the infants. However, frightening behaviour was linked to disorganised attachment irrespective of maternal attachment security.

780 **Spangler G and Zimmerman P (1999) 'Attachment representation and emotion regulation in adolescents: a psychobiological perspective on internal working models',** *Attachment and Human Development*, 1:3, pp. 270–90

This theoretical article discusses the development of internal working models within a developmental framework. The authors argue that the primary attachment system in the newborn infant operates at the level of reflexes. This will change initially to a sensory/motor or procedural level of operation and subsequently to levels of representation. These different systems may operate independently. A securely attached adult with an insecure attachment history may demonstrate behaviour in highly stressful situations or towards specific people reminiscent of these early experiences. These preliminary data lend support to the hypothesis that assessment of different levels of attachment behaviour may yield different results. This has important implications for how the stability in attachment patterns is measured.

781 **Solomon J and George C (eds.) (1999) Attachment Disorganization.** New York: *Guilford Press*

This book is the first edited volume to focus specifically on attachment disorganisation. It includes contributions from leading researchers and clinicians and presents an up-to-date view of theoretical and empirical developments in relation to the development and consequences of disorganised attachment in infancy. Contains a specific chapter in relation to attachment disorganisation among children with neurological problems.

782 **Stovall K and Dozier M (1998) 'Infants in foster care: an attachment theory perspective',** *Adoption Quarterly*, 2:1, pp. 55–88
A literature review that highlights how the foster infant's previous attachment experiences may affect their adaptation to foster care. The article is important in describing how different attachment experiences (neglect/abuse/separation) may affect the strategies an infant develops to ensure their needs are met. These strategies may, however, result in behaviour which is experienced as difficult and alienating by foster carers. This behaviour is especially evident in infants placed after 12 months of age and requires particular sensitivity on the part of the carer to ensure that the infant's needs for support/nurturance are met.

783 **Stovall K and Dozier M (2000) 'The development of attachment in new relationships: single subject analyses for 10 foster infants',** *Development and Psychopathology*, 12:2, pp. 133–56
This article presents the findings of a small-scale study analysing the development of attachment in ten infant caregiver dyads. Assessment of infants using the "strange situation procedure" and of the caregivers using the adult attachment interview were supplemented by a diary completed daily over a two-month period. The development of secure attachment was evident in those infants

placed before 12 months of age but not in those placed later, even if they were placed with carers with secure attachment patterns. The authors argue that insecure attachment may develop when foster parents do not respond to the underlying neediness masked by avoidant and resistant behaviour. In these situations there is a risk that the carer will perpetuate a model of parenting that is perceived by the infant to be unavailable or rejecting.

784 **van IJzendoorn M H, Goldberg S, Kroonenberg P M and Frenkel O J (1992) 'The relative effects of maternal and child problems on the quality of attachment: a meta-analysis of attachment in clinical samples',** *Child Development*, 63:4, pp. 840–58

This article comprises a meta-analysis of 34 clinical studies of attachment. The aim of the study was to assess the relative importance of mother- and child-related problems in determining attachment status. Mother-related problems included mothers with mental health problems or situations of maltreatment. Child-related problems included prematurity, deafness or developmental delay. The findings suggest that, in clinical samples, the mother appears to play a more important role than the infant in shaping the quality of infant/mother attachment. In situations where the infant has problems the mother appears to be able to adapt to the infant's needs and behaviour. These findings are consistent with the predictions of attachment theory.

785 **van IJzendoorn M H (1995) 'Adult attachment representations, parental responsiveness and infant attachment: a meta-analysis on the predictive validity of the adult attachment**

interview', *Psychological Bulletin*, 117:3, pp. 387–403
This important article reports the findings of two meta-analyses in relation to the adult attachment interview (AAI). The aim was to test the predictive validity of the AAI in relation to two key areas. The first concerned the association between the parent's attachment representation and the infant's attachment pattern. The second focused on the question of how this association occurred. The findings suggest that the predictive validity of the AAI is not restricted to the secure/insecure distinction but extends further to the three insecure AAI classifications. This appears to be more evident in infant/mother than infant/father dyads. There are unanswered questions both about the role of fathers and how infants deal with the complicated network of attachment relationships within the family. The second question of how attachment patterns are transmitted from mother to infant remains unclear.

786 van IJzendoorn M H, Juffer F and Duyvesteyn M G (1995) 'Breaking the intergenerational cycle of insecure attachment: a review of the effects of attachment–based interventions on maternal sensitivity and infant security', *Journal of Child Psychology & Psychiatry*, 36:2, pp. 225–48
A review of the evidence of the effects of attachment-based interventions on maternal sensitivity and infant attachment security. Sixteen studies were reviewed and 12 were included in a quantitative meta-analysis. The findings suggest that short-term interventions are more effective than long-term, more intensive programmes. Increased sensitivity on the part of the parent did not necessarily succeed in changing the child's insecure attachment pattern. Changes in parents were evident at

the behavioural but not necessarily at the representational level. The article demonstrates the complex nature of the process of change in attachment relationships.

787 **van IJzendoorn M H and de Wolff M S (1997) 'In search of the absent father: meta-analyses of infant–father attachment: a rejoinder to our discussants',** *Child Development*, 68:4, pp. 604–09
This article describes the findings of two meta-analyses examining the role of fathers in the development of attachment security. Given the predominance of studies in relation to mother–infant attachment this is an important addition to the literature. The first analysis is based on eight studies examining the role of fathers; the second is based on 14 studies examining the association between infant–mother and infant–father attachment. The findings suggest fathers do shape the infant's attachment but to a lesser extent than mothers (p. 607). In addition, they imply that attachment security is relationship specific. Infants may therefore experience a secure attachment with one parent but an insecure attachment with the other.

788 **van IJzendoorn M H, Schuengel C and Bakermans-Kranenburg M J (1999) 'Disorganized attachment in early childhood: meta-analysis of precursors, concomitants and sequelae',** *Development and Psychopathology*, 11:2, pp. 225–49
Summarises the evidence from a series of meta-analyses undertaken to test the validity of the construct of disorganised attachment. Almost 80 studies were included in the analysis. The findings confirm the reliability and discriminate validity of disorganised attachment, though the authors acknowledge that the manifestations are

subtle and not necessarily easy to observe. There is an established link with maltreatment. The impact of disorganised attachment can be observed in heightened levels of stress, a greater risk of developing externalising behaviour difficulties and a tendency to develop dissociative behaviour later in life.

789 **Zeanah C H (1996) 'Beyond insecurity: a reconceptualization of attachment disorders in infancy',** *Journal of Consulting and Clinical Psychology*, 64:1, pp. 42–52
The author critically reviews the construct of attachment disorder. He suggests that the current criteria required by ICD10 and DSMIV for diagnosis of attachment disorder require revision to take into account current research and asks three important questions: Is it reactive? Is it attachment? Is it a disorder? He argues that the current definitions refer more generally to the social consequences of maltreatment rather than attachment *per se*. The definition should be based on specific attachment constructs. Important distinctions are made between insecure attachment and attachment disorder. Zeanah suggests an alternative conceptualisation which would include the differentiation of three different types of disorder: non-attachment, disordered attachment and disrupted attachment.

790 **Zimmerman P (1999) 'Structure and functions of internal working models of attachment and their role for emotion regulation',** *Attachment and Human Development*, 1:3, pp. 291–306
Explores the structure and function of internal working models with specific reference to their role in emotional regulation. Internal working models regulate emotional

communication both within individuals and between individuals and their attachment figures. The article includes empirical data examining the hypothesis that differences in attachment representation, as measured by the AAI, would lead to differences in key aspects of emotion regulation. The findings, based on a sample of adolescents, provide preliminary support for the hypothesis that a secure working model of attachment is related to adaptive emotional regulation.

Therapeutic and practice developments

791 **Archer C (2004) 'Substance misuse, attachment disorganisation and adoptive families', in Phillips R (ed.) Children Exposed to Parental Substance Misuse: Implications for family placement.** London: *BAAF*

Advocates the importance of adoptive families understanding the effects on children of being raised within a substance-misusing household, including attachment patterns and physical and mental health.

792 **Archer C and Burnell A (eds.) (2003) Trauma, Attachment and Family Permanence: Fear can stop you loving.** London: *Jessica Kingsley*

Explores ways of integrating attachment theory and developmental psychology into effective practice with fostered and adopted children and their families and carers. The second part of the book uses the example of a fictionalised family to illustrate the Family Futures' inclusive approach, where adoptive and foster parents become pivotal members of the therapeutic team. Contributions from actual case studies are also included to demonstrate how this approach has benefited families. Also see refs. 475 and 476.

793 **Beek M (1999) 'Parenting children with attachment difficulties: views of adoptive parents and implications for post-adoption services',** *Adoption & Fostering*, 23:1, pp. 16–23

Describes a post-adoption service established to meet the needs of adoptive parents caring for children with attachment difficulties. The service included an ongoing support group and "surgery" for families who were experiencing difficulties. The group was influenced by ideas drawn from attachment theory. The adoptive parents identified a number of key themes that they felt were particularly important, including acknowledgement that attachment theory could help them to understand their children's needs. In turn, this meant they could adapt their parenting strategies to meet these needs more effectively. Other key themes included acknowledgement of the painful adjustment in expectations for parents and an understanding of their need to nurture themselves and their families.

794 **Cairns K (2002) Attachment, Trauma and Resilience: Therapeutic caring for children.** London: *BAAF*

The author shares her experience as a foster carer caring for children with troubled early histories. The book is written in a personal style and provides vivid insights into life within the family. The author also shares her understanding of theoretical ideas that have helped her to make sense of her experiences.

795 **Courtney A (2000) 'Loss and grief in adoption: the impact of contact',** *Adoption & Fostering*, 24:2, pp. 33–44
See ref. 410.

796 **Daniel B, Wassell S and Gilligan R (1999) ' "It's just common sense isn't it?" Exploring ways of putting the theory of resilience into action',** *Adoption & Fostering*, 23:3, pp. 6–15

This article describes a small pilot project established to explore the feasibility of developing guidelines for practitioners based on the concept of resilience. Six domains of functioning were identified: a secure base, education, friendship, talents and interests, positive values and social competencies. Although a number of these areas have been influenced by attachment theory, the authors argue that there is a different emphasis in an approach based on resilience. In contrast to permanency planning, for example, the emphasis is on small steps and achievements. Through the use of tools such as ecomaps a child can be helped to reflect on who the significant people are in their life. Families can be supported to find even 'small but significant ways' of contributing to the child's security (p. 7).

797 **Edens J F and Cavell T A (1999), 'A review and reformulation of adoptive relationships from an attachment perspective',** *Adoption Quarterly*, 3:2, pp. 43–70

Examines a number of key aspects of the adoption experience through the lens of attachment theory. The authors utilise the Categorical Model of Attachment Styles, which has specific relevance to adult attachment. They consider whether this framework can provide useful insight into some of the key tasks for adoptive parents and adoptive adults. Of particular interest is the application of this model to discussions about motivation to adopt and the issues involved in searching. A number of tentative hypotheses are suggested which could provide the basis for future research.

798 **Fearnley S (1996) The Extra Dimension.** Rawtenstall: *Keys Attachment Centre*
An account of attachment theory as used in an intervention for children and young people who have severe difficulties in attachment. The book is written by one of the directors of Keys, the independent project offering the services. It provides a clear formulation of the services provided, describing both principles and practice. In some of its elements, the interventive methods are "intrusive" and involve holding techniques, which are subject of some controversy.

799 **Frederici R (1998) Help for the Hopeless Child: A guide for families.** Alexandria, VA: *Frederici & Associates*
The author's approach to therapy is based on strongly directive physical control for autistic-like behaviour, but applied also to what are described as "attachment disorders". Rutter *et al* (2000 – ref. 578) quote his recommendation for a graded introduction of institutionalised children into "normal" UK and US life.

800 **Gilligan R (2001) Promoting Resilience: A resource guide on working with children in the care system.** London: *BAAF*
Examines the concept of resilience and explains how it can be applied in practice with young people in public

care. Gilligan uses his considerable experience to develop a range of practical ideas on how to improve the quality of life for children in care using relationship opportunities in their family and social networks, and school and leisure activities.

801 **Golding K (2003) 'Helping foster carers, helping children: using attachment theory to guide practice',** *Adoption & Fostering*, 27:2, pp. 64–73
This article, written by a consultant clinical psychologist, describes an interagency project established to provide support and training for foster carers of children within the Looked After System. In the main, the emphasis is on work with carers but in a small number of instances there is also work with the children themselves. There are a number of different aspects to the service including a consultation service and group work. Theoretical ideas, drawn largely from attachment theory, are used to help carers develop strategies to assist the children in developing a secure base 'within which the child can learn emotional regulation and the ability to be reflective' (p. 69).

802 **Golding K and Picken W (2004) 'Group work for foster carers caring for children with complex problems',** *Adoption & Fostering*, 28:1, pp. 25–37
Describes the use of two different types of groups developed by the Primary Care and Support Team in Worcestershire. The first is based on a parent training programme and helps foster carers consider different ways of dealing with their foster children's challenging behaviour. The second group focuses on the children's attachment difficulties and helps foster carers to adapt their parenting to respond to these problems. Routine,

practice-based evaluation suggests that group interventions can help carers to increase their understanding of the needs of foster children and their skill in managing them on a day-to-day basis.

803 **Gordon C (1999) 'A parenting programme for parents of children with disturbed attachment patterns',** *Adoption & Fostering*, 23:4, pp. 49–56
A description of a parenting programme established to meet the needs of adoptive parents caring for children with attachment difficulties. The intervention is based on ideas based broadly on attachment theory. The programme combines theoretical and practical input. The aim is to enable adopters to gain insight into the impact of early neglect and trauma and to develop practical strategies for parenting on a day-to-day basis. The author is an adoptive parent and Co-director of Family Futures, an attachment centre based in London.

804 **Haight W L, Doner Kagle J and Black J E (2003) 'Understanding and supporting parent–child relationships during foster care visits: attachment theory and research',** *Social Work*, 48:2, pp. 195–207
Uses attachment theory to identify strategies for promoting more positive parent–child interactions during foster care visits.

805 **Hart A, Luckock B and Gerhardt C (2002) The Attachment Project in Context: Developing therapeutic and social support services for adoptive and long-term foster families in Brighton and Hove: A research-based evaluation.** Brighton: *University of Brighton Faculty of Health*
Research report examining the effectiveness of a par-

ticular (attachment therapy) approach to effective service provision for adoptive and long-term foster families. Finds some effectiveness but concludes, in particular, that a fresh model of support is required at a national policy level – one which recognises that all families offering "permanent" substitute homes are entitled to specific services which do not fit easily into models of assessment, and targeted provision designed for families vulnerable to social exclusion.

806 **Hart A and Thomas H (2000) 'Controversial attachments: the indirect treatment of fostered and adopted children via parent co-therapy',** *Attachment and Human Development*, 2:3, pp. 306–27
This article describes a model for clinical practice with foster/adopted children within a child mental health setting. The model, described as parent co-therapy (PCT), is based broadly on attachment theory. The basic premise is that when attachment issues are paramount indirect work with parents is likely to be more effective than direct work with children in the early years of placement. The central focus of treatment is to facilitate the development of secure attachments within the adoptive/foster family. Direct involvement with the child is undertaken by the carer acting as co-therapist. The model challenges traditional roles within multidisciplinary teams. The method is described by reference to a single case study based on a sibling group.

807 **Hendry A and Vincent J (2002) 'Supporting adoptive families: an interagency response',** *Representing Children*, 15:2, pp. 104–17
A description of a service established to meet the needs

of adoptive families caring for "attachment disordered children". The service is based not only on an understanding of attachment and trauma but also specific adoption issues such as identity and loss. There is also an awareness of the impact of caring for children with troubled histories. Parents are vulnerable to the projection of issues arising from the child's disordered working models (p. 115) and may need help in their own right to manage this process.

808 **Hill A (2003) 'Issues facing brothers of sexually abused children: implications for professional practice',** *Child & Family Social Work*, 8:4, pp. 281–90
It is recognised that abuse interferes with the development of a coherent life narrative, in particular about abusive events. This paper draws on the author's experience of undertaking play therapy with the brothers of sexually abused children. It illustrates the range of difficulties that such boys may face and identifies implications for professional practice. Their experience is influenced by the nature of the child's attachment relationships with his non-abusing parents or carers, his abused sibling and with the abuser himself. This struggle for a coherent narrative about the sexual abuse can have a significant impact on the development of a sense of masculine identity, especially when the abuser is the boy's own father and/or the abused child is male. In the context of increasing professional awareness of the need to support siblings of sexually abused children, it is argued that there should be a specific focus on gender and identity issues for boys.

809 **Hobday A, Kirby A and Oller K (2002) Creative Therapy for Children in New Families.** Oxford: *Blackwell*
Provides information and insights into the problems faced by children who have moved to new families through fostering or adoption. It contains a broad range of activities designed to help children overcome emotional and behavioural difficulties including guidelines about how, when, where and at what age to use them.

810 **Hopkins J (2000) 'Overcoming a child's resistance to late adoption: how one new attachment can facilitate another',** *Journal of Child Psychotherapy*, 26:3, pp. 335–47
This article, written by a psychotherapist, movingly describes the process of healing and emotional growth in a nine-year-old boy placed for adoption following a history of adversity. The construct of disorganised attachment is used to provide insight into the boy's behaviour and the defensive strategies developed in response to early trauma. Despite a long period of initial rejection, change became possible through the therapist's containment of negative feelings. This in turn influenced the development of more positive relationships within the adoptive family.

811 **Hopkirk E (2002) 'Adoption after bereavement',** *Adoption & Fostering*, 26:1, pp. 15–24
An exploration of the issues of loss for adoptive parents, with specific reference to the loss of a previous child (stillbirth or death). The author reports the findings of a small-scale, qualitative study comparing the views of family placement and childcare workers with those of adoptive families. The findings challenge established

views about the need for adoptive parents to grieve for the loss of their child before they are emotionally able to move on to adoption. The families themselves report that grieving is a life-long process, that memories will continue to be triggered but this does not preclude the ability or desire to parent another child.

812 **Howe D and Fearnley S (1999) 'Disorders of attachment and attachment therapy',** *Adoption & Fostering*, 23:2, pp. 19–30
Attachment therapies based on "cognitive structuring" and "therapeutic holding" appear to be having some success with children who have failed to respond to other treatments employed by the child mental health services. The authors describe different patterns of attachment and the behaviours associated with children classified as disorganised and disordered in their attachment behaviours. They outline therapeutic interventions based on developmental attachment theory using a case sample.

813 **Hughes D (1999) 'Adopting children with attachment problems',** *Child Welfare*, pp. 541–60
This practice-based article describes a framework for working with children with attachment difficulties. The article is written in an accessible style by a clinical psychologist in private practice in the USA. The author offers a useful description of the dynamics that may occur when adoptive parents offer nurture and care to a child with significant attachment problems. He suggests that children may appear superficially friendly when they do not have any real understanding of reciprocal relationships and that they develop patterns of control and self-reliance as a means of surviving neglectful and abuseful

experiences. The article includes a useful description of parenting and treatment strategies, including holding therapy.

814 **Hunter M (2001) Psychotherapy with Young People in Care: Lost and found.** Hove: *Routledge*
A thoughtful and practical guide that draws lightly on the deep theoretical understanding which informs the author's work.

815 **Jewett C (1995) Helping Children Cope with Separation and Loss.** London: *Batsford*
Children may experience the pain of loss in a wide variety of situations. In this book, Claudia Jewett has developed simple techniques that any adult can use to help children through their grief. Using case histories and sample dialogues, she explains how to help children come to a timely resolution of their grief.

816 **Kenrick J (2000) ' "Be a kid": the traumatic impact of repeated separations on children who are fostered and adopted',** *Journal of Child Psychotherapy*, 26:3, pp. 393–412
An account by a psychotherapist of a long-term therapeutic intervention with a young child, 'helping him to make sense' of his previous experiences of separation. The author argues that it is important to recognise the therapeutic needs of looked after children, particularly children who have experienced repeated separations and are living in transitional placements within the care system. Many of these children have experienced abuse and/or deprivation prior to entry into care. Without therapeutic support children can find themselves alone and 'unable to process or to attach meaning to experience' (p. 393).

817 **Mercer J (2001) ' "Attachment therapy" using deliberate restraint: an object lesson on the identification of unvalidated treatments',** *Journal of Child and Adolescent Psychiatric Nursing*, 14:3, pp. 105–14

A review of attachment therapies involving "therapeutic holding". The author insists that this is more accurately described as "restraint" and is strongly critical of the therapies.

818 **Prynn B (2001) 'Family building in adoption',** *Adoption & Fostering*, 25:1, pp. 33–43

A report of the findings of a small-scale, qualitative study examining factors that might explain why some placements seem more "successful" than others. The study design was based on concepts derived from attachment and psychodynamic theory. A judgement was made about the degree of comfort/discomfort the adopters described in relation to their experience of adoptive parenting. Particular note was made of their description of their attachment history. Factors associated with positive outcomes included the degree of coherence with which adoptive parents described their personal history, their sensitivity to feelings of loss and their openness to support from family, friends and community.

819 **Schofield G (2001) 'Resilience and family placement: a lifespan perspective',** *Adoption & Fostering*, 25:3, pp. 6–19

Schofield explores the construct of resilience and illustrates this through selective examples from a qualitative study of 40 adults who grew up in foster care. She argues that it is important to view resilience within a developmental perspective. Rather than a static trait within the child, resilience develops as a result of the interaction of a child's internal and external worlds. The author considers the conceptual overlap between resilience and attachment. A key construct linking the two themes is the internal working model, which develops as the child adapts to their caregiving environment. Although there are differences, the two theories are not incompatible and therefore practitioners should feel comfortable in using both frameworks to guide their practice.

820 Seden J (2002) 'Parenting and the Harry Potter stories: a social care perspective', *Children & Society*, 16:5, pp. 295–305

This article analyses the capacities of the parents in the Harry Potter stories, written by J K Rowling, from a social care perspective. It argues that there is a synergy between what the social sciences have discovered about "good enough parenting" and the insights that can be gathered from entering the imaginative world of literature. This is illustrated by a discussion of the qualities of the parents and parent substitutes in the four books published between 1997 and 2000. It concludes that fictional experiences of childhood create empathy in the reader and enable us to confront the need for imagination as parents and practitioners, while the social sciences keep knowledge grounded and evidenced.

821 Steele H (2003) 'Holding therapy is not attachment therapy: Editor's introduction to this invited Special Issue', *Attachment and Human Development*, 5:3, pp. 219

Steele introduces the reader to an important special issue of *Attachment and Human Development* examining current perspectives on the identification and treatment of attachment disorders. This particular edition was compiled because of concern about the 'misguided use of attachment theory and research by some clinicians working with highly vulnerable children and their parents (often adopted)' (p. 219). The author reminds the reader of the core constructs of attachment theory, i.e. the provision of a secure base and sensitive attunement. This, he argues, forms the key components of therapeutic interventions informed by attachment theory.

The journal includes a target article (see ref. 771) and a number of short commentaries by academic researchers and clinicians from developmental and clinical psychology, child psychiatry and social work, in relation to this controversial area of practice.

822 **Thompson S (2003) 'Attachment or trauma? Factors mediating the impact of early maltreatment in adopted children',** *Representing Children*, 16:2, pp. 104–21

A review of the literature in relation to outcomes in adoption suggests that a child's early history of maltreatment continues to affect the psychosocial development of some children despite good-quality care within the adoptive family. The author draws on attachment theory, particularly developments in the theory base underlying the construct of internal working models, to explore the process by which this occurs. Particular focus is given to the role of disorganised attachment in view of an established link both with maltreatment and externalising behaviour difficulties. The article concludes with implications for post-placement work with adoptive families.

823 **Tyrell C and Dozier M (1999) 'Foster parents' understanding of children's problematic attachment strategies: the need for therapeutic responsiveness',** *Adoption Quarterly*, 2:4, pp. 49–64
This article reports the findings of a small-scale study examining foster parents' understanding of children's insecure attachment strategies. A sample of 25 foster mothers was compared to a sample of 25 biological mothers in relation to a number of aspects of parenting, including their understanding of insecure attachment strategies. As expected, the foster mothers reported significantly more attachment-related difficulties with their foster children than the biological mothers in relation to their birth children. Foster mothers did not, however, demonstrate a greater understanding of attachment constructs. The authors conclude that foster parents need specialised knowledge and skills if they are to relate therapeutically with the special needs of many foster children.

824 **Whelan D J (2003) 'Using attachment theory when placing siblings in foster care',** *Child & Adolescent Social Work Journal*, 20:1, pp. 21–36
This article, written by a treatment foster care manager in Wisconsin USA, draws on attachment theory to develop a framework for decision-making in relation to sibling placements. The author argues that an examination of the child's attachment history and behaviour will assist the practitioner in determining whether placement of the siblings together will detract from or contribute to the provision of a secure caregiving environment for each of the children. Includes cases vignettes to illustrate the main argument.

Life story work

825 Betts B and Ahmed A (2003) My Life Story CD Rom. Orkney: *Information Plus*
This interactive CD ROM guides worker and child through a range of activities to assemble key information, process current situations and consider what the future might hold. Using a colourful and interactive menu system based on a treasure island (palm trees, sailing galleon and a treasure chest), it opens into seven interactive sections with a wide range of activities, user input, printable worksheets and help.

826 Bond H (2000) 'Who am I?', *Foster Care*, 103, pp. 12–14
Reports on the use of life work by foster carers to help children who have had disjointed lives.

827 Camis J (2001) My Life and Me. London: *BAAF*
An illustrated workbook to help children separated from their birth families to maintain or develop their knowledge of their life history. Contains space for photographs, drawings and other documents, etc. and comes already set up for some major divisions: my health, birth family, school and so on. Includes guidelines for use that are suitable for adoptive parents, social workers or others.

828 Clegg P and Toll K (1996) 'Videotape and the memory visit: a living lifebook for adopted children', *Child Welfare*, 75:4, pp. 311–19
The Michigan Adoption Resource Exchange in collaboration with the Jackson County Department of Social

Services, USA, has introduced "Living Lifebooks", a channel for communication. Shows how a sample videotape of biological parents can open up avenues of development and self-exploration for an adopted person that are unavailable in other forms.

829 **Gray B and Ridden G (1999) Lifemaps of People with Learning Disabilities.** London: *Jessica Kingsley*
Presents 14 biographies written by people of all ages who have a learning disability. Discusses how these stories might be representative of other people with learning difficulties and what key themes may be identified from the stories. Outlines the use of lifemaps and discusses their use for carers, educators, care managers and others.

830 **Hanney L and Kozlowska K (2002) 'Healing traumatised children: creating illustrated story books in family therapy',** *Family Process*, 41:1, pp. 37–65
The authors describe the therapeutic practice of creating illustrated storybooks in family therapy with traumatised children. Illustrated stories offer a predictable structure to sessions and facilitate engagement and participation of children in therapy. The therapeutic emphasis of storybooks can be adjusted to take into account a child's life story, verbal capacity, level of anxiety and traumatic hyperarousal. The creation of storybooks is an active process that embraces important aspects of trauma-specific interventions, including expression of trauma-related feelings, clarification of erroneous beliefs about the self, others or the traumatic event, and externalisation of traumatic stimuli into artwork, allowing for exposure and habituation of the arousal response. A

focus on visual images alongside narrative takes advantage of children's developmental capacities and spontaneous pleasure in the creation of art, thus minimising anxiety and enhancing feelings of mastery, competence and hope.

831 Harper J (1996) 'Recapturing the past: alternative methods of life story work in adoption and fostering', *Adoption & Fostering*, 20:3, pp. 21–28
The traditional method of using photos, drawings, writings and memorabilia from the child's past to create a life story book may not always be possible or appropriate. Harper presents four case studies in which, for various reasons, it was necessary to pursue alternative methods of life story work, for instance through play and the exploration of dreams. She underlines the importance of truthfulness, sensitivity and flexibility on the part of the therapist, and the need to constantly watch out for clues from the child. In following their lead, she asserts, the most constructive path towards rebuilding their sense of self will be found.

832 Holody R and Maher S (1996) 'Using lifebooks with children in family foster care: a here-and-now process model', *Child Welfare*, 75:4, pp. 321–35
Lifebooks are well established as effective tools for helping children in family foster care in the USA cope with past events and future plans. The here-and-now process described in this article focuses on the child's present life being more accessible for both the child and the worker than traditional lifebooks. Case examples demonstrate the model's effectiveness in each phase of the worker's encounters with the child. Limitations of the model are discussed.

833 **Kahn H (2002) 'Filling the gaps',** *Community Care*, 1414, 21 March, p. 42
Argues that life story work with children should be seen as a necessary part of helping fostering and adoption placements.

834 **Nicholls E (2003) 'Model answer',** *Community Care*, 1479, 31 July, pp. 32–34
The author suggests that life story work has not evolved to meet the changing needs in practice, legislation and of looked after children. Such work helps to retain and record the history and significant moments of a child's life and this article describes a new model for practice – the "new life work model" – applicable to all looked after children. The model's dimensions are the preservation of children's memories, preparing the child to move onto permanency and promoting identity by providing a comprehensive family history book.

835 **Ryan T and Walker R (1993) Life Story Work.** London: *BAAF*
Practical guide, with examples, to making and using life story books with adopted children.

836 **Streng I C (2002) 'Group work with children and adolescents using lifegames',** *Groupwork*, 13:2, pp. 49–71
This paper is a practice account of groupwork with children using a board-game format. Four different board games encourage the understanding and disclosure of the complex feelings experienced by children and young people when they are confronted with traumatic life events. Lifegames have been devised to help children and adolescents who have encountered adversity in their

lives as a consequence of bereavement, family break-up, poor peer relationships or bullying. Combining the principles of groupwork and games helps engage and motivate them to address and work through their difficulties. Lifegames are a means to assist professionals in their work with children and young people.

837 **Treacher A and Katz I (2001) 'Narrative and fantasy in adoption',** *Adoption & Fostering*, 25:3, pp. 20–28
Adoption touches on basic personal and cultural narratives, emotions and fantasies surrounding the self and family. The authors explore the narratives of all those involved in the process, both professionals and those with personal investments. They draw on contemporary theory of narrative and psychoanalytic theory of fantasy in order to explore and understand some of the issues arising in adoption. A central contention is that all identity, whether adopted or not, is multifaceted, inherently conflicted and constantly developing. The theoretical and emotional endeavour is to place this view of identity as a central backbone to understanding adoption. Treacher and Katz argue that many narratives and fantasies function to pass over problematic feelings and fantasies. For example, life story books can silence the difficulties experienced for the adoptee and may not allow space for an exploration of troublesome feelings and fantasies. They contend that maturity is based on the capacity to face up to contradictions and conflict, and to allow for such complex narratives.

838 **Turner A (2000) 'Use of computers to enhance the story-telling of young people with learning difficulties',** *Mental Health and Learning Disabilities Care*, 3:5, pp. 160–64

The author describes a pilot project to explore the use of computer technology to promote the story-telling abilities of children with learning difficulties. Using computers the children produced far longer and more complex stories and interacted more vigorously with the process than they did with single still pictures.

839 **Usher J (1993) Life Story Work: A therapeutic tool for social work.** Norwich: *University of East Anglia*

Research study focusing on life story work with children. Looks at the theory behind this type of work, using it in practice and practical issues for social workers and line managers.

840 **Wingham G (2003) 'This is your life',** *Care and Health*, 27, 15 January, pp. 34–35

Explores the role and practice of life story work with children and young people.

Title index*

A

* Some titles have been abbreviated in the Index – see main entry for full titles. In keeping with normal practice, titles of books, reports and legal frameworks, such as acts and regulations, appear in italics while titles of articles in journals/periodicals and websites appear in roman.

B

C

D

E

F

G

H

I

M

N

O

P

Q

R

S

T

U

V

W

Y

Author index

C

D

E

F

G

H

I

J

K

L

M

N

O

S

U

V

W

Y

Z